I0413212

Land-Use Analysis and Simulated Effects of Land-Use Change and Aggregate Mining on Groundwater Flow in the South Platte River Valley, Brighton to Fort Lupton, Colorado

By L.R. Arnold, C.S. Mladinich, W.H. Langer, and J.S. Daniels

Prepared in cooperation with the City of Fort Lupton and the City of Brighton

Scientific Investigations Report 2010–5019

U.S. Department of the Interior
U.S. Geological Survey

U.S. Department of the Interior
KEN SALAZAR, Secretary

U.S. Geological Survey
Marcia K. McNutt, Director

U.S. Geological Survey, Reston, Virginia: 2010

For more information on the USGS—the Federal source for science about the Earth, its natural and living resources, natural hazards, and the environment, visit http://www.usgs.gov or call 1-888-ASK-USGS

For an overview of USGS information products, including maps, imagery, and publications, visit http://www.usgs.gov/pubprod

To order this and other USGS information products, visit http://store.usgs.gov

Suggested citation:
Arnold, L.R., Mladinich, C.S., Langer, W.H., and Daniels, J.S., 2010, Land-use analysis and simulated effects of land-use change and aggregate mining on groundwater flow in the South Platte River valley, Brighton to Fort Lupton, Colorado: U.S. Geological Survey Scientific Investigations Report 2010–5019, 117 p.

Contents

Figures

Tables

Conversion Factors

Inch/Pound to SI

Multiply	By	To obtain
Length		
inch (in.)	2.54	centimeter (cm)
foot (ft)	0.3048	meter (m)
mile (mi)	1.609	kilometer (km)
Area		
acre	0.4047	hectare (ha)
square foot (ft^2)	0.09290	square meter (m^2)
square mile (mi^2)	2.590	square kilometer (km^2)
Volume		
acre-foot (acre-ft)	1,233	cubic meter (m^3)
Flow rate		
cubic foot per day (ft^3/d)	0.02832	cubic meter per day (m^3/d)
cubic foot per second (ft^3/s)	0.02832	cubic meter per second (m^3/s)
gallon per minute (gal/min)	0.06309	liter per second (L/s)
acre-foot per year (acre-ft/yr)	1,233	cubic meter per year (m^3/yr)
Specific capacity		
gallon per minute per foot [(gal/min)/ft)]	0.2070	liter per second per meter [(L/s)/m]
Hydraulic conductivity		
foot per day (ft/d)	0.3048	meter per day (m/d)
Hydraulic gradient		
foot per mile (ft/mi)	0.1894	meter per kilometer (m/km)
Transmissivity*		
foot squared per day (ft^2/d)	0.09290	meter squared per day (m^2/d)

Temperature in degrees Fahrenheit (°F) may be converted to degrees Celsius (°C) as follows:

$$°C=(°F-32)/1.8$$

Vertical coordinate information is referenced to the National Geodetic Vertical Datum of 1929 (NGVD 29) unless otherwise noted.

Horizontal coordinate information is referenced to the North American Datum of 1983 (NAD 83).

Altitude, as used in this report, refers to distance above the vertical datum.

*Transmissivity: The standard unit for transmissivity is cubic foot per day per square foot times foot of aquifer thickness [(ft^3/d)/ft^2]ft. In this report, the mathematically reduced form, foot squared per day (ft^2/d), is used for convenience.

Other abbreviations used in this report:

L   Length

T   Time

L/T   Length per time

Land-Use Analysis and Simulated Effects of Land-Use Change and Aggregate Mining on Groundwater Flow in the South Platte River Valley, Brighton to Fort Lupton, Colorado

By L.R. Arnold, C.S. Mladinich, W.H. Langer, and J.S. Daniels

Abstract

Land use in the South Platte River valley between the cities of Brighton and Fort Lupton, Colo., is undergoing change as urban areas expand, and the extent of aggregate mining in the Brighton–Fort Lupton area is increasing as the demand for aggregate grows in response to urban development. To improve understanding of land-use change and the potential effects of land-use change and aggregate mining on groundwater flow, the U.S. Geological Survey, in cooperation with the cities of Brighton and Fort Lupton, analyzed socio-economic and land-use trends and constructed a numerical groundwater flow model of the South Platte alluvial aquifer in the Brighton–Fort Lupton area. The numerical groundwater flow model was used to simulate (1) steady-state hydrologic effects of predicted land-use conditions in 2020 and 2040, (2) transient cumulative hydrologic effects of the potential extent of reclaimed aggregate pits in 2020 and 2040, (3) transient hydrologic effects of actively dewatered aggregate pits, and (4) effects of different hypothetical pit spacings and configurations on groundwater levels. The SLEUTH (Slope, Land cover, Exclusion, Urbanization, Transportation, and Hillshade) urban-growth modeling program was used to predict the extent of urban area in 2020 and 2040. Wetlands in the Brighton–Fort Lupton area were mapped as part of the study, and mapped wetland locations and areas of riparian herbaceous vegetation previously mapped by the Colorado Division of Wildlife were compared to simulation results to indicate areas where wetlands or riparian herbaceous vegetation might be affected by groundwater-level changes resulting from land-use change or aggregate mining.

Analysis of land-use conditions in 1957, 1977, and 2000 indicated that the general distribution of irrigated land and non-irrigated land remained similar from 1957 to 2000, but both land uses decreased as urban area increased. Urban area increased about 165 percent from 1957 to 1977 and about 56 percent from 1977 to 2000 with most urban growth occurring east of Brighton and Fort Lupton and along major transportation corridors. Land-use conditions in 2020 and 2040 predicted by the SLEUTH modeling program indicated urban growth will continue to develop primarily east of Brighton and Fort Lupton and along major transportation routes, but substantial urban growth also is predicted south and west of Brighton.

Steady-state simulations of the hydrologic effects of predicted land-use conditions in 2020 and 2040 indicated groundwater levels declined less than 2 feet relative to simulated groundwater levels in 2000. Groundwater levels declined most where irrigated land was converted to urban area and least where non-irrigated land was converted to urban area. Simulated groundwater-level declines resulting from land-use conditions in 2020 and 2040 are not predicted to substantially affect wetlands or riparian herbaceous vegetation in the study area because the declines are small and wetlands and riparian herbaceous vegetation generally are not located where simulated declines occur.

Transient simulations of the cumulative hydrologic effects of multiple reclaimed pits in 2020 and 2040 indicated that lined and fines-backfilled pits caused groundwater levels to decline downgradient from pits and to rise upgradient from pits, whereas unlined pits had the opposite effect. The maximum decline resulting from the cumulative effects of reclaimed pits in 2020 and 2040 ranged from about 9 to 11 feet, and the maximum rise was about 5 to 9 feet. Groundwater levels changed most during the first year, and groundwater levels ceased to change substantially in most areas of the simulated aquifer within about 10 years. Some wetlands or areas of riparian herbaceous vegetation are located where simulated groundwater levels resulting from the effects of reclaimed pits in 2020 and 2040 changed more than 2 feet, indicating that groundwater-supported wetlands or riparian herbaceous vegetation at these locations might be affected by the changed groundwater levels. Some areas where groundwater-level rises resulting from the cumulative effects of reclaimed pits in 2020 and 2040 occurred where the simulated depth to water is less than 5 feet, potentially creating conditions favorable to the formation of new wetlands at these locations.

Transient simulations of hypothetical actively dewatered pits were used to predict the magnitude and extent of drawdown resulting from a single pit, two closely spaced pits, two widely spaced pits, and three closely spaced pits. The maximum extent of drawdown of 2 or more feet ranged from about 12,400 feet for a single dewatered pit to about 13,100 feet for three closely spaced dewatered pits. Most drawdown occurred during the first year, and drawdown extent after 1 year was almost as great as after 15 years. Because dewatering typically occurs for multiple years and most drawdown occurs rapidly during the first year, groundwater-supported wetlands in areas of 2 or more feet of drawdown might be affected by lower groundwater levels resulting from pit dewatering.

Transient simulations of three hypothetical lined pits were used to evaluate the effect that pit spacing and configuration have on groundwater-level changes resulting from lined pits. Simulations indicated that groundwater-level changes resulting from lined pits became larger as pit size increased and became smaller as pit spacing increased. Groundwater-level changes resulting from lined pits decreased by successively smaller amounts as the distance between pits was increased. Offsetting the center pit upgradient or downgradient from other pits decreased the hydrologic effects of lined pits to a greater extent than increasing the distance between aligned pits. Simulations indicated that offset pits with a spacing of 200 to 400 feet provide a configuration that reduces the hydrologic effects of lined pits by the greatest amount while minimizing the distance between pits.

Introduction

The South Platte River valley between the cities of Brighton in Adams County and Fort Lupton in Weld County, Colo. (fig. 1), is underlain by an extensive unconfined alluvial aquifer and is undergoing land-use change as urban areas expand and the extent of aggregate mining increases in response to urban development. Changes in land use and land cover can have substantial influence on economic and environmental conditions at multiple scales and can affect the distribution and quantity of aquifer recharge (Bauer and Vaccaro, 1990; Harbor, 1994; Scanlon and others, 2005), which can alter groundwater levels and flow directions in shallow alluvial aquifers underlying areas of land-use change. The presence of large aggregate-mining pits excavated below the water table also can affect groundwater levels and flow directions in shallow alluvial aquifers. When a pit is mined in a dry condition (dry mining), groundwater is pumped or otherwise removed from the pit, and drawdown occurs in the surrounding aquifer as the pit is deepened (Knepper, 2002). When aggregate mining is completed, pits typically are either backfilled, allowed to refill with water, or lined with a low-permeability barrier to create reservoirs for water storage. Pits

backfilled with fine sediments can alter local aquifer hydraulic conductivity and also can affect the direction of groundwater flow. Pits allowed to refill with water create areas of evaporation, causing groundwater losses to the atmosphere. Pits lined with low-permeability material create barriers to groundwater flow that can cause groundwater levels to rise upgradient from pits and decline downgradient from pits (Arnold and others, 2003). Groundwater levels near aggregate pits commonly are monitored during the life of mining operations, but isolating the hydrologic effects of pits, whether active or reclaimed, can be difficult because multiple pits can affect groundwater levels and flow directions in a complex manner along an entire river reach. In addition, other hydrologic stresses, such as well pumping, can affect groundwater levels near pits. Where the water table is near land surface, wetlands might depend on groundwater to support vegetation, and large changes in groundwater levels resulting from land-use change or aggregate mining could adversely affect wetlands. Groundwater-level declines could cause wetlands to dry up, and groundwater-level rises could flood wetlands or create conditions favorable for the formation of wetlands at new locations.

In 2004, the U.S. Geological Survey (USGS), as part of the Central Region Integrated Science Partnership program, initiated a study of land-use change and the cumulative effects of land-use change and aggregate mining on groundwater flow in the alluvial aquifer of the South Platte River valley between the cities of Brighton and Fort Lupton. As part of the study, a numerical groundwater flow model of the South Platte alluvial aquifer was developed to simulate the steady-state hydrologic effects of land-use change and multiple reclaimed pits, and wetlands were mapped to indicate areas where wetlands might be affected by changes in groundwater levels. In 2005, the study was expanded in cooperation with the City of Fort Lupton and the City of Brighton to include simulation of short-term transient hydrologic effects of both active and reclaimed pits and the effects of different hypothetical pit spacings and configurations on groundwater flow.

Purpose and Scope

The purpose of this report is to present results of the land-use analysis and the simulated effects of land-use change and aggregate mining on groundwater flow in the South Platte River valley between the cities of Brighton and Fort Lupton, Colo. Results also provide an indication of areas where wetlands and areas of riparian herbaceous vegetation might be affected by groundwater-level changes.

Socioeconomic and land-use data were compared and analyzed to improve understanding of the kinds and locations of changes that are taking place and the rate at which changes are occurring. Historical land-use data were used as input to the urban-growth modeling program SLEUTH (Slope, Land cover, Exclusion, Urbanization, Transportation, and Hill-shade) (U.S. Geological Survey and University of California at Santa Barbara, 2001) to predict the potential extent of urban

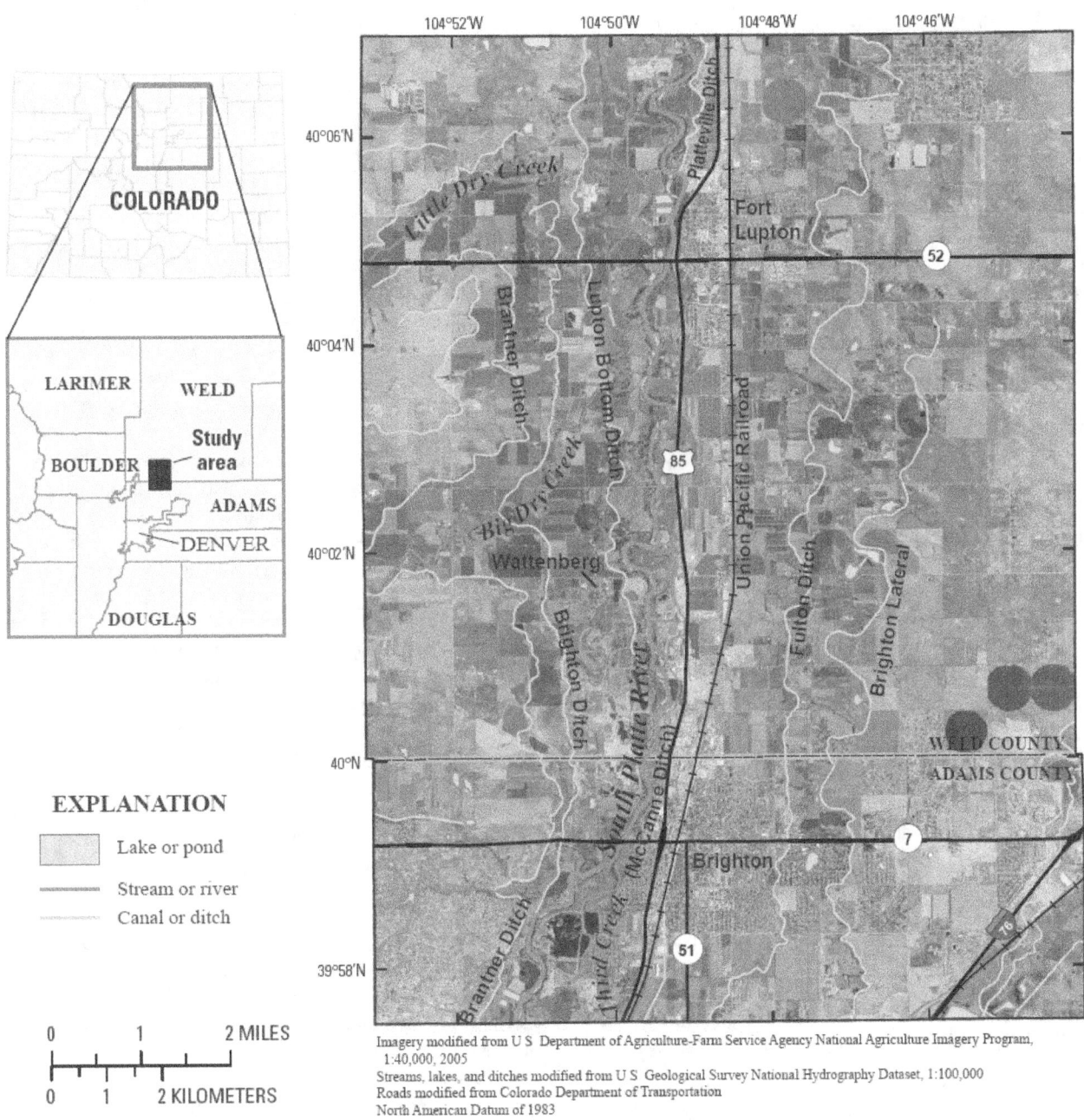

Imagery modified from U S Department of Agriculture-Farm Service Agency National Agriculture Imagery Program,
   1:40,000, 2005
Streams, lakes, and ditches modified from U S Geological Survey National Hydrography Dataset, 1:100,000
Roads modified from Colorado Department of Transportation
North American Datum of 1983

Figure 1.   Location of South Platte study area. Brighton to Fort Lupton, Colorado.

development in the study area in 2020 and 2040. Land-use conditions in 1957, 1977, and 2000 were selected for use in analyzing historical land-use change because spatial datasets (U.S. Geological Survey, 1999, 2001b, c) were available for these time periods. Wetland locations were mapped by using false-color infrared aerial photographs (appendix) to identify probable wetland areas, and those areas were subsequently verified by field inspection.

The USGS modular groundwater modeling program MODFLOW-2000 (Harbaugh and others, 2000) was used to simulate the potential effects of land-use change and aggregate mining on groundwater flow. The model was calibrated to land-use and hydrologic conditions representative of 1957, 1977, and 2000 to facilitate simulations concerning the effects of land-use change. Hydrologic data for 3 years before and after each calibration year were used as input to the model to better represent average hydrologic conditions in each time period. Simulations include (1) steady-state hydrologic effects of predicted land-use conditions in 2020 and 2040, (2) transient cumulative hydrologic effects of the potential extent of reclaimed aggregate pits (lined, unlined, and backfilled with fine sediments) in 2020 and 2040, (3) transient hydrologic effects of actively dewatered aggregate pits, and (4) effects of different pit spacings and configurations on groundwater levels.

Areas of simulated groundwater-level decline and rise were compared to wetland locations mapped by this study and to areas of riparian herbaceous vegetation mapped by the Colorado Division of Wildlife (2007a, b) to indicate areas where groundwater-supported wetlands or riparian herbaceous vegetation might be adversely affected by groundwater-level changes or conditions might be favorable for the formation of new wetlands. The South Platte River valley between the cities of Brighton and Fort Lupton was selected for study because it is experiencing substantial land-use changes as agricultural land is converted to urban and suburban areas and is undergoing rapid development of new aggregate mines.

Study Area Description

Physiography and Climate

The study area (fig. 1) is an 88-mi^2 region along an 11-mi reach of the South Platte River in northeastern Colorado, approximately 20 mi northeast of the city of Denver. The study area consists of river valley and alluvial terrace landforms with relief generally less than about 250 ft between the valley floor and adjacent upland areas (Robson, 1996; Robson and others, 2000). Land-surface altitude along the river valley ranges from about 4,870 ft at the northern boundary of the study area to about 4,980 ft at the southern boundary. The historically agricultural region also is part of the Wattenberg field, Colorado's second-largest and the Nation's eighth-largest gas field (Energy Information Administration, 2006) and part of the last major source of gravel aggregate in the

Denver metropolitan area (Lindsey and others, 1998). The South Platte River, its tributaries, and irrigation ditches dissect the agricultural landscape. There are two main municipalities in the study area. In the south is the city of Brighton, which straddles Adams and Weld Counties, and in the north is the city of Fort Lupton, in Weld County. Both Brighton and Fort Lupton are situated primarily along the east side of the South Platte River and along U.S. Highway 85. Between Brighton and Fort Lupton, on the west side of the South Platte River, is the small town of Wattenberg. Many farmsteads dot the landscape surrounding these municipalities. Both dry-land farming and irrigated agriculture are practiced in the study area. Irrigated agricultural land is supported by surface-water diversions from the South Platte River and by groundwater pumped from the alluvial aquifer. Flood irrigation is the most common method of irrigation used in the study area, but irrigation using center-pivot sprinklers also is common (Colorado Decision Support Systems, 2004). For the purposes of this report, the irrigation season is considered to be the period May through October. The region typifies a rural agricultural landscape transitioning to become a suburban extension of the greater Denver metropolitan area.

Temperature and precipitation data are available for two National Weather Service stations (Fort Lupton 2 SE and Brighton; fig. 2) in or near the study area (Western Regional Climate Center, 2007). Data from the Fort Lupton 2 SE station are available for the period 1948 to 1976. Data from the Brighton station are available for the period 1973 to the present (2007). Based on the period of record for the two stations, the mean July maximum temperature in the study area is 89.6°F, and the mean July minimum temperature is 56.3°F (Western Regional Climate Center, 2007). The mean January maximum temperature is 42.7°F, and the mean January minimum temperature is 13.2°F. Mean annual precipitation in the study area is 13.3 in. with about 67 percent of precipitation occurring during the irrigation season from May through October (Western Regional Climate Center, 2007).

Pan-evaporation data are available in the vicinity of the study area from two weather stations (Fort Collins and Wiggins 7 SW; fig. 2) (Western Regional Climate Center, 2007). Mean annual pan evaporation in the study area estimated on the basis of data from these two stations and the U.S. Department of Commerce (1968) is about 48 in., which greatly exceeds mean annual precipitation. About 82 percent of the pan evaporation occurs during the irrigation season from May through October.

Streams and Ditches

The primary surface-water feature in the study area is the South Platte River. Streamflow data collected by the U.S. Geological Survey (2006a) and the Colorado Division of Water Resources (2006a) indicate streamflow in the South Platte River varies throughout the year with highest flows generally in May and June resulting from snowmelt from the

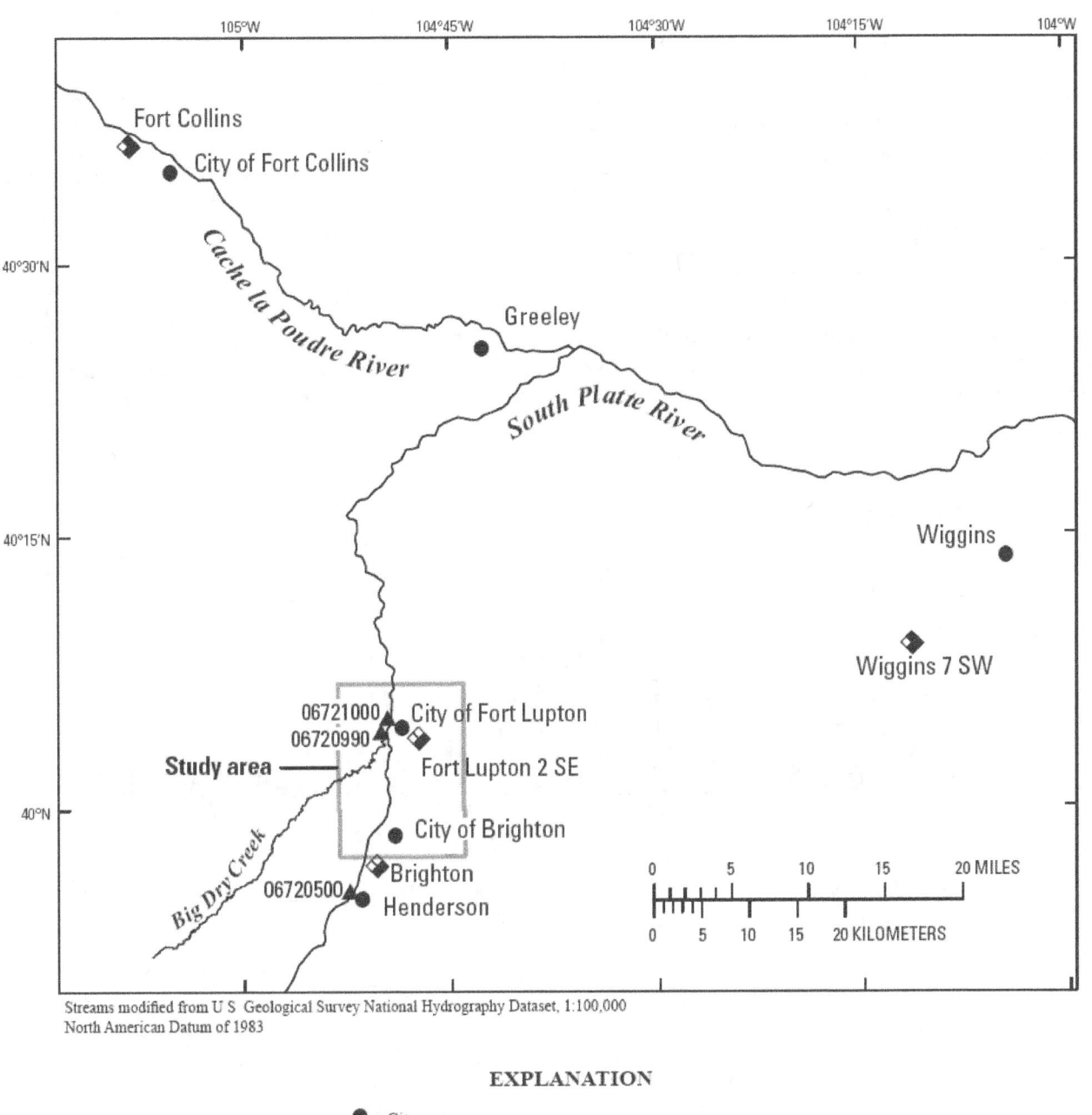

Streams modified from U S Geological Survey National Hydrography Dataset, 1:100,000
North American Datum of 1983

EXPLANATION

●   City or town

Fort Lupton 2 SE ◈   Weather station and station name–Precipitation and temperature

Wiggins 7 SW ◆   Weather station and station name–Precipitation, temperature, and evaporation

06721000 ▲   Stream gage and station number

Figure 2. Location of weather stations and stream gages used by the study.

nearby Rocky Mountains. Mean monthly streamflow in the South Platte River at Fort Lupton (station number 06721000) (fig. 3) ranges from about 63 to 106 million ft³/d (728–1,230 ft³/s) during May–June for the time periods (1954–1960, 1974–1980, and 1997–2003) analyzed by this study. After peak runoff, mean monthly streamflow generally decreases throughout the summer to a value ranging from about 11 to 33 million ft³/d (128–387 ft³/s). Mean monthly streamflow generally was greatest for the period 1997–2003 and least for the period 1954–1960. River stage based on mean monthly streamflow at Fort Lupton varies by less than 2 ft throughout the year for the time periods compared; however, river stage temporarily can increase as much as about 4 ft during periods of high runoff. Flow in the South Platte River through the

study area is regulated by upstream diversions and releases and is not representative of natural conditions.

Water is diverted from the South Platte River to irrigate crops in the study area primarily from about mid-April to mid-October (Colorado Division of Water Resources, 2006b; fig. 4). Brighton Ditch, Lupton Bottom Ditch, and Platteville Ditch divert water from the South Platte River in the study area; although no longer in use, McCanne Ditch (now occupied by Third Creek) historically diverted water from the South Platte River in the study area. Brantner Ditch and Fulton Ditch divert water from the South Platte River upstream from the study area but supply water to fields in the study area. During the periods 1954–1960, 1974–1980, and 1997–2003, the mean of total diversions by the Brighton, McCanne, Lupton Bottom, and Platteville Ditches was about

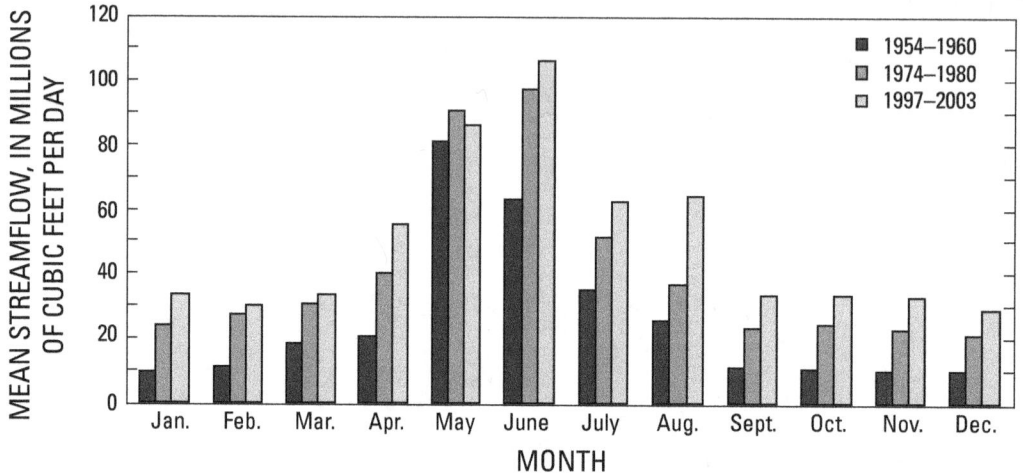

Figure 3.   Mean monthly streamflow of the South Platte River at Fort Lupton, Colorado (station 06721000), for the periods 1954–1960, 1974–1980, and 1997–2003.

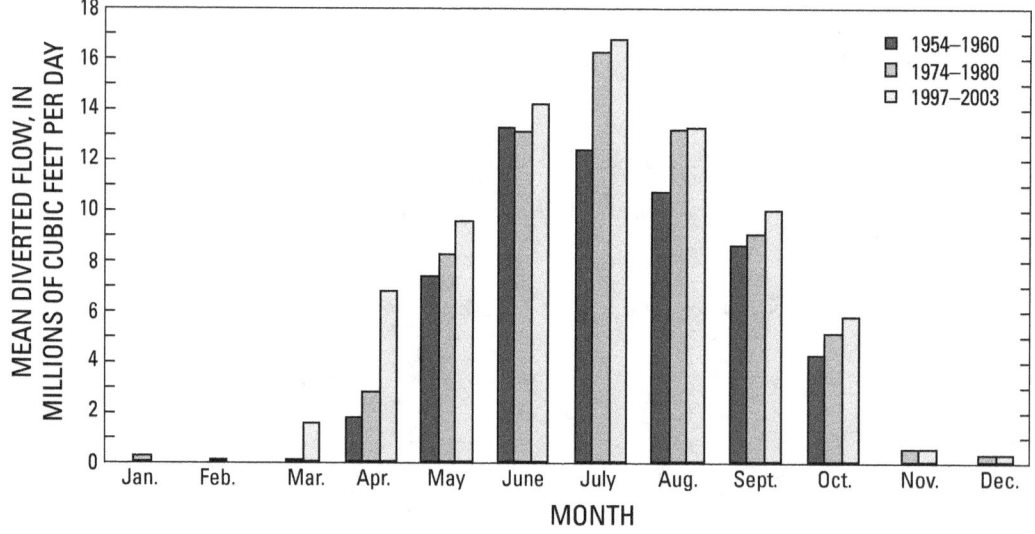

Figure 4.   Sum of mean monthly diversions from the South Platte River by Brighton, McCanne, Lupton Bottom, and Platteville Ditches for the periods 1954–1960, 1974–1980, and 1997–2003.

2.1 billion ft³ (48,600 acre-ft). These diversions were used to irrigate an average of about 16,500 acres (Colorado Division of Water Resources, 2006b), resulting in average water application of about 3 ft during the irrigation season. Ditches in the study area generally are unlined (Bob Stahl, Division 1 Water Commissioner, oral commun., 2004) and above the water table.

Tributaries to the South Platte River in the study area include Big Dry Creek, Little Dry Creek, and Third Creek (fig. 1). Big Dry Creek is the largest tributary in the study area with mean monthly flow ranging from about 2 to 5 million ft³/d (23–60 ft³/s) (U.S. Geological Survey, 2006a) near the creek's confluence with the South Platte River (station number 06720990). Little Dry Creek and Third Creek flow intermittently. Flow in Little Dry Creek is intercepted by Lupton Bottom Ditch before it reaches the South Platte River.

Aggregate Mining

Second only to crushed stone, more sand and gravel is produced in the United States than any other nonfuel mineral commodity in terms of volume and value. During 2005, about 1.4 billion tons of sand and gravel, with a value of $7.46 billion were produced by about 3,800 companies from more than 6,000 operations in 50 States (Bolen, 2005). In Colorado, about 46.6 million tons of sand and gravel (about 10 tons per capita) worth about $256 million were produced during 2005 (Bolen, 2005).

Most sand and gravel is used as construction aggregate and can be prepared from deposits containing a wide range of particle sizes. To be an economically valuable resource, the deposits need to be minable and accessible to nearby markets. The mining site needs to qualify for all necessary land-use and environmental permits, and the operation needs to meet or exceed all costs including acquisition, operation, compliance with regulations, and reclamation in order to be profitable. Permit applications and reclamation plans need to consider many factors including hydrology, geology, land use and zoning, air quality, cultural and scenic features, vegetation, and wildlife habitat (Knepper, 2002). Several years may be required to consider all factors before a permit is issued.

Site preparation for aggregate mining includes removing vegetation and stripping sufficient overburden to access the resource. Topsoil commonly is separated from the overburden and stockpiled for reclamation activities. Site preparation also includes construction of access roads, fences, berms, haul roads, drainage ditches, culverts, settlement ponds, processing and maintenance facilities, and other plant infrastructure (Langer and others, 2004). The life of an aggregate operation is variable. Mining plans on file with the Colorado Division of Mining Reclamation and Safety (CDMRS) indicate aggregate mining operations in the study area plan to operate from 6 to 29 years with an average life of about 14 years. During the life of the operation, aggregate within the permitted boundaries typically will be mined in phases lasting an average of about 3 years each.

Sand and gravel can be mined wet by dredging from water-filled pits, or groundwater can be removed from the pit so that the materials can be mined dry using conventional earth moving equipment. Some pits are dewatered by collecting groundwater in drains in the floor of the pit and pumping the water out of the pit (Langer and others, 2004; fig. 5A). This dewatering technique generally continues for the life of the pit and may be completed in phases for large pits as mining progresses. As the pit is dewatered, the water table in the vicinity of the pit is lowered, and drawdown resulting from the dewatering can affect nearby wetlands, wells, and streams. In some instances, slurry walls are used to isolate the pit from groundwater during dewatering (Knepper, 2002; fig. 5B). Once the slurry wall is in place, the pit can be dewatered without substantially affecting the surrounding aquifer. However, the slurry wall creates a barrier to groundwater flow that causes groundwater levels to rise on the upgradient side of the pit and decline on the downgradient side of the pit.

Following excavation, sand and gravel is processed to remove unwanted material. If the gravel has a diameter larger than about 1.5 in., it commonly is crushed and screened to create properly sized particles. Depending on the product, the gravel may be washed to remove fine particles, and waste fines typically are sent to a settling pond. Conveyors move the sorted sand and gravel to separate stockpiles awaiting sale (Langer and others, 2004).

Excavation area varies depending on distribution of the gravel, the amount of permitted land, and existing infrastructure, such as roads, buildings, and oil and gas transmission lines. Pits generally range in size from about 3 acres to more than 300 acres. Because of the start-up costs of permitting and operating sand and gravel operations, pits generally are larger than 10 acres. Based on mining plans for 58 existing or proposed pits on file with the CDMRS for the study area as of October 2006, 81 percent of pits are larger than 10 acres and 50 percent are larger than 25 acres (fig. 6). Mining phases for pits range from about 6 to 81 acres with an average phase size of about 34 acres. Pits in the study area typically are excavated down to the bedrock surface.

Following the excavation of available sand and gravel, pits in the study area may be left unlined and allowed to refill with water, backfilled with sediments, or lined or surrounded with a low-permeability barrier, such as a slurry wall or clay liner, to isolate the pit from the surrounding aquifer (fig. 6). Pits left open and allowed to refill with water can alter groundwater flow by creating large areas where sediments comprising the aquifer have been removed, and groundwater is exposed to evaporation. Pits backfilled with overburden sediments having hydraulic conductivity similar to the surrounding aquifer typically have little long-term effect on groundwater flow. Pits backfilled with fine sediments from aggregate processing can alter groundwater flow because of decreased hydraulic conductivity within the area of the backfilled pit. Pits lined or surrounded with a low-permeability barrier at the conclusion of mining can have the same effect on groundwater levels and flow as pits surrounded with slurry walls prior to dewatering

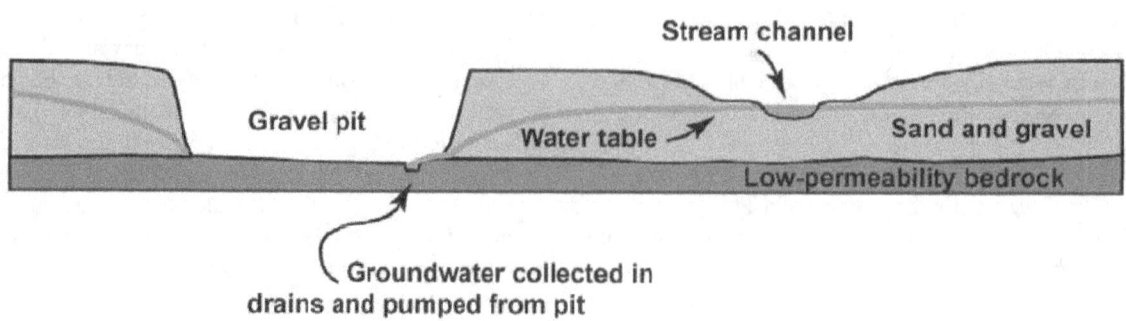

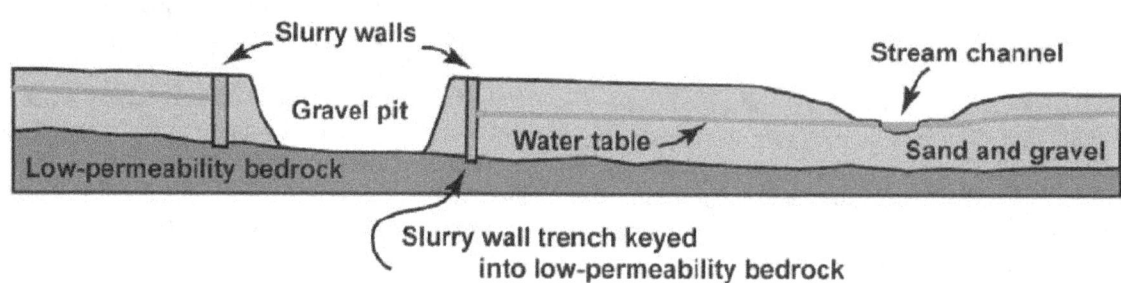

Figure 5.   Two methods of dry-mining aggregate below the water table: (*A*) Pit dewatered without a slurry wall; (*B*) Pit dewatered after installing a slurry wall.

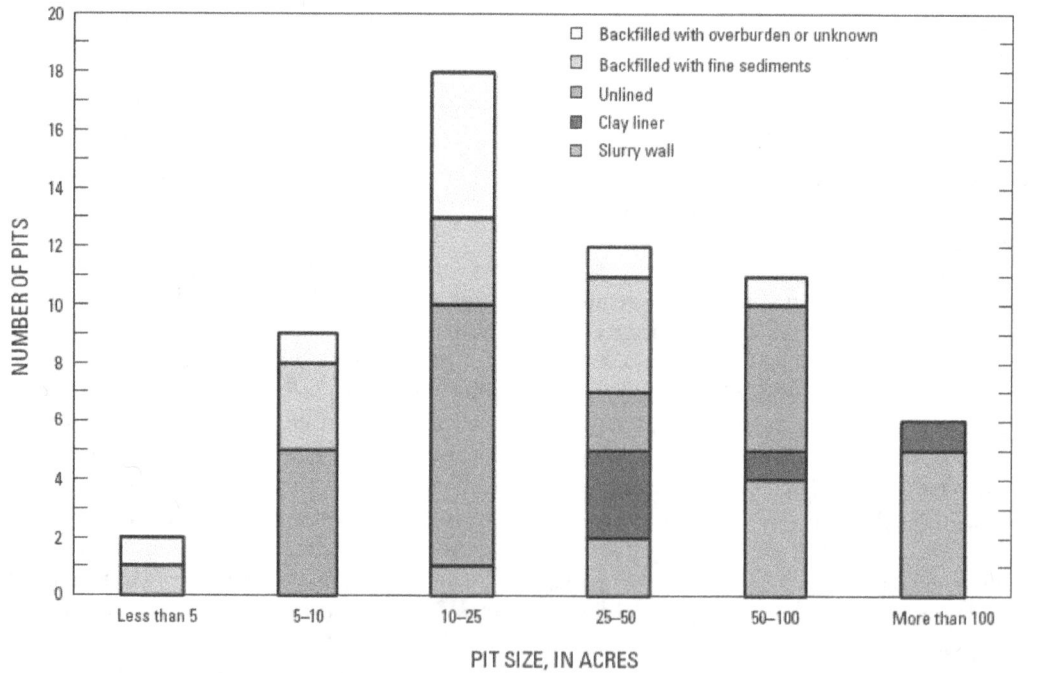

Figure 6.   Distribution of pit sizes and methods used to reclaim pits, Brighton to Fort Lupton, Colorado.

at the start of mining. After reclamation, former aggregate pits can be used for a variety of applications including residential or commercial property, recreation, natural areas such as wetlands, or water storage (Knepper, 2002). Reclamation plans on file with the CDMRS indicate that about 50 percent of backfilled pits in the Brighton-Fort Lupton area will be reclaimed as wetlands.

Wetlands

The term *wetlands* collectively includes all ecosystems that contain transitional zones between land and water, encompassing many different ecosystem types throughout the world (Verhoeven, 2003; Mitsch and Gosselink, 2000). A number of classification systems for wetlands have been developed for different purposes. One widely used classification system was prepared by the U.S. Fish and Wildlife Service (USFWS) and described in a report by Cowardin and others (1979). Five general wetland systems were identified and divided into 10 subsystems, 55 classes, and 121 subclasses, all of which are characterized by examples of dominant types of plants or animals. Another widely used classification system was developed to legally define wetlands in the United States in order to delineate areas that are under the jurisdiction of Section 404 of the Clean Water Act. The term *jurisdictional wetland* comes from that classification system. Various formal definitions of wetlands have been developed for scientific and management purposes over the years (Mitsch and Gosselink, 2000), but generally they all include the presence of standing water for some period during the growing season, hydric soils (with evidence of reducing conditions), and vegetation adapted to, or tolerant of, saturated conditions. Within the study area, small wetlands are common along the South Platte River, irrigation ditches, and around surface-water bodies. Larger wetlands occur in topographic depressions away from the river, particularly in abandoned oxbows formed by the South Platte River. Cottonwood trees and other riparian vegetation also commonly grow along the South Platte River and within abandoned oxbows.

In general, wetlands are among the most productive natural ecosystems on Earth (Hammer, 1991). Wetlands are valuable for the commercial products they provide, such as food, fiber, lumber, and energy resources, and for recreational endeavors, such as boating, hiking, hunting, fishing, and bird-watching. However, wetlands also provide food, shelter, nesting areas, breeding grounds, and stopovers for many types of resident and migratory forms of life, and they support a large diversity of plants, birds, microbes, invertebrates, amphibians, reptiles, fish, and mammals, many of which could not live anywhere else. In addition, wetlands are valuable because they are capable of flood mitigation, storm abatement, erosion control, aquifer recharge, and water-quality improvement (Louisiana Coastal Wetlands Conservation and Restoration Task Force, 2007). At an even larger and more complex scale, wetlands influence the global cycles of nitrogen, sulfur, methane, and carbon dioxide (Louisiana Coastal Wetlands Conservation and Restoration Task Force, 2007; Mitsch and Gosselink, 2000).

Specific vegetation thrives in wetlands because it has special adaptations to survive the anaerobic rooting environment and fluctuating groundwater levels that can flood emergent plant parts. Wetland plants have the unique ability to enhance oxygen transport below ground through aerenchyma (an airy root tissue), grow taller in deeper water through development of elongate leaf stalks, and even stimulate shallow and above-ground rooting in deep water so the roots can be in contact with oxygen-containing water higher in the water column (Cronk and Fennessy, 2001).

Although wetland plants have adapted to surviving in saturated soils, they are similar to terrestrial plants in that they cannot survive long without water. Length of survival time depends on the species, its general health, and on numerous environmental factors, such as temperature, humidity, soil type, and available nutrients. Plant species that can survive in saturated conditions for lengthy periods but can also tolerate drier soil conditions for part of their growing season are called facultative wetland plants (Reed, 1988).

Wetlands can be supported by surface water, groundwater, or both. If groundwater levels decline only slightly beneath groundwater-supported wetlands, effects such as plant death or a change in plant species composition might not occur for some time, depending on the water-holding capacity of the soil, the plant species present, and the weather. Even periodic rain events can substantially delay or mitigate the effects of slightly lower groundwater levels on upland facultative wetland plants. However, if groundwater levels decline substantially, such as below root depth, the effects can occur much faster. A large decline in groundwater levels for an extended period of time could lead to changes in plant species community composition, wildlife and fish use, and functions performed by the original wetland communities. Once the original plants show substantial signs of water stress, the wetland and all its associated functions likely will change permanently. On the other hand, if groundwater levels rise to near land surface, hydrologic conditions favorable to the formation of new wetlands could be created or the hydrology of existing wetlands could be altered. The ability of a wetland to adapt to changes in hydrologic conditions is affected by the timing and rate of the changes. Many wetland species can migrate with changing hydrologic conditions if the rate of change is slow.

Groundwater Hydrology

Geologic Setting

Three categories of alluvial landforms occur along the South Platte River based on age, relative elevation, and degree of dissection (fig. 7). From oldest (highest) to youngest (lowest), they are (1) dissected alluvial fans and terraces

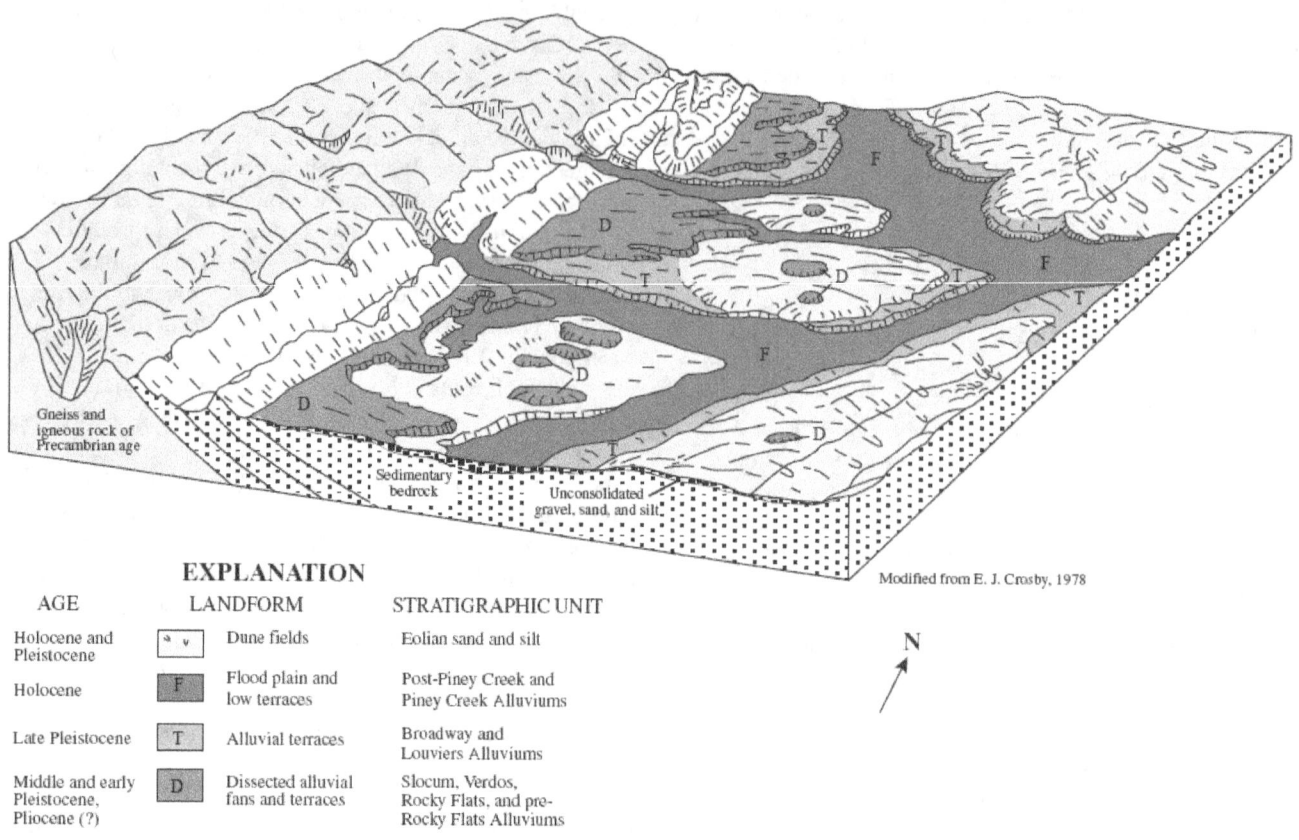

Modified from E. J. Crosby, 1978

EXPLANATION

AGE	LANDFORM		STRATIGRAPHIC UNIT
Holocene and Pleistocene		Dune fields	Eolian sand and silt
Holocene	F	Flood plain and low terraces	Post-Piney Creek and Piney Creek Alluviums
Late Pleistocene	T	Alluvial terraces	Broadway and Louviers Alluviums
Middle and early Pleistocene, Pliocene (?)	D	Dissected alluvial fans and terraces	Slocum, Verdos, Rocky Flats, and pre-Rocky Flats Alluviums

N

Figure 7. Landforms and stratigraphic units of the South Platte River valley and its tributaries.

located near the mountain front and on divides between major streams, (2) alluvial terraces located along the margins of major stream valleys, and (3) flood plains and low terraces that compose the modern South Platte River valley and the valleys of its tributaries (Lindsey and others, 2005). In the Brighton-Fort Lupton area, dissected alluvial fans and terraces commonly are composed of sediments of inferior quality for construction purposes and seldom are mined for aggregate. Furthermore, they generally are small, topographically high relative to modern streams, well-drained, and isolated from the South Platte alluvial aquifer and South Platte River. Therefore, these landforms are not included in the aquifer extent simulated in this study.

Sediments of the alluvial terrace (Broadway terrace) and low terrace associated with the modern flood plain (post-Piney Creek terrace) in the study area (fig. 8) generally constitute the South Platte alluvial aquifer and are included in simulations of groundwater flow by this study. The Broadway terrace forms a broad alluvial plain that extends along the eastern side of the South Platte River from Denver to downstream from Greeley (Lindsey and others, 2005). In the Brighton–Fort Lupton area, the Broadway terrace is about 20 ft above the flood plain of the South Platte River (fig. 8). Alluvial sediments of the Broadway terrace consist of laterally extensive layers of gravel, sand, silt, and clay, but clay layers thicker than about 2

ft generally are discontinuous. Gravel of the Broadway terrace is as much as 50 ft thick near Brighton (fig. 8, section L–L').

The flood plain and post-Piney Creek terrace occupy a narrow, modern valley, which is less than one-half the width of the valley defined by the Broadway terrace. Three gravel units have been identified within the post-Piney Creek terrace in the study area (Lindsey and others, 2005). The gravel units are, from bottom to top, a basal, yellowish-brown coarse gravel; a middle, yellowish-brown sandy gravel; and an upper, grayish-brown gravel. The basal gravel rests on the valley floor incised through the Broadway terrace and into the underlying bedrock. The upper gravel contains interbedded sand in places and locally contains cottonwood and willow logs. The three gravel units can be traced in borehole logs and gravel pits as far north as Fort Lupton, where all three are sandy (Lindsey and others, 1998).

Total thickness of unconsolidated sediments in the South Platte River valley between Brighton and Fort Lupton ranges from 0 ft in areas where bedrock crops out along valley margins to about 70 ft where the valley of Little Dry Creek joins the main valley of the South Platte River (Robson, 1996; Robson and others, 2000, sheet 1). Sediment thickness beneath the South Platte River generally is 20–40 ft, whereas sediment thickness between the South Platte River and the valley margins commonly is 40–60 ft (Robson, 1996; Robson and others, 2000, sheet 1).

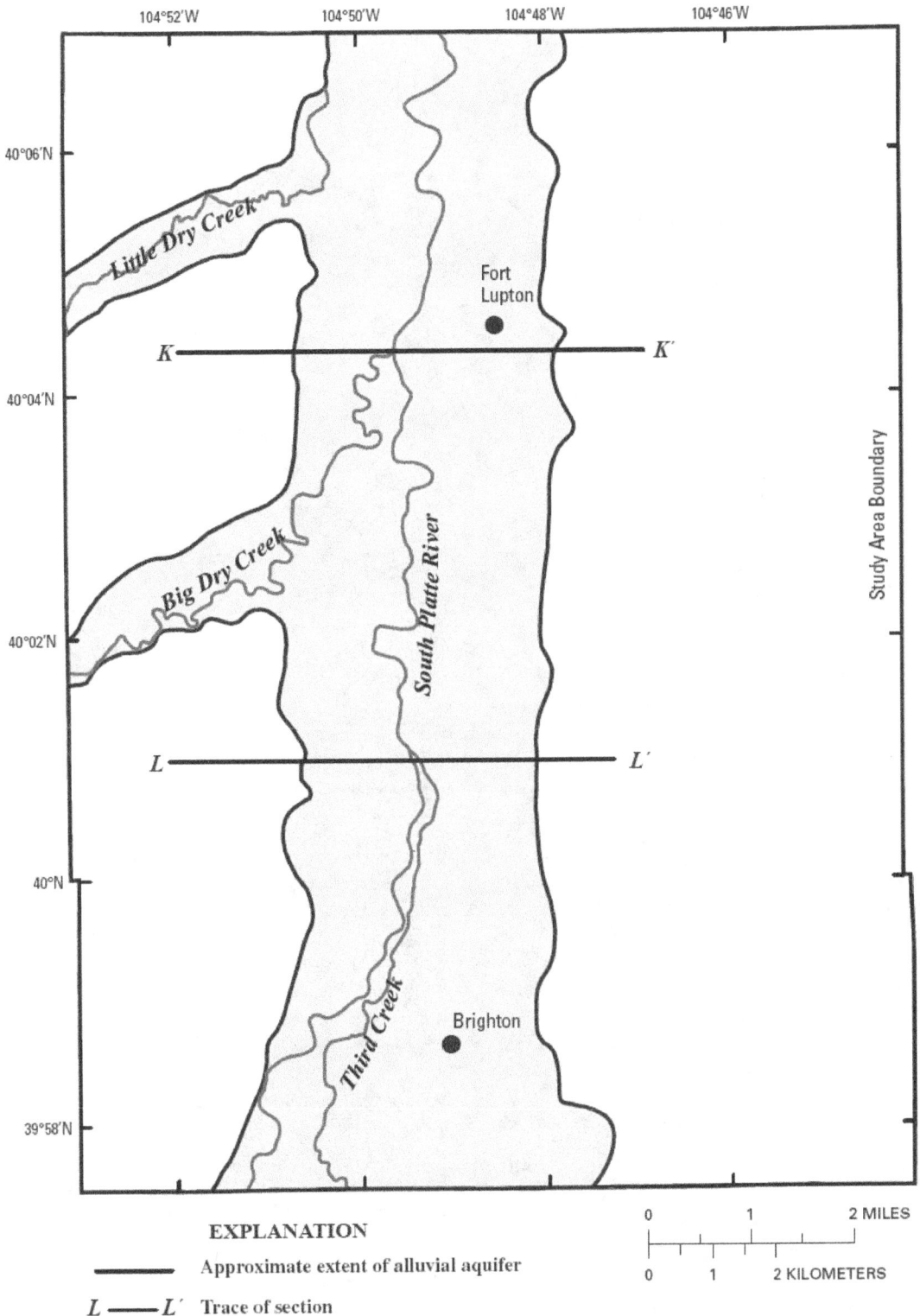

Figure 8. Geologic sections through alluvium of the South Platte River valley, Brighton to Fort Lupton, Colorado.

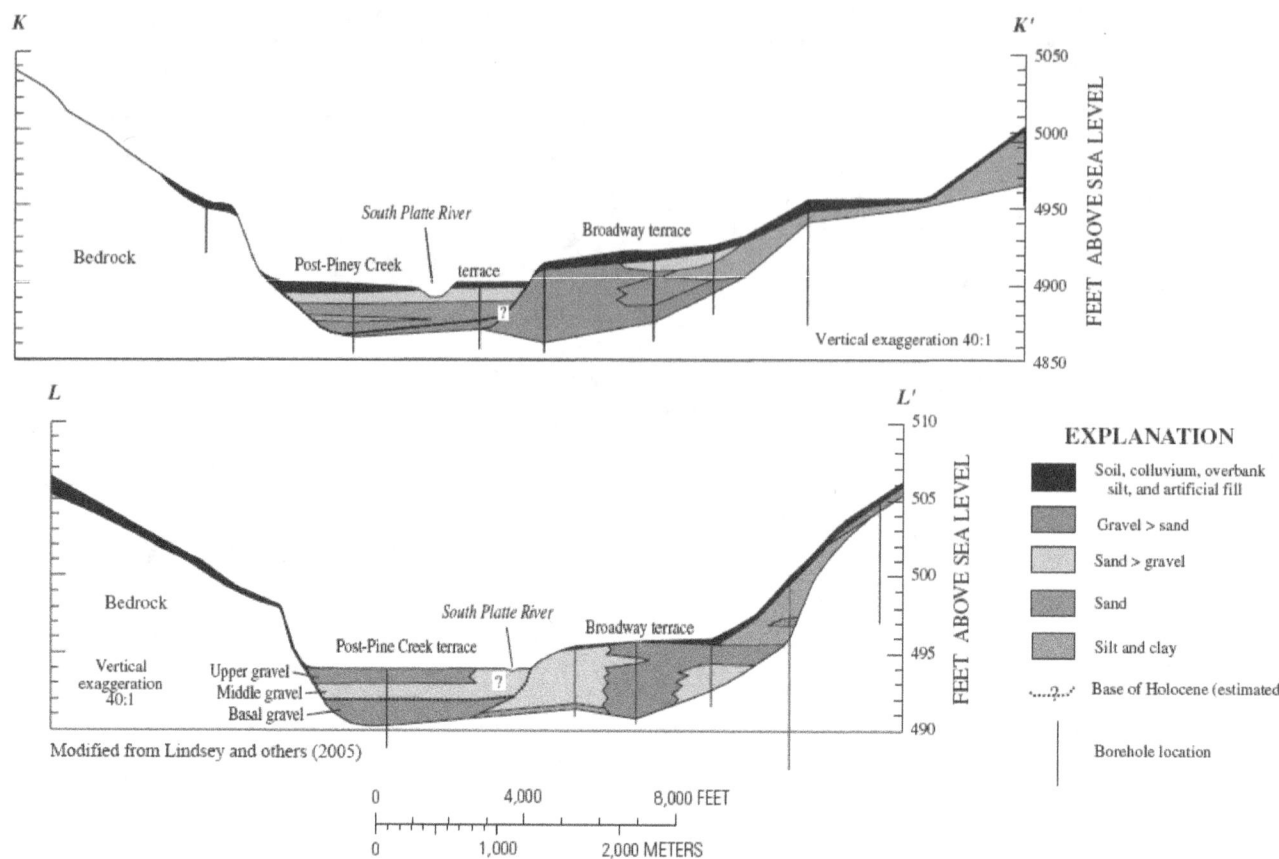

Figure 8.   Geologic sections through alluvium of the South Platte River valley, Brighton to Fort Lupton, Colorado.—Continued

Nearly all alluvium in the study area overlies bedrock of the Arapahoe Formation of Cretaceous age (Robson, 1983, sheet 1). The Arapahoe Formation consists of 400 to 700 ft of interbedded conglomerate, sandstone, siltstone, and shale. Lithologic logs of wells and test holes in the study area indicate that bedrock directly beneath alluvium of the South Platte River valley in the Brighton-Fort Lupton area generally is composed of dark blue-gray to black shale that provides a sharp contact between the bedrock and alluvium. Eolian (wind-blown) sand and silt, generally less than 3 ft thick, covers the alluvium in some places and much of the bedrock outside main stream valleys (Colton, 1978; Trimble and Machette, 1979).

Aquifer Characteristics

The South Platte alluvial aquifer ranges from about 2 mi wide near the northern end of the study area to about 4 mi wide near its southern end (Robson, 1996; Robson and others, 2000). The aquifer boundary is well-defined in most places by bedrock that crops out to form upland areas along both sides of the valley. Saturated thickness generally is 20–40 ft but commonly is 10–20 ft along valley margins and locally might be as much as 60 ft, particularly along a paleochannel on the

west side of the valley between Big and Little Dry Creeks (fig. 9). Depth to water generally is less than 20 ft in the study area and typically is less than 10 ft near the South Platte River; however, depth to water commonly is 20–40 ft along the eastern side of the valley (Robson, 1996; Robson and others, 2000, sheet 5). The South Platte alluvial aquifer generally is unconfined, but small areas of semi-confined conditions can exist where clay and sand layers are well stratified. Ground-water flow in the aquifer predominantly is down valley and toward the South Platte River and its tributaries (Robson, 1996; Robson and others, 2000, sheet 3) (fig. 9). The water-table gradient generally is 0.002–0.003 (10–15 ft/mi) down the South Platte River valley and averages about 0.005 (25 ft/mi) from the valley margins toward the river.

Groundwater Levels

The water table in the study area generally is highest in summer and early fall, likely as a result of increased aquifer recharge from infiltration of irrigation water applied to fields, seepage from unlined ditches, and greater precipitation. Groundwater levels generally decline throughout the non-irrigation season (November to April) and reach their lowest levels in the spring prior to the irrigation season. However, in

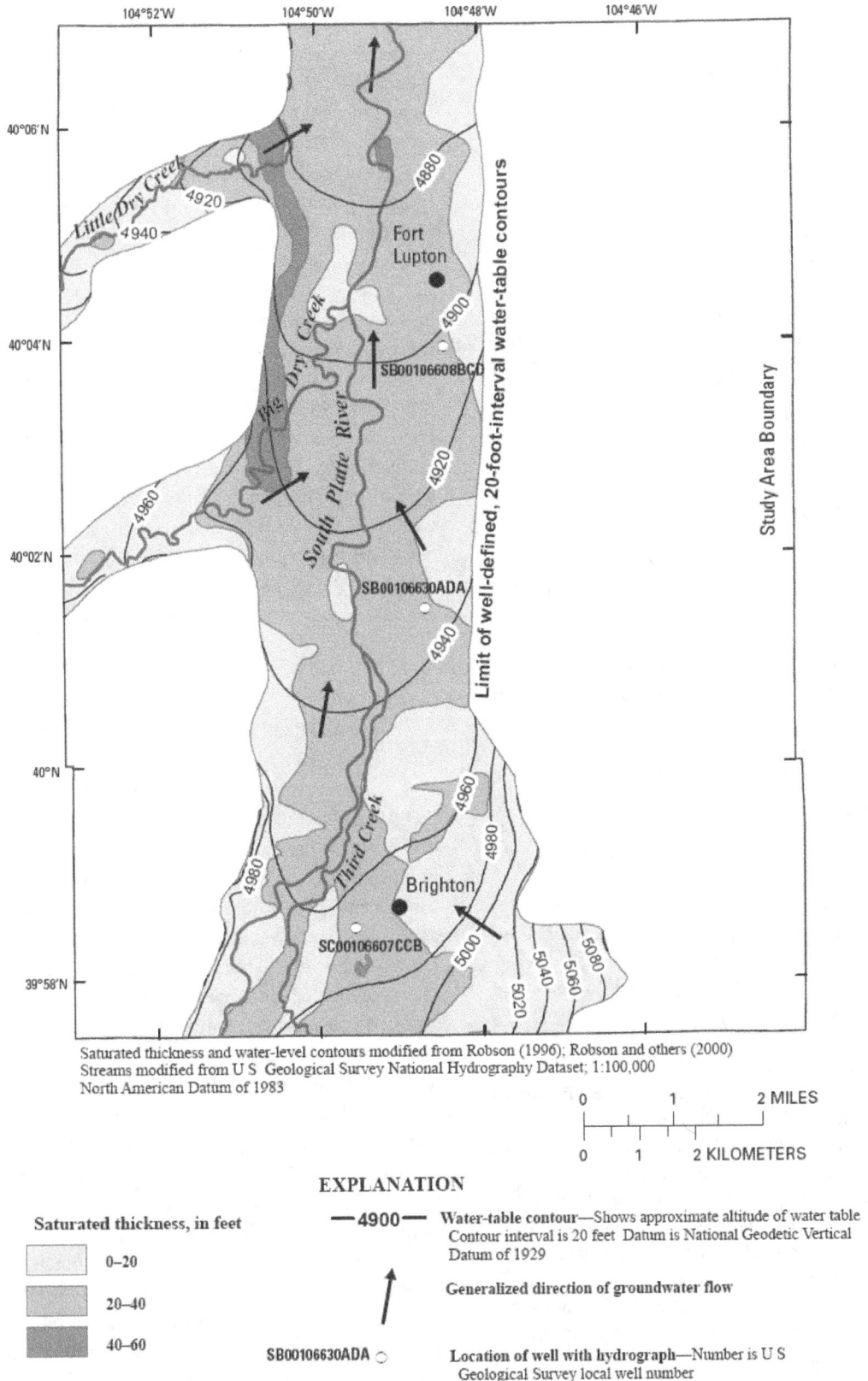

Figure 9. Saturated thickness and generalized water-table conditions of the South Platte alluvial aquifer, Brighton to Fort Lupton, Colorado.

localized areas of heavy well pumping, groundwater levels could be lower during the irrigation season than at other times of the year. The magnitude of seasonal groundwater-level fluctuations (fig. 10) varies by location and from year to year. Groundwater-level data (U.S. Geological Survey, 2006b; Michael Schaubs, Colorado Division of Water Resources, written commun., 2006) indicate groundwater-level fluctuations between the irrigation season and the non-irrigation season during 1954–2003 generally ranged from about 0 to 7 ft. Groundwater-level fluctuations near the South Platte River generally were less than near valley margins because of the stabilizing influence of the river. The magnitude of annual (year to year) groundwater-level fluctuations commonly was about one-half the magnitude of the groundwater-level fluctuation between the irrigation season and the non-irrigation season. Annual groundwater levels generally were stable or slightly declining during the periods of measurement at each location.

Hydraulic Properties

Transmissivity of the alluvial aquifer was estimated from aquifer-test results presented in published reports (Wilson, 1965; Smith and others, 1964) and from specific-capacity data reported by McConaghy and others (1964), Schneider (1962), and well-construction records on file with USGS and the Colorado Division of Water Resources. The method of Theis and others (1963, p. 331–341) was used to estimate aquifer transmissivity from specific-capacity data using a modified form of Theis's equation 1 as presented by Prudic (1991). The modified form of the equation is given as:

$$T = 15.32(Q/s)(-0.577 - \ln[r^2S/4Tt]) \qquad (1)$$

where

T is aquifer transmissivity, in feet squared per day,

Q/s is specific capacity of the pumped well, in gallons per minute per foot,

r is effective radius of the pumped well, in feet,

S is storage coefficient of the aquifer (dimensionless), and

t is elapsed pumping time, in days.

Given input values of Q/s, r, S and t, aquifer transmissivity (T) can be determined by providing an initial estimate of T in the right side of the equation and iteratively substituting calculated T from the left side of the equation back into the right side until the values for T on both sides of the equation are essentially the same. Because the South Platte alluvial aquifer generally is unconfined, specific yield was substituted for S in equation 1. The value of specific yield in equation 1 was estimated to be 0.25 from data provided by Johnson (1967), who reported specific yield values ranging from 0.12 to 0.35 with a mean value of about 0.25 for materials ranging from medium sand to coarse gravel. A diameter of 18 in. was assumed for wells without casing information, based on the most common well diameter reported on well-construction records. Because storage coefficient (S) and well radius (r) are

within the natural-log term of equation 1, calculated transmissivity is relatively insensitive to errors in estimates of S and r. Transmissivities calculated by using specific capacity of wells with small pumping rates typically were found by this study to be an order of magnitude less than those with large pumping rates. Therefore, only wells with pumping rates greater than 100 gal/min (similar to aquifer-test conditions) were used to estimate transmissivity from specific capacity.

Comparison of transmissivities calculated using equation 1 to transmissivities determined by aquifer tests indicates that transmissivities based on specific capacity generally are less than those from aquifer tests. To improve the accuracy of transmissivity estimates based on specific capacity, transmissivity values from aquifer-test results provided by Wilson (1965) and Smith and others (1964) for 27 wells in the South Platte alluvial aquifer between Denver and Greeley were regressed (fig. 11) against transmissivity estimates based on specific capacity, and the resulting linear regression equation was used to adjust the transmissivity estimates. The regression has a correlation coefficient of 0.89 and a coefficient of determination (R^2) of 0.80. The equation used to adjust transmissivities calculated from specific capacity data is:

$$T_{adj} = 1.2\,T_{sc} + 7{,}755 \qquad (2)$$

where

T_{adj} is the final, adjusted transmissivity value, in feet squared per day, and

T_{sc} is transmissivity estimated from specific capacity, in feet squared per day.

Because the regression line of the equation does not intercept the graph origin, the regression equation is not valid for transmissivity values substantially less than the smallest transmissivity value determined from specific capacity. Only wells with construction similar to those used to develop the regression equation were used in the estimation of final, adjusted transmissivity values (table 1).

Hydraulic conductivity was estimated by dividing calculated transmissivity by the length of the perforated interval at each well location (table 1). The hydraulic-conductivity distribution and location of wells used to estimate hydraulic conductivity are shown in figure 12. Estimated hydraulic conductivity ranges from 390 ft/d at one location near the margin of the aquifer to 2,100 ft/d in a small area near the center of the aquifer south of Brighton. Most estimated hydraulic-conductivity values range from about 600 to 1,400 ft/d with the greatest values generally along the central part of the valley. Aquifer tests conducted in the Arapahoe bedrock aquifer underlying the study area indicate hydraulic conductivity values ranging from 0.3 to 1.5 ft/d (Robson, 1983), which is 2 to 3 orders of magnitude less than the hydraulic conductivity of the alluvial aquifer.

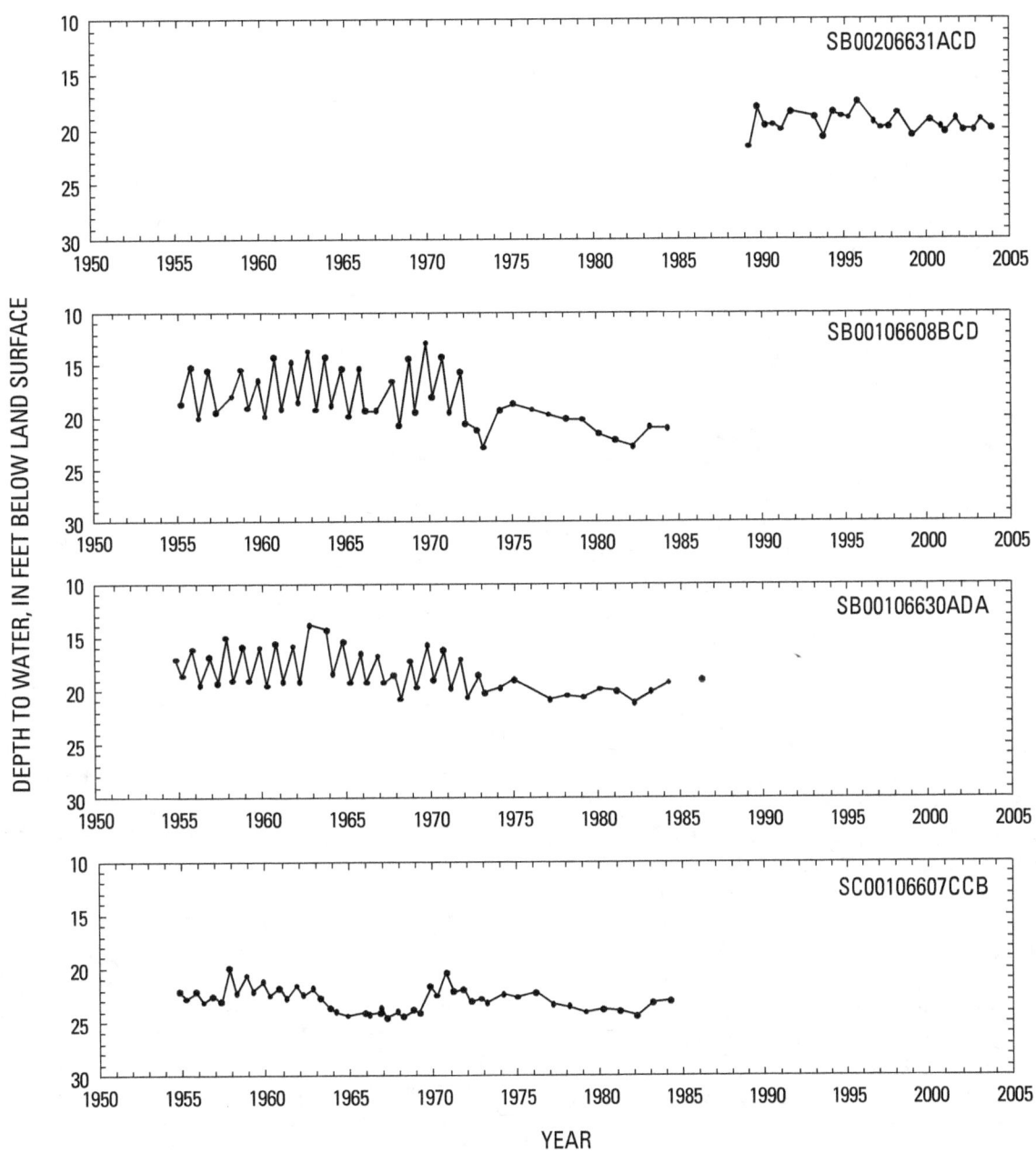

Figure 10.   Groundwater-level fluctuations in four wells completed in the South Platte alluvial aquifer, Brighton to Fort Lupton, Colorado, 1954–2003. (The 13-digit well identifier is the U.S. Geological Survey site name or the Colorado Division of Water Resources location number.)

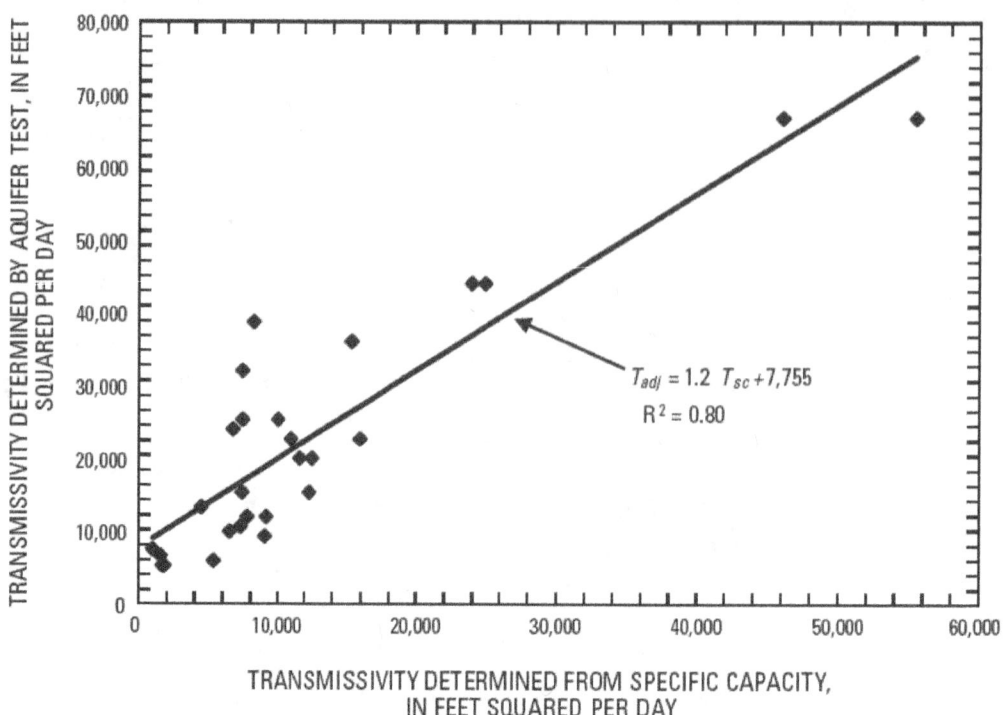

Figure 11. Relation of transmissivity determined by aquifer tests to transmissivity determined from specific capacity for 27 wells in the South Platte alluvial aquifer between Denver and Greeley, Colorado.

Aquifer Inflows

Inflows to the South Platte alluvial aquifer in the study area are primarily from infiltration of precipitation and water applied to irrigated agricultural fields, seepage from irrigation ditches, and subsurface inflow from the upgradient end of the aquifer and tributary valleys. Depending on the hydraulic gradient between the alluvial aquifer and the underlying Arapahoe bedrock aquifer, the South Platte alluvial aquifer also could receive groundwater inflow from the Arapahoe aquifer, but because the hydraulic conductivity of the Arapahoe aquifer is much less than that of the alluvial aquifer, inflow from the Arapahoe aquifer likely is a small component of the total water budget for the alluvial aquifer.

Recharge

Recharge from infiltration at the land surface varies spatially and temporally and depends on many factors, such as the amount, rate, and timing of precipitation and applied water; evapotranspiration; surface cover (including vegetation); soil type; geology; and slope of the land surface. For the purposes of this study, recharge in the Brighton–Fort Lupton area was distributed by land use (native and non-irrigated land, irrigated agricultural land, and urban areas) because land use generally considers differences in applied water, evapotranspiration,

and surface cover. Precipitation, soils, geology, and slope are considered to be substantially uniform with respect to recharge within the extent of the South Platte alluvial aquifer in the study area and are not used as discriminating factors for recharge.

Recharge beneath native and non-irrigated land. Recharge from infiltration of precipitation beneath native grasslands and shrublands in arid and semiarid regions, where evaporation exceeds precipitation most days of the year, typically is small (Scanlon and others, 2005). A synthesis of 26 recharge studies by Scanlon and others (2006) indicates mean annual recharge beneath predominantly natural ecosystems in semiarid and arid regions ranges from about 0.008 to 1.4 in., which represents 0.1–5 percent of precipitation. When native vegetation is converted to dry-land (non-irrigated) agriculture, recharge can increase because tilled and fallow fields may allow more infiltration, or it can decrease because crops with deeper roots might more efficiently capture water infiltrating down through the soil. Recharge estimates for native grassland converted to dry-land agriculture computed using a deep-percolation model indicated little change for semi-arid conditions similar to those in the study area (Bauer and Vaccaro, 1990). Based on those results, recharge for native land and non-irrigated land was considered to be equal for the purpose of this study.

Because topography in the study area generally is gently sloping and sediments of the South Platte alluvial aquifer are

Table 1. Aquifer transmissivity and hydraulic conductivity estimated from aquifer tests and specific capacity of wells completed in the South Platte alluvial aquifer, Brighton to Fort Lupton, Colorado.

[CDWR, Colorado Division of Water Resources; USGS, U.S. Geological Survey; (gal/min)/ft, gallons per minute per foot; ft, feet; ft/d, feet per day; ft²/d, feet squared per day]

Well identifier[1]	Specific capacity [(gal/min)/ft]	Transmissivity value estimated from specific capacity (ft²/d)	Transmissivity value from aquifer test (ft²/d)	Adjusted transmissivity value from linear regression (ft²/d)	Saturated thickness[2] (ft)	Estimated hydraulic conductivity (ft/d)	Source
15273RF	32	4,100		12,600	33	390	CDWR
SC00106701CCA1	17	2,200		10,400	22	470	USGS
20026RF	53	7,200		16,400	34	480	CDWR
B1-66-8bcd	37		10,000		18	560	Wilson (1965)
SB00206736ACC1	31	3,300		11,700	12	600	USGS
B1-66-18ddc	70		20,100		33	610	Wilson (1965)
B1-66-31ada	49	3,200		11,600	19	610	Schneider (1962)
C1-66-6abb	58		9,400		15	630	Wilson (1965)
13409F	15	2,200		10,400	16	650	CDWR
B1-66-19bbc	57		10,700		16	670	Wilson (1965)
B1-67-12acc	76	8,500		17,900	27	680	Schneider (1962)
962RF	33	5,000		13,800	20	690	CDWR
B1-66-30dad	49		15,400		22	700	Wilson (1965)
24152F	37	5,700		14,500	20	730	CDWR
B1-67-13bdd	69		22,700		30	760	Wilson (1965)
11749RF	45	5,200		14,000	17	820	CDWR
6818R	52	8,200		17,500	20	880	CDWR
C1-66-18bbd	116	10,200		19,900	22	910	Schneider (1962)
SC00106605BBB1	53	5,000		13,800	15	920	USGS
13413F	28	3,200		11,600	12	970	CDWR
7110RF	45	7,000		16,100	16	1,010	CDWR
11082F	53	6,100		15,100	15	1,010	CDWR
B1-66-18ddd	49		24,100		23	1,050	Smith and others (1964)
11383R	56	8,600		18,100	17	1,060	CDWR
B1-67-25acc	63	4,500		13,100	12	1,100	Schneider (1962)
11083RF	41	4,700		13,300	12	1,110	CDWR
C1-67-13dcc	58	4,600		13,300	12	1,110	Schneider (1962)
6588R	39	6,600		15,700	14	1,120	CDWR
B1-66-8bdc			20,100		17	1,180	Wilson (1965)
19805F	38	5,800		14,700	12	1,220	CDWR
B1-67-36cdd2	60	5,700		14,600	12	1,220	Schneider (1962)
SB00106607ACD1	60	8,300		17,700	14	1,270	USGS
SC00106617CBD2	25	4,300		12,800	10	1,280	USGS

Table 1.   Aquifer transmissivity and hydraulic conductivity estimated from aquifer tests and specific capacity of wells completed in the South Platte alluvial aquifer, Brighton to Fort Lupton, Colorado.—Continued

[CDWR, Colorado Division of Water Resources; USGS, U.S. Geological Survey; (gal/min)/ft, gallons per minute per foot; ft, feet; ft/d, feet per day; ft²/d, feet squared per day]

Well identifier[1]	Specific capacity [(gal/min)/ft]	Transmissivity value estimated from specific capacity (ft²/d)	Transmissivity value from aquifer test (ft²/d)	Adjusted transmissivity value from linear regression (ft²/d)	Saturated thickness[2] (ft)	Estimated hydraulic conductivity (ft/d)	Source
C1-66-7dacd	42	8,000		17,400	13	1,290	McConaghy and others (1964)
C1-67-12ccdb	92	10,900		20,800	15	1,390	McConaghy and others (1964)
20138R	89	14,300		24,900	13	1,910	CDWR
C1-66-7dbb	294		66,800		34	2,010	Smith and others (1964)
C1-67-13aac	55	4,100		12,600	6	2,100	Schneider (1962)

[1]Identifier for USGS wells and Smith and others (1964) is local well number. Identifier for CDWR wells is well permit number. Identifier for McConaghy and others (1964), Schneider (1962), and Wilson (1965) is location number.

[2]Saturated thickness estimated as saturated thickness within perforated interval of well.

moderately to highly permeable, mean annual recharge from infiltration of precipitation likely is near the upper end of the range indicated by Scanlon and others (2006). Based on long-term mean annual precipitation of 13.3 in., mean annual recharge beneath native and non-irrigated areas in the study area is estimated to be 0.3–0.7 in. (about 2–5 percent of precipitation), or about 0.5 in.

Recharge beneath irrigated agricultural land. Recharge beneath irrigated agricultural land in the study area includes infiltration of precipitation, infiltration of water applied to irrigated fields, and seepage losses from irrigation ditches. Net recharge beneath irrigated agricultural land was estimated by using the water-table-fluctuation method (WTF) described by Healy and Cook (2002). The WTF method is based on the premise that rises in groundwater levels in unconfined aquifers are caused by recharge water arriving at the water table and that no other sources or sinks affect groundwater levels during the recharge event. Recharge is calculated as:

$$R = S_y \, (dh/dt) \tag{3}$$

where

R is aquifer recharge, in length per time,
S_y is specific yield (dimensionless), and
dh/dt is the change in water-table hydraulic head over time, in length per time.

Typically, the WTF method is applied over short time periods to estimate recharge that occurs from individual recharge events. However, the method also can be used to provide an estimate of seasonal or annual net recharge to an aquifer. Seasonal groundwater-level changes in 18 wells

located on irrigated agricultural land were used to estimate net recharge during the irrigation season in the study area (table 2). Groundwater-level rises during the irrigation season measured during various years from 1955 through 1991 ranged from 0 to about 9 ft with a mean of about 3 ft. Because recharge from infiltration of precipitation is estimated to be small, groundwater-level rises beneath irrigated land during the irrigation season are assumed to be primarily caused by infiltration of irrigation water applied to agricultural fields and seepage from irrigation ditches. However, seasonal net recharge estimated by using the WTF method also includes any other sources of recharge active in areas of irrigated agriculture during the irrigation season, such as from farm septic systems. Similarly, seasonal net recharge estimated by using the WTF method includes losses to the aquifer, such as from well pumping. Because the South Platte alluvial aquifer in the study area has high hydraulic conductivity, the water table recovers rapidly from the local effects of well pumping, and groundwater-level measurements made before and after the irrigation season (when pumping is inactive) likely do not reflect the localized effects of drawdown resulting from pumping. Therefore, groundwater-level rises observed in the study area are assumed to be representative of seasonal water-table fluctuations in the aquifer and not representative of localized groundwater-level recovery after seasonal pumping ceases. Using an assumed specific-yield value of 0.25 (based on the mean value for medium sand to coarse gravel sediments reported by Johnson, 1967), mean net recharge beneath irrigated land in the study area during the irrigation season is estimated to be 8.0 in. with a standard deviation of 5.1 in. (table 2). Compared to an average surface-water application

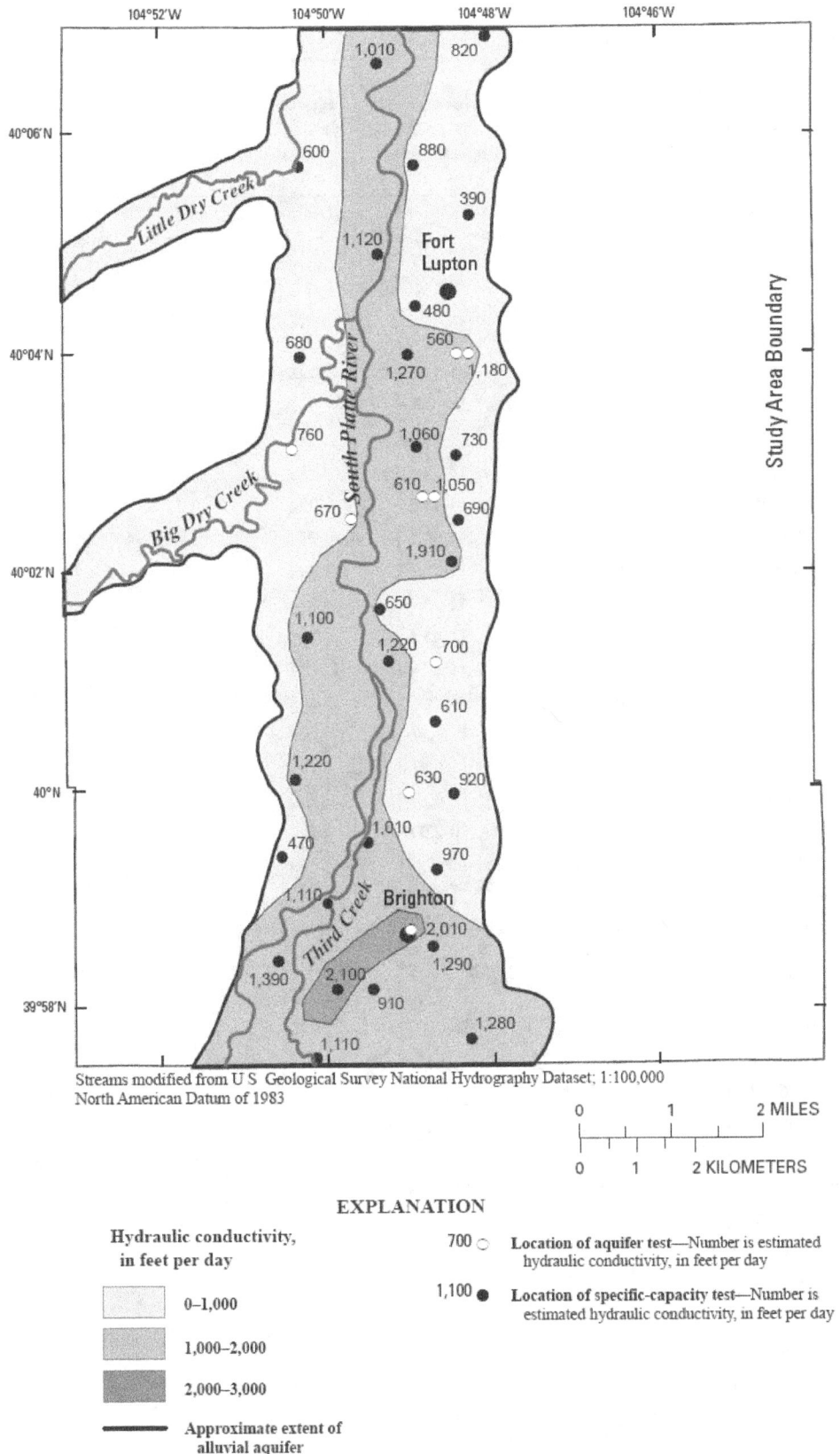

Figure 12. Hydraulic-conductivity distribution and location of wells used to estimate hydraulic conductivity of the South Platte alluvial aquifer, Brighton to Fort Lupton, Colorado.

Table 2. Seasonal groundwater-level rises and estimated recharge from applied irrigation water, Brighton to Fort Lupton, Colorado.

Well identifier[1]	Date of first water-level measurement	Date of second water-level measurement	Elapsed time (days)	Groundwater-level rise[2] (feet)	Estimated recharge[3] (inches)
SB00106608BAD2	03/20/67	11/01/67	226	4.56	13.7
SB00106608BAD2	03/18/68	11/04/68	231	7.18	21.5
SB00106608BAD2	03/11/69	11/03/69	237	8.81	26.4
SB00106608BAD2	03/16/70	10/23/70	221	4.69	14.1
SB00106608BAD2	03/23/71	11/02/71	224	5.05	15.2
SB00106608BAD2	03/23/72	11/24/72	246	5.29	15.9
SB00106608BCD	04/04/55	11/08/55	218	3.54	10.6
SB00106608BCD	04/17/56	11/13/56	210	4.58	13.7
SB00106608BCD	04/15/58	11/13/58	212	2.56	7.7
SB00106608BCD	04/01/59	11/11/59	224	2.72	8.2
SB00106608BCD	04/05/60	11/02/60	211	5.67	17.0
SB00106608BCD	03/31/61	11/08/61	222	4.47	13.4
SB00106608BCD	03/26/62	11/05/62	224	4.87	14.6
SB00106608BCD	04/12/63	11/05/63	207	5.03	15.1
SB00106608BCD	03/18/64	11/10/64	237	3.43	10.3
SB00106608BCD	04/12/65	11/26/65	228	4.50	13.5
SB00106608BCD	03/16/66	11/17/66	246	0	0
SB00106608BCD	03/18/68	11/04/68	231	6.47	19.4
SB00106608BCD	03/11/69	11/03/69	237	6.65	20.0
SB00106608BCD	03/16/70	10/23/70	221	3.82	11.5
SB00106608BCD	03/23/71	11/02/71	224	3.83	11.5
SB00106608BCD	03/23/72	11/24/72	246	0	0
SB00106608CCD	03/20/67	11/01/67	226	4.31	12.9
SB00106608CCD	03/18/68	11/04/68	231	5.32	16.0
SB00106608CCD	03/11/69	11/03/69	237	3.35	10.1
SB00106608CCD	03/16/70	10/23/70	221	3.35	10.1
SB00106608CCD	03/23/71	11/02/71	224	2.15	6.5
SB00106608CCD	03/23/72	11/24/72	246	3.08	9.2
SB00106617CCD2	03/20/67	11/01/67	226	2.92	8.8
SB00106617CCD2	03/18/68	11/04/68	231	4.26	12.8
SB00106617CCD2	03/11/69	11/03/69	237	2.94	8.8
SB00106617CCD2	03/16/70	10/23/70	221	3.47	10.4
SB00106617CCD2	03/23/71	11/02/71	224	1.19	3.6
SB00106620CBD	03/20/67	11/01/67	226	4.24	12.7
SB00106620CBD	03/18/68	11/05/68	232	3.96	11.9
SB00106620CBD	03/11/69	11/03/69	237	4.16	12.5
SB00106620CBD	03/16/70	10/23/70	221	2.87	8.6
SB00106620CBD	03/23/71	11/09/71	231	2.53	7.6
SB00106620CBD	03/23/72	11/24/72	246	2.99	9.0
SB00106630ACA	03/27/89	10/30/89	217	0.85	2.5
SB00106630ACA	03/20/90	11/12/90	237	4.70	14.1

Table 2. Seasonal groundwater-level rises and estimated recharge from applied irrigation water, Brighton to Fort Lupton, Colorado.—Continued

Well identifier[1]	Date of first water-level measurement	Date of second water-level measurement	Elapsed time (days)	Groundwater-level rise[2] (feet)	Estimated recharge[3] (inches)
SB00106630ACA	03/13/91	12/17/91	279	2.25	6.8
SB00106630ADA	04/05/55	11/08/55	217	2.48	7.4
SB00106630ADA	04/17/56	11/13/56	210	2.62	7.9
SB00106630ADA	05/07/57	11/12/57	189	4.25	12.8
SB00106630ADA	04/07/58	11/13/58	220	3.24	9.7
SB00106630ADA	04/01/59	11/11/59	224	3.12	9.4
SB00106630ADA	04/12/60	11/02/60	204	3.98	11.9
SB00106630ADA	03/31/61	11/08/61	222	3.28	9.8
SB00106630ADA	03/26/62	11/05/62	224	5.38	16.1
SB00106630ADA	03/18/64	11/10/64	237	3.00	9.0
SB00106630ADA	04/12/65	11/26/65	228	2.73	8.2
SB00106630ADA	03/16/66	11/18/66	247	2.49	7.5
SB00106630ADA	03/22/67	11/01/67	224	0.77	2.3
SB00106630ADA	03/18/68	11/05/68	232	3.61	10.8
SB00106630ADA	03/11/69	11/03/69	237	3.92	11.8
SB00106630ADA	03/16/70	10/23/70	221	2.76	8.3
SB00106630ADA	03/23/71	11/02/71	224	2.75	8.3
SB00106630ADA	03/23/72	11/24/72	246	2.08	6.2
SB00106632CDC	03/20/67	10/31/67	225	3.69	11.1
SB00106632CDC	03/18/68	11/04/68	231	4.08	12.2
SB00106632CDC	03/11/69	11/03/69	237	5.71	17.1
SB00106632CDC	03/16/70	10/23/70	221	4.89	14.7
SB00106632CDC	03/22/71	11/02/71	225	2.52	7.6
SB00106632CDC	03/23/72	11/24/72	246	2.39	7.2
SB00106701BDC	04/15/68	10/14/68	182	0.39	1.2
SB00106701BDC	03/10/69	11/04/69	239	2.01	6.0
SB00106701BDC	03/17/70	10/23/70	220	0.88	2.6
SB00106701BDC	03/22/71	11/04/71	227	1.08	3.2
SB00106701BDC	03/23/72	11/19/72	241	1.32	4.0
SB00106712ACC	03/20/67	10/31/67	225	1.92	5.8
SB00106712ACC	03/18/68	11/04/68	231	1.98	5.9
SB00106712ACC	03/10/69	11/04/69	239	2.66	8.0
SB00106712ACC	03/17/70	10/23/70	220	1.58	4.7
SB00106712ACC	03/22/71	11/04/71	227	2.02	6.1
SB00106712ACC	03/23/72	11/19/72	241	1.16	3.5
SB00106713BDD	03/20/67	10/31/67	225	1.97	5.9
SB00106713BDD	03/18/68	11/04/68	231	2.07	6.2
SB00106713BDD	03/17/70	10/23/70	220	1.23	3.7
SB00106713BDD	03/22/71	11/04/71	227	1.38	4.1
SB00206629ABC2	03/20/67	11/01/67	226	3.45	10.4
SB00206629ABC2	03/19/68	11/05/68	231	3.19	9.6
SB00206629ABC2	03/11/69	11/04/69	238	5.13	15.4

Table 2. Seasonal groundwater-level rises and estimated recharge from applied irrigation water, Brighton to Fort Lupton, Colorado.—Continued

Well identifier[1]	Date of first water-level measurement	Date of second water-level measurement	Elapsed time (days)	Groundwater-level rise[2] (feet)	Estimated recharge[3] (inches)
SB00206629ABC2	03/17/70	10/23/70	220	2.79	8.4
SB00206629ABC2	03/23/71	11/06/71	228	2.12	6.4
SB00206629ABC2	03/21/72	11/21/72	245	1.02	3.1
SB00206629CCD	04/04/55	11/08/55	218	1.49	4.5
SB00206629CCD	04/17/56	11/13/56	210	0.94	2.8
SB00206629CCD	05/06/57	11/12/57	190	3.90	11.7
SB00206629CCD	04/02/58	11/12/58	224	2.24	6.7
SB00206629CCD	04/01/59	11/11/59	224	1.21	3.6
SB00206629CCD	04/05/60	11/02/60	211	2.14	6.4
SB00206629CCD	03/31/61	11/08/61	222	2.44	7.3
SB00206629CCD	03/26/62	11/05/62	224	1.96	5.9
SB00206629CCD	04/12/63	11/05/63	207	0.93	2.8
SB00206629CCD	03/18/64	11/10/64	237	1.67	5.0
SB00206629CCD	04/12/65	11/21/65	223	1.99	6.0
SB00206629CCD	03/16/66	11/18/66	247	0.04	0.1
SB00206629CCD	03/22/67	11/01/67	224	1.19	3.6
SB00206629CCD	03/19/68	11/05/68	231	0.80	2.4
SB00206629CCD	03/11/69	11/04/69	238	3.01	9.0
SB00206629CCD	03/17/70	10/23/70	220	1.96	5.9
SB00206629CCD	03/23/71	11/06/71	228	0.35	1.1
SB00206629CCD	03/23/72	11/21/72	243	0.56	1.7
SB00206630ADD	03/20/67	11/01/67	226	0.47	1.4
SB00206630ADD	03/19/68	11/05/68	231	0.70	2.1
SB00206630ADD	03/11/69	11/04/69	238	2.42	7.3
SB00206630ADD	03/17/70	10/23/70	220	1.10	3.3
SB00206630ADD	03/23/71	11/06/71	228	0	0
SB00206630ADD	03/23/72	11/11/72	233	4.35	13.1
SB00206631BDA	03/20/67	11/01/67	226	0	0
SB00206631BDA	03/19/68	11/05/68	231	0	0
SB00206631BDA	03/11/69	11/04/69	238	1.63	4.9
SB00206631BDA	03/17/70	10/23/70	220	0.38	1.1
SB00206631BDA	03/23/71	11/04/71	226	0.13	0.4
SB00206631BDA	03/23/72	11/19/72	241	0.16	0.5
SB00206725CDC	03/20/67	11/01/67	226	2.58	7.7
SB00206725CDC	03/19/68	11/05/68	231	3.18	9.5
SB00206725CDC	03/11/69	11/04/69	238	2.36	7.1
SB00206725CDC	03/17/70	10/23/70	220	1.72	5.2
SB00206725CDC	03/23/71	11/04/71	226	1.53	4.6
SB00206725CDC	03/23/72	11/19/72	241	0	0
SB00206736DBB	03/20/67	11/01/67	226	2.18	6.5
SB00206736DBB	03/19/68	11/05/68	231	1.44	4.3
SB00206736DBB	03/11/69	11/04/69	238	1.53	4.6

Table 2. Seasonal groundwater-level rises and estimated recharge from applied irrigation water, Brighton to Fort Lupton, Colorado.—Continued

Well identifier[1]	Date of first water-level measurement	Date of second water-level measurement	Elapsed time (days)	Groundwater-level rise[2] (feet)	Estimated recharge[3] (inches)
SB00206736DBB	03/17/70	10/23/70	220	0.59	1.8
SB00206736DBB	03/23/71	11/09/71	231	0.25	0.8
SC00106618CDC1	03/20/67	10/31/67	225	2.18	6.5
SC00106618CDC1	03/18/68	11/04/68	231	3.41	10.2
SC00106618CDC1	03/10/69	11/03/69	238	3.95	11.9
SC00106618CDC1	03/16/70	10/01/70	199	3.85	11.6
SC00106618CDC1	03/22/71	10/30/71	222	0.69	2.1
SC00106618CDC1	04/04/72	11/22/72	232	3.64	10.9
Mean				2.67	8.0
Standard Deviation				1.69	5.1

[1] Well identifier is site name in the U.S. Geological Survey National Water Information System (http://waterdata.usgs.gov/co/nwis/gw).

[2] Water-level-rise values equal to 0 indicate altitude of the second water-level measurement is less than or equal to the altitude of the first water-level measurement.

[3] Estimated recharge represents net recharge during the irrigation season and is calculated using the water-table fluctuation method described by Healy and Cook (2002) with an assumed specific-yield value of 0.25.

of about 3 ft, mean recharge from irrigation represents about 22 percent of applied irrigation water and about 18 percent of applied irrigation water (3 ft) and precipitation during the irrigation season (67 percent of mean annual precipitation, or about 9 in.) combined.

Recharge estimated beneath irrigated fields represents average conditions and does not distinguish between recharge beneath flood- and sprinkler-irrigated sites, which can have substantially different recharge rates. Susong (1995) used a water-budget method to estimate that about 49 percent of applied irrigation water and precipitation became recharge beneath a flood-irrigated field, whereas about 10 percent became recharge beneath a sprinkler-irrigated field when crop water requirements were exceeded. Similarly, Roark and Healy (1998) estimated recharge beneath two flood-irrigated alfalfa fields to be 14–43 percent of applied water and precipitation, depending on soil permeability. Recharge beneath a sprinkler-irrigated site about 7 mi north of the Brighton–Fort Lupton study area was estimated to be about 12 percent of applied water and precipitation for soils similar to those in the study area (Gaggiani, 1995).

Seepage losses from ditches in the study area likely are substantial. Average seepage loss for Lupton Bottom Ditch is estimated to be about 30 percent of the diverted inflow based on flow measurements along the ditch (Lupton Bottom Ditch Company, oral commun., 2004). A study of Fulton Ditch indicated overall seepage loss is about 20 percent of the diverted inflow (George McDonnell, Fulton Irrigating Ditch Company, oral commun., 2004).

Recharge beneath urban areas. Recharge beneath urban areas commonly is assumed to be less than recharge beneath native and non-irrigated areas (Savini and Kammerer, 1961; Harbor, 1994; Arnold and Friedel, 2000) because greater impervious cover—such as roads, parking lots, rooftops, and driveways—increases runoff (Leopold, 1968; Barfield and others, 1981) and prevents infiltration of water at the land surface. However, Lerner (2002) presents results of several studies that indicate recharge beneath urban areas might be greater than beneath native and non-irrigated land because of leaky water mains and sewers and overirrigation of lawns, trees, and gardens. In areas of commercial development, impervious surfaces generally compose a large percentage of the land cover, and irrigated landscapes occupy only small areas. Conversely, residential areas generally have moderate impervious cover, and irrigated lawns and landscaping occupy substantial area. Therefore, recharge beneath commercial areas is likely to be less than recharge beneath native and non-irrigated land, whereas recharge beneath residential areas might be greater. The amount of impervious area in the study area was estimated from 2006 images of the Brighton–Fort Lupton area viewed by using Google Earth (accessed August 1, 2006, at *http://earth.google.com*) at scales ranging from about 1:750 to 1:2,000. Based on visual inspection of the images, commercial areas in Brighton and Fort Lupton are estimated to have about 50–95 percent impervious cover, and residential areas are estimated to have about 20–50 percent impervious cover. However, commercial and residential areas are combined in the analysis of land-use change (see "Land-Use Analysis"), and average combined recharge beneath urban areas might be less than or greater than recharge beneath native and non-irrigated land.

Subsurface Inflow

Subsurface inflow to the South Platte alluvial aquifer in the study area can be estimated using a form of Darcy's Law (Fetter, 1994):

$$Q = -KA \, (dh/dl) \qquad (4)$$

where

Q	is subsurface inflow, in cubic feet per day,
K	is aquifer hydraulic conductivity, in feet per day,
A	is aquifer cross-sectional area, in square feet, and
dh/dl	is water-table hydraulic gradient (dimensionless).

Using values representative of average hydraulic conductivity (1,000 ft/d), cross-sectional area (550,000 ft^2), and hydraulic gradient (−0.003), subsurface inflow at the upgradient end of the South Platte alluvial aquifer in the study area is calculated using equation 4 to be 1,650,000 ft^3/d (19.1 ft^3/s). Combined subsurface inflow from the tributary valleys of Big and Little Dry Creeks (assuming K = 450 ft/d, A = 150,000 ft^2, dh/dl = −0.005) calculated using equation 4 is 337,500 ft^3/d (3.9 ft^3/s). Total estimated subsurface inflow from the upgradient end of the South Platte alluvial aquifer and tributary valleys is then 1,987,500 ft^3/d (23.0 ft^3/s). In addition to subsurface inflow from the upgradient end of the aquifer and tributary valleys, inflow also likely occurs along the east aquifer boundary from return flow of irrigation water applied upgradient and outside the eastern limit of the aquifer. Assuming average hydraulic conductivity at the valley margin is 650 ft/d, saturated cross-sectional area is 580,000 ft^2, and hydraulic gradient is −0.005, average subsurface return flow along the east side of the aquifer calculated using equation 4 is about 1,885,000 ft^3/d (21.8 ft^3/s) during the irrigation season. Inflow along the west aquifer boundary is considered negligible because unconsolidated sediments on hillslopes west of the aquifer commonly are thin or absent (fig. 8), limiting subsurface return flow of irrigation water applied upgradient and outside the western limit of the aquifer.

Aquifer Outflows

Outflows from the alluvial aquifer in the study area primarily are discharge to the South Platte River, well withdrawals, phreatophyte evapotranspiration, aggregate-pit dewatering, and subsurface outflow at the downgradient end of the aquifer.

Flow to the South Platte River

The direction of flow between the South Platte River and the alluvial aquifer within the hyporheic zone near the river is highly variable (McMahon and others (1995), but, overall, the general direction of flow is from groundwater to the river. A monthly mass-balance analysis of streamflow and diversion data (table 3) (U.S. Geological Survey, 2006a; Colorado Division of Water Resources, 2006a, b) for substantial inflows (Big Dry Creek) and outflows (Brighton Ditch, McCanne Ditch, Lupton Bottom Ditch, and Platteville Ditch) along the South Platte River between stream gages located at Henderson (station 06720500) (fig. 2) and Fort Lupton (station 06721000) indicates that the river generally gains groundwater in all months of the year (fig. 13). For the time periods analyzed (1954–1960, 1974–1980, and 1997–2003), streamflow gains generally were greatest during the irrigation season from May through October and least during the non-irrigation season from November through April when groundwater levels decline, reducing the aquifer hydraulic gradient toward the river. During the irrigation season, mean monthly gains to the South Platte River ranged from about 3.0 to 21.0 million ft^3/d (35–243 ft^3/s) with a mean value of about 9.0 million ft^3/d (104 ft^3/s). During the non-irrigation season, mean monthly flow to and from the South Platte River ranged from a loss of about 1.1 million ft^3/d (13 ft^3/s) to a gain of about 6.4 million ft^3/d (74 ft^3/s). Streamflow gains correlate with the magnitude and timing of diversions from the South Platte River for irrigation (fig. 4), indicating that water diverted for irrigation possibly infiltrates rapidly to the water table and increases discharge to the river during the irrigation season. However, streamflow gains appear to begin declining sooner than diversions during the irrigation season, possibly because groundwater withdrawals from irrigation wells generally are greatest in mid to late summer (Hurr and others, 1975), and groundwater withdrawals can capture recharge from seepage of diverted surface water applied to fields.

Well Withdrawals

Irrigation-well withdrawals from an area of the South Platte alluvial aquifer that encompasses the study area were estimated by Smith and others (1964) to be about 17,900 ft^3/d (150 acre-ft/yr) per well in 1956 and about 7,160 ft^3/d (60 acre-ft/yr) per well in 1957. Hurr and others (1975) estimated mean irrigation withdrawals from the South Platte alluvial aquifer between Henderson and the Colorado-Nebraska State line to range from about 14,320 to 26,260 ft^3/d (120 to 220 acre-ft/yr) per well for the period 1960–70. Withdrawals from irrigation wells in the study area during the time periods considered (1954–1960, 1974–1980, and 1997–2003) are estimated to be within the range (7,160–26,260 ft^3/d per well) indicated by these studies for other wells in the South Platte aquifer. However, because withdrawal rates and the number and location of irrigation wells active during each irrigation

Table 3.   Mass-balance estimation of gain or loss of water along the South Platte River between stream gages located near Henderson and Fort Lupton for the periods 1954–60, 1974–80, and 1997–2003.

[All values are mean monthly streamflow in cubic feet per day]

Month	South Platte River at Henderson (06720500)[1]	South Platte River at Fort Lupton (06721000)[2]	Big Dry Creek (06720990)[2]	Brighton Ditch (810)[3]	McCanne Ditch (868)[3]	Lupton Bottom Ditch (812)[3]	Platteville Ditch (813)[3]	Gain or loss Henderson to Fort Lupton[4]
				1954–60				
January	5,947,751	9,011,904	1,986,728	0	0	0	0	1,077,425
February	8,215,646	10,710,577	1,955,577	0	0	0	0	539,354
March	14,263,773	17,956,660	2,159,487	0	0	0	0	1,533,400
April	19,357,503	20,638,133	4,146,215	249,741	0	822,046	680,924	−1,112,874
May	78,915,009	80,877,552	3,368,800	1,397,152	0	3,275,284	2,686,403	5,952,583
June	66,702,596	62,868,025	3,196,041	2,499,465	0	5,924,246	4,799,796	6,192,895
July	39,363,937	35,146,201	3,023,282	2,307,750	0	5,283,616	4,794,275	5,144,623
August	28,099,123	25,288,893	2,936,902	1,972,895	0	4,582,453	4,114,611	4,922,826
September	11,855,487	11,071,293	3,800,697	1,547,817	0	3,745,289	3,283,659	3,991,874
October	8,532,224	10,231,678	2,936,902	762,481	0	2,146,494	1,334,243	3,005,770
November	7,219,237	9,847,745	2,418,625	0	0	0	0	209,882
December	6,387,721	9,587,254	1,986,728	0	0	0	0	1,212,806
				1974–80				
January	21,582,398	23,859,887	1,986,728	0	205,552	0	0	496,313
February	23,986,779	27,156,402	1,955,577	0	30,105	0	0	1,244,151
March	27,859,031	30,754,071	2,159,487	0	0	71,669	0	807,222
April	39,064,478	40,342,805	4,146,215	856,195	0	1,180,406	757,040	−74,248
May	82,410,476	90,310,819	3,368,800	1,942,635	33,446	3,270,905	2,952,773	12,731,302
June	91,101,899	97,414,541	3,196,041	2,814,624	66,241	5,008,805	5,196,008	16,202,278
July	58,133,714	51,473,651	3,023,282	3,285,239	86,401	6,494,429	6,369,405	6,552,129
August	40,468,041	36,581,179	2,936,902	2,602,788	36,233	5,282,422	5,258,930	6,356,608
September	23,527,475	23,487,566	3,800,697	1,795,090	0	3,203,018	4,039,053	5,196,555
October	22,620,806	24,389,045	2,936,902	1,155,069	199,977	1,499,082	2,210,598	3,896,064
November	19,449,335	22,579,118	2,418,625	15,635	316,805	19,338	134,539	1,197,474
December	17,485,306	20,943,745	1,986,728	0	316,804	0	0	1,788,515
				1997–2003				
January	31,140,687	33,630,870	2,417,603	0	0	0	0	72,581
February	28,005,362	30,013,766	2,110,272	0	0	0	0	−101,868
March	30,826,138	33,278,261	2,935,254	394,539	0	292,044	848,404	1,051,857
April	50,413,078	55,192,626	5,146,141	1,784,034	0	1,732,501	3,251,485	6,401,427
May	77,964,196	86,120,025	4,939,604	2,132,562	0	3,284,309	4,141,885	12,774,981
June	95,962,587	106,253,626	3,486,826	2,479,140	0	4,787,001	6,923,745	20,994,098
July	56,950,774	62,563,978	3,976,369	3,013,238	0	6,472,664	7,258,821	18,381,558
August	58,298,951	64,075,285	3,580,436	2,257,486	0	5,005,307	5,985,577	15,444,267
September	30,998,304	33,428,664	3,309,374	1,541,329	0	3,637,651	4,778,566	9,078,532
October	30,987,791	33,459,475	3,145,882	794,489	0	1,546,379	3,374,717	5,041,387
November	30,290,224	32,634,907	2,812,896	61,139	0	204,113	227,894	24,932
December	26,930,118	28,910,823	2,171,578	0	0	319,438	0	128,564

[1]Number is station identifier. Data from Colorado Division of Water Resources (2006a).

[2]Number is station number. Data from U.S. Geological Survey (2006).

[3]Number is structure identifier. Data from Colorado Division of Water Resources (2006b).

[4]Positive values indicate gain to river from groundwater. Negative values indicate loss from river to groundwater.

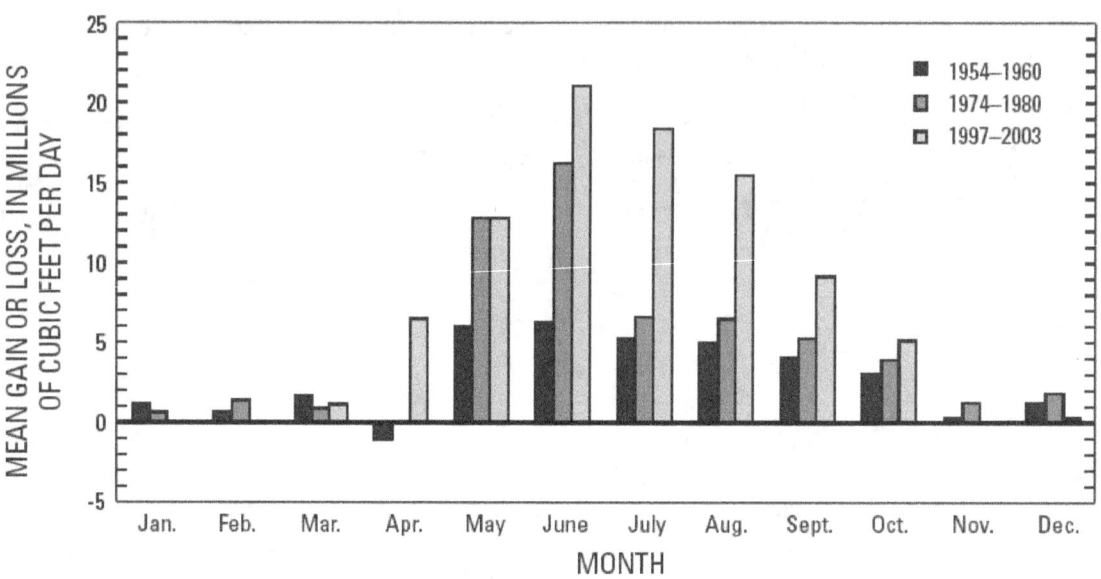

Figure 13. Mean monthly gain or loss in flow of the South Platte River between stream gages located near Henderson and Fort Lupton, Colo., for the periods 1954–1960, 1974–1980, and 1997–2003. [Streamflow and diversion data used to estimate gain or loss are from U.S. Geological Survey (2006) and Colorado Division of Water Resources (2006a,b).]

season have large uncertainty, total irrigation-well withdrawals are largely uncertain.

Municipal-well withdrawals are estimated based on pumping data provided by the two main municipalities in the study area and historical population estimates. Data provided by the city of Fort Lupton (Steve Nguyen, Clear Water Rights, Inc., written commun., 2005) and the city of Brighton (Dawn Hessheimer, city of Brighton, written commun., 2007) indicate municipal-well withdrawals during the irrigation season from May through October are 2 to 3 times greater than those during the non-irrigation season from November through April (fig. 14). The sum of mean withdrawals from all municipal wells during May–October for the years considered (1954–1960, 1974–1980, and 1997–2003) range from about 976,000 to 1,550,000 ft^3/d (22.4–35.6 acre-ft/yr), whereas the sum of mean withdrawals from all municipal wells during November–April range from about 376,000 to 752,000 ft^3/d (8.6–17.3 acre-ft/yr). Municipal-withdrawal data prior to 2000 were not available for Fort Lupton; so mean withdrawals for Fort Lupton during 1997–2003 reflect mean withdrawals from only 2000 to 2003. Historical (1954–1960 and 1974–1980) municipal withdrawals for Fort Lupton were estimated based on per capita use during 2000–2003 multiplied by population estimates (Colorado State Demography Office, 2007) provided by State censuses taken in 1960 and 1980. Mean municipal withdrawals for Brighton are based on withdrawal data provided for each year considered.

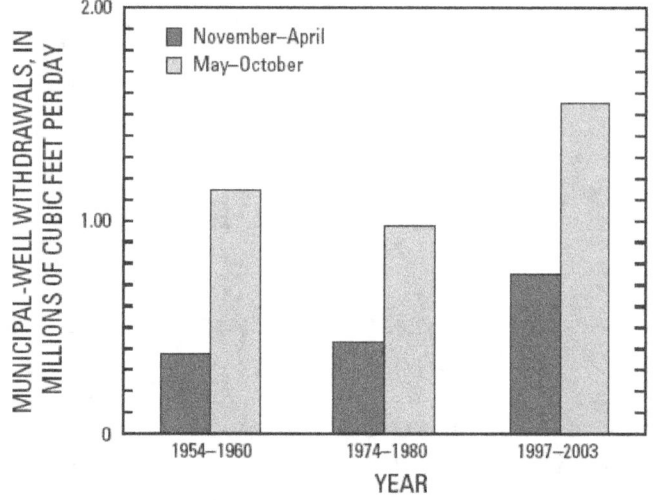

Figure 14. Sum of mean municipal-well withdrawals by Brighton and Fort Lupton during the irrigation season (May–October) and non-irrigation season (November–April) for the periods 1954–1960, 1974–1980, and 1997–2003. [Withdrawal data provided by Dawn Hessheimer, city of Brighton, written commun. (2007) and Steve Nguyen, Clear Water Rights, Inc., written commun. (2005).]

Phreatophyte Evapotranspiration

Phreatophyte evapotranspiration occurs when plants or trees have roots deep enough to penetrate the water table and use water directly from the aquifer. Phreatophytes in the South Platte study area consist primarily of cottonwood trees (Colorado Division of Wildlife, 2007a, b), however, Russian olive and willow trees also are present in the study area. Annual evapotranspiration by phreatophytes consisting primarily of cottonwood and cottonwood-willow trees has been estimated to range from about 24 to 36 in. in the North Platte basin of Wyoming (VanKlaveren and others, 1975) and the South Platte River valley (Hurr and others, 1975). Most of the evapotranspiration occurs concurrently with the irrigation season from May through October. Phreatophyte evapotranspiration from the South Platte alluvial aquifer in the study area is assumed to fall within this range on the basis of similar climatic and hydrologic conditions.

Mine Dewatering and Subsurface Outflow

The rate of mine dewatering for individual aggregate pits in the study area is highly variable depending on the size and timeframe of the mining operation but typically is greater than 192,500 ft^3/d (1,000 gal/min) and can be continuous for several years. Subsurface outflow at the downgradient end of the alluvial aquifer is estimated using equation 4 as −1,200,000 ft^3/d (−13.9 ft^3/s), assuming average hydraulic conductivity is 1,000 ft/d, cross-sectional area is 400,000 ft^2, and hydraulic gradient is 0.003. The negative sign denotes that the direction of groundwater flow is out of the aquifer.

Land-Use Analysis

Socioeconomic Trends

In the early 1990s population growth in northeastern Colorado was largest in Douglas County to the south of Denver (Douglas County, 2002). Since about 2000, substantial growth has shifted to the agricultural region north of Denver in Adams, Weld, Boulder, and Larimer Counties. Proximity to Denver, access to major transportation corridors and an international airport, moderate land values, and most importantly, the availability of water are the prime drivers for urban growth in this region (Mladinich, 2006). Water supply, largely in the form of reservoirs (from early irrigation development and aggregate mining) and groundwater, already is in place in the region, which is one of the main reasons for the shifting growth from Douglas County (Wagner, 2002; Parton and others, 2003).

The South Platte study area is in the northern growth area, but the degree of growth in Brighton has been different than that of Fort Lupton. Growth in Brighton (at the southern end of the study area) has been larger and faster than in Fort

Lupton because Brighton is closer to Denver, has a railway stop, and is the seat of Adams County (Wagner, 2002). Both cities were incorporated between 1887 and 1890 and were trading centers whose production and service industries grew to support the surrounding agricultural region. The main economic drivers in the region historically have been agriculture and mineral extraction, and the region has followed the typical cycles of economic booms and busts experienced throughout Colorado (Kendall, 2002; Parton and others, 2003). These cycles have resulted from national and international economic trends and also have corresponded with drought cycles. Each drought period has led to a downturn in agriculture and the industries supporting them.

The population of Brighton and Fort Lupton increased gradually through the early to mid-1900s and began to increase more rapidly during the second half of the century (Colorado State Demography Office, 2007) (fig. 15). Rapid population growth began in Brighton around 1960, whereas rapid population growth in Fort Lupton began around 1980. Rapid population growth in both cities continued through 2000.

Starting in the mid-1960s through the mid-1980s, the region reflected the shift in the State's economy from traditional resource-based industries, including agriculture and mineral extraction, to high technology, energy, and service industries (Kendall, 2002). Land values rose and farm incomes fell during the 1970s and 1980s, resulting in a downturn for farmers and ranchers in the region and throughout the State. In the vicinity of the study area, the number of farm owners and farm employment were declining during this time period (U.S. Department of Commerce, 2007) (fig. 16), and by the 1970s, all the sugar-beet mills in the region had closed (Kendall, 2002).

The State's economic rebound in the 1990s in the high-technology and communications industries were reflected by an economic upturn in the region. However, in the late 1990s, declining prices and cutbacks in Federal farm programs reduced farm incomes. Since the late 1990s, the region has attracted retirees and high-technology and service-industry employees because of its small-town atmosphere, moderate land values, and relatively low cost of living (Kendall, 2002).

Land-Use Trends

Land-use/land-cover data sets for 1957, 1977, and 1997 (U.S. Geological Survey, 1999, 2001b, c,) were analyzed and compared to determine the type, extent, and rate of land-use change in the study area. The land-use/land-cover data set for 1997 was used to represent approximate land-use conditions in 2000. Land use in the study area was classified into three major types based on similarity of recharge conditions for input to the numerical groundwater flow model. The three major land-use classifications used in the study are (1) urban areas, (2) irrigated agriculture, and (3) non-irrigated land. Urban areas include all land uses related to urban

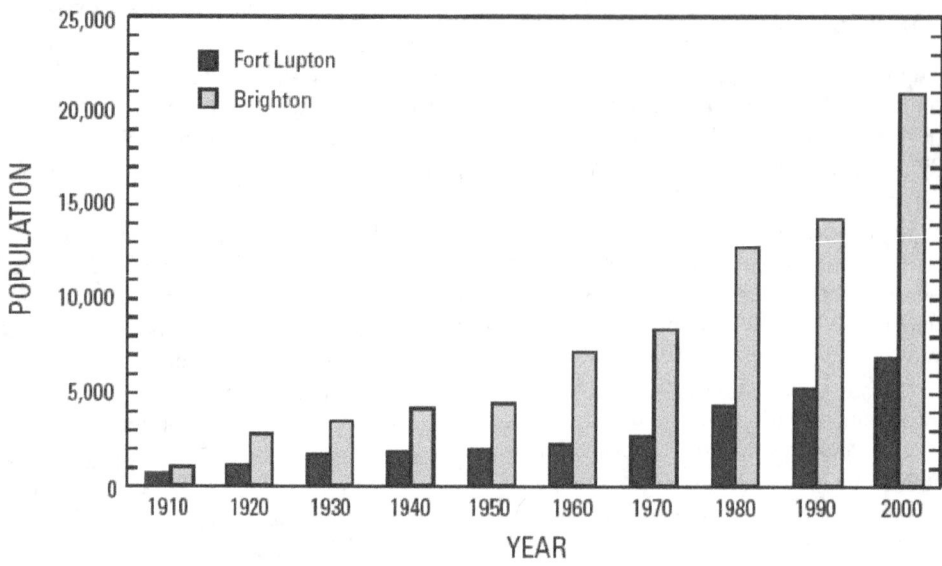

Figure 15. Populations of Brighton and Fort Lupton, Colo., 1910–2000. [Data from Colorado State Demography Office (2007)].

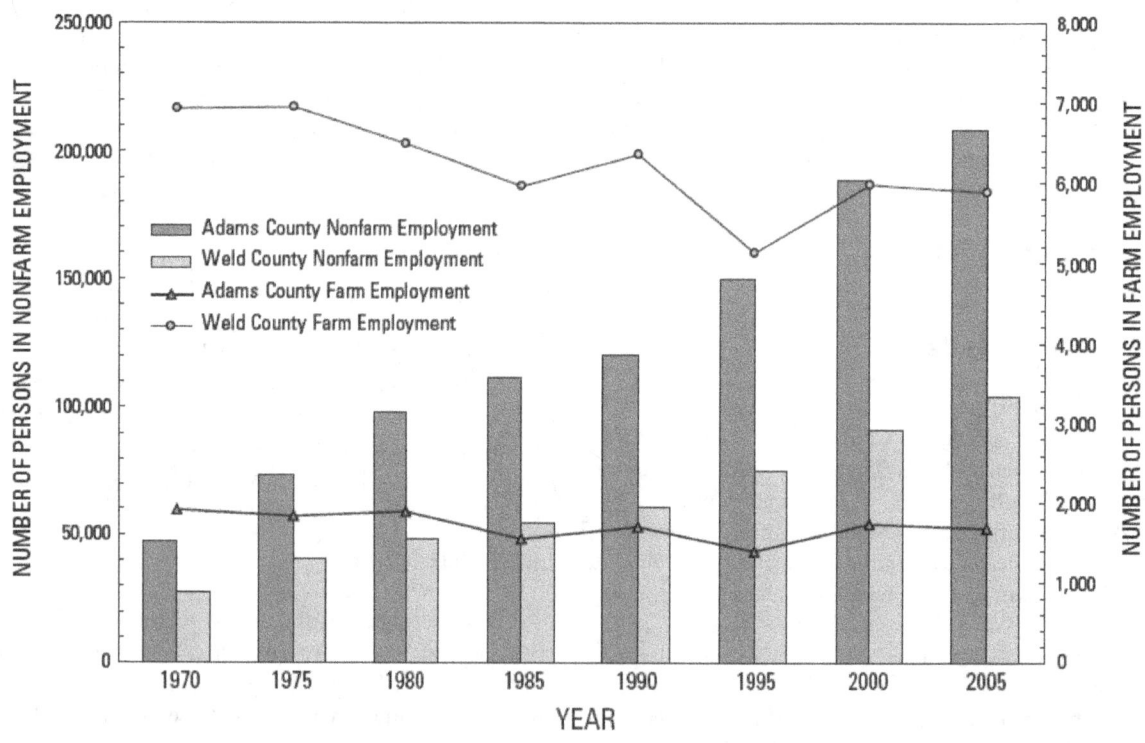

Figure 16. Farm and nonfarm employment in Adams and Weld Counties, Colo., 1970–2005. [Data from Colorado State Demography Office (2007)].

development, such as commercial, industrial, and residential areas. Irrigated agricultural areas represent cultivated land irrigated for crop production. Within the classification, no distinction is made between areas irrigated by surface water or groundwater. Similarly, no distinction is made between irrigation methods used, such as sprinkler or flood irrigation. Non-irrigated land includes all other land uses in the study area, primarily dry-land agriculture and native land. Small farm plots indicated as residential areas were included as part of the dominant land use (irrigated agriculture or non-irrigated land) surrounding the farm.

The general distribution of irrigated and non-irrigated land in 1957, 1977, and 2000 (figs. 17A–C) is similar for each year. Non-irrigated land generally is located near the South Platte River and on upland areas outside the limits of the alluvial aquifer, whereas irrigated agricultural land generally is located on well-drained soils away from the river and along tributaries to the South Platte River. Locally, relatively small conversions between irrigated agricultural land and non-irrigated land have occurred. In some places, irrigated land in 1957 was converted to non-irrigated land by 1977 and converted back again to irrigated land by 2000. Similar conversions of non-irrigated land to irrigated land also occurred between 1957 and 2000. Overall, the total area of non-irrigated and irrigated land decreased slightly from 1957 to 2000 (table 4), and the reduction in irrigated land was slightly larger than that for non-irrigated land. Irrigated land use decreased 6–7 percent between each time period compared, and non-irrigated land use decreased about 4 percent between each time period. By contrast, urban land use increased about 165 percent between 1957 and 1977 and about 56 percent between 1977 and 2000. Although urban development increased greatly between 1957 and 2000, the total land area covered by urban development in the study area in 2000 was relatively small (about 13 percent) compared to irrigated land (about 38 percent) and non-irrigated land (about 50 percent). Most urban development in the study area is associated with the cities of Brighton and Fort Lupton. Urban growth of both cities between 1957 and 2000 primarily has been to the east (away from the South Platte River) and along the corridor of U.S. Highway 85 and the Union Pacific Railroad line.

Predictions of Land-Use Change

Predictions of future urban extent in the study area in 2020 and 2040 were made using the SLEUTH urban-growth modeling program (U.S. Geological Survey and University of California at Santa Barbara, 2001). SLEUTH is a cellular automaton-based modeling program that derives its name from input required to conduct simulations (Slope, Land cover, Exclusions, Urbanization, Transportation, and Hillshade). Slope and land cover provide information about the likelihood of urban growth occurring in an area, whereas exclusions define areas where urban growth will not likely occur because

Table 4. Area and percent change of urban, irrigated, and non-irrigated land uses, 1957–2000, and predicted urban land use in 2020 and 2040, Brighton to Fort Lupton, Colorado.

[--, not applicable]

Land Use	1957		1977			2000			2020			2040		
	Area (acres)	Percent of total land area	Area (acres)	Percent of total land area	Percent change 1957–77	Area (acres)	Percent of total land area	Percent change 1977–2000	Area (acres)	Percent of total land area	Percent change 2000–20	Area (acres)	Percent of total land area	Percent change 2020–40
Urban	1,740	3.1	4,610	8.2	165.0	7,180	12.8	55.7	14,510	25.9	102.1	20,570	36.7	41.8
Irrigated	24,050	42.9	22,430	40.0	-6.7	21,040	37.5	-6.2	--	--	--	--	--	--
Non-irrigated	30,290	54.0	29,040	51.8	-4.1	27,860	49.7	-4.1	--	--	--	--	--
Total	56,080	100.0	56,080	100.0	0.0	56,080	100.0	-0.0	--	--	--	--	--

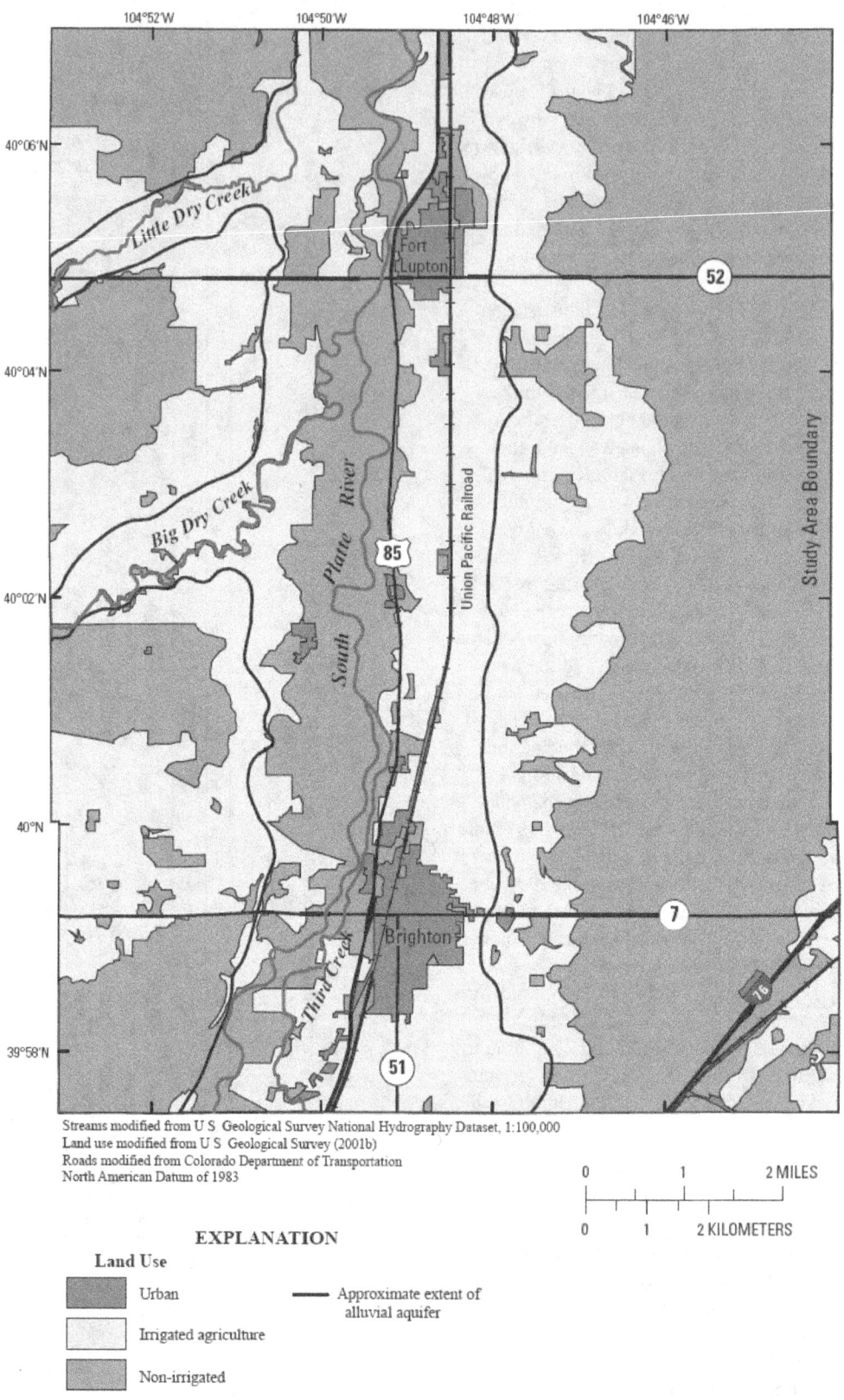

Figure 17A.   Generalized land use in 1957, Brighton to Fort Lupton, Colorado.

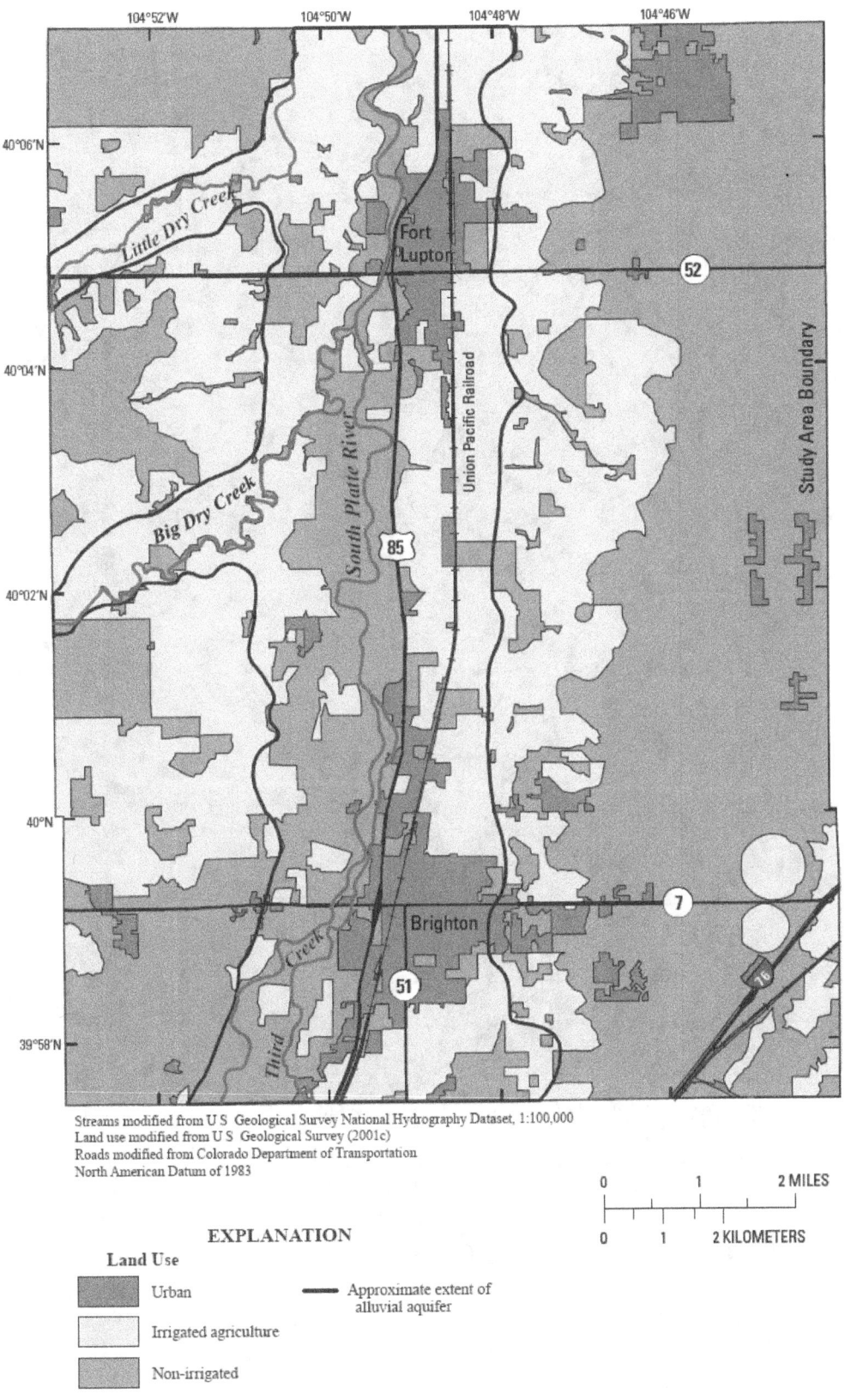

Streams modified from U S Geological Survey National Hydrography Dataset, 1:100,000
Land use modified from U S Geological Survey (2001c)
Roads modified from Colorado Department of Transportation
North American Datum of 1983

EXPLANATION

Land Use

Urban

Irrigated agriculture

Non-irrigated

Approximate extent of alluvial aquifer

Figure 17B. Generalized land use in 1977, Brighton to Fort Lupton, Colorado.

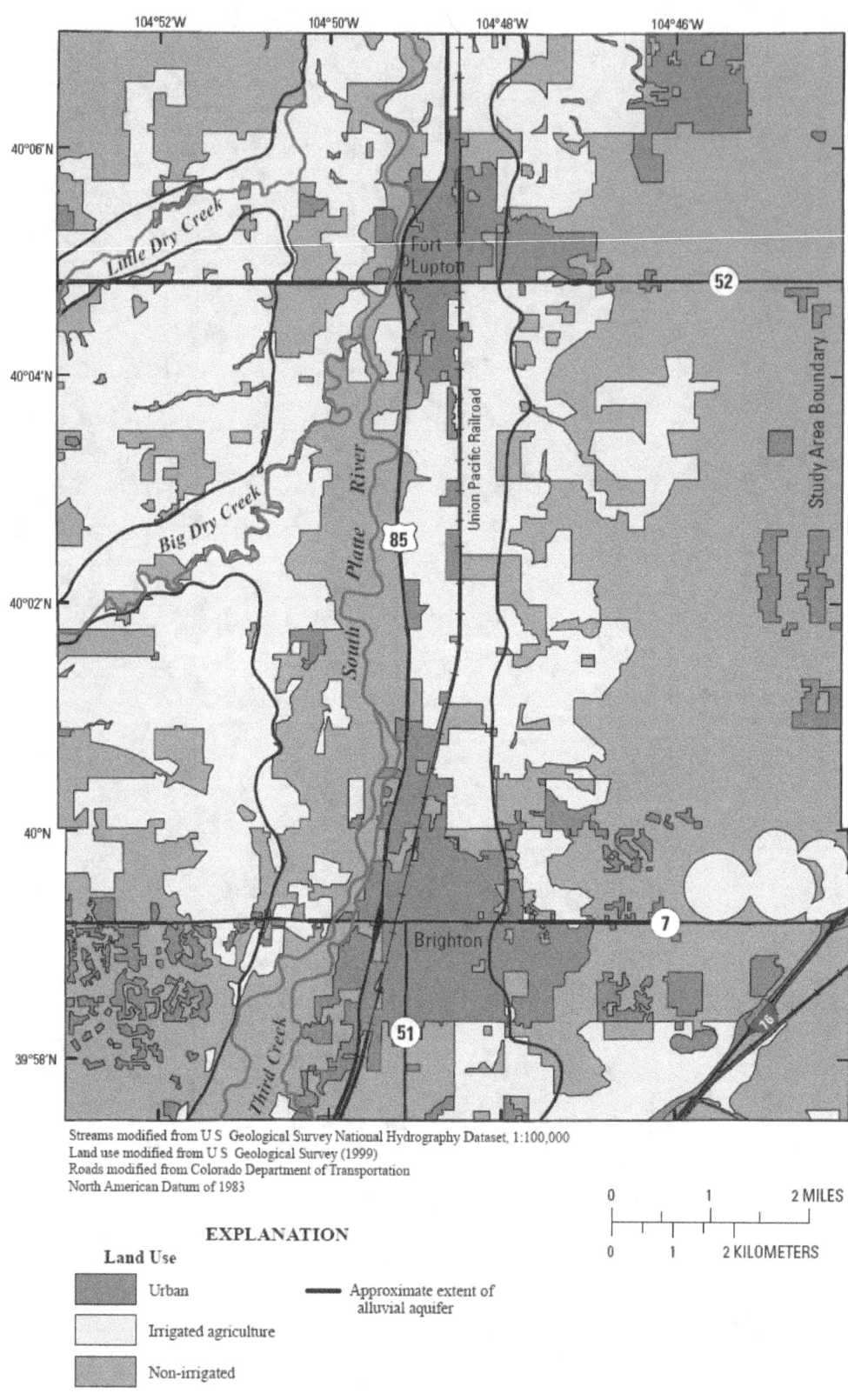

Streams modified from U S Geological Survey National Hydrography Dataset, 1:100,000
Land use modified from U S Geological Survey (1999)
Roads modified from Colorado Department of Transportation
North American Datum of 1983

EXPLANATION

Land Use

Urban

Irrigated agriculture

Non-irrigated

Approximate extent of alluvial aquifer

Figure 17C.   Generalized land use in 2000, Brighton to Fort Lupton, Colorado.

of development restrictions or physical limitations, such as water bodies. Transportation is used to define the location of roads along which urban development commonly proceeds. Hillshade is used to provide spatial context to simulations. SLEUTH predicts urban growth by comparing historical urban extent and growth over time to determine a set of coefficients that represent different factors contributing to urban growth. The probability that existing urban areas will expand and the probability that new urban areas will develop are considered in the modeling program based on the coefficients determined during calibration to historical urban development.

In this study, slope and hillshade were determined for SLEUTH model input by using a USGS Digital Elevation Model (DEM) with 30-m resolution (accessed June 10, 2005 at *http://rockyweb.cr.usgs.gov/elevation*). Land cover was defined as either urban or nonurban for the model on the basis of land-use categories indicated by U.S. Geological Survey (1999, 2001a, b, c). Areas of irrigated agriculture and non-irrigated land were not changed in the simulation except where urbanization was predicted to occur. Exclusion areas were defined on the basis of water bodies indicated by U.S. Geological Survey (2001d). Land-use zoning maps were not used to define exclusion areas because such maps were not available in digital format suitable for SLEUTH model input. Transportation corridors were defined on the basis of roads and railroads indicated by U.S. Geological Survey (2001e, f). The SLEUTH model was calibrated to urban extent in 1937, 1957, 1977, and 2000 (U.S. Geological Survey, 1999, 2001a, b, c) using a 50-m by 50-m cell size to determine characteristics of urban growth in the study area. Coefficients determined by calibration then were used to predict urban extent in 2020 and 2040. Because land-use zoning was not considered in model input, predicted urban extent was compared to city and county zoning maps and development plans (city of Brighton, 2003; city of Fort Lupton, 2006; Weld County, 2006) at the conclusion of the simulation, and predicted urban extent was modified to reflect areas most likely to be developed on the basis of the maps and plans. The modified results of the SLEUTH simulations (figs. 18A and 18B) generally indicate areas where the predicted probability of urban growth is 70 percent or more. Similar to historical trends, urban growth is predicted to occur predominantly to the east of Brighton and Fort Lupton and along major transportation routes (U.S. Highway 85, Interstate 76, and Union Pacific Railroad). However, substantial growth also is predicted to the south and west of Brighton as areas of low urban density are more fully developed. The amount of urban area predicted in 2020 and 2040 is provided in table 4. The modified results of the model simulations represent one possible outcome of urban growth in the study area based on historical trends. Actual urban growth could be substantially different from that shown in figures 18A and 18B if factors affecting future urban growth are different than those used by the simulation. Errors associated with predictions of urban growth by the SLEUTH model simulations are difficult to quantify and were not estimated as part of this study.

As of late 1999, five aggregate mining operations were evident in the study area (Google Earth, accessed January 4, 2007, at *http://earth.google.com*). To estimate the potential extent of future aggregate mining in the study area, mining and reclamation plans on file with the CDMRS were reviewed in October 2006. At the time of the review, 58 aggregate pits were either reclaimed, active, or planned for development by 2020. The potential extent of aggregate mining in 2020 and planned methods of reclamation based on permit records is shown in figure 19A. A proposed lined water-storage facility unrelated to aggregate mining is included in figure 19A because its effect on groundwater flow would be the same as that of a lined pit. Although actual mining extents and methods of reclamation are subject to change based on market conditions and the needs of mining companies, results shown in figure 19A provide an indication of how mining might develop in the Brighton-Fort Lupton area.

The potential extent of aggregate mining in 2040 (fig. 19B) is not based on existing mining plans but rather on extrapolation of the size, spacing, and density of pit development in 2020. Aggregate-mining extent in 2040 represents potential conditions when mining within the study area is approximately fully developed. Pits generally were added and shaped with consideration of existing roads, ditches, houses, and oil wells shown on USGS 7.5-minute topographic quadrangle maps (1994) at a scale of 1:24,000 and with consideration of wetlands mapped as part of this study (see "Wetland Mapping") and areas of riparian herbaceous vegetation indicated by the Colorado Division of Wildlife (2007a, b). Aggregate in the tributary valleys of Big and Little Dry Creeks was assumed to not be of sufficient quality to mine; therefore no pits were added at these locations. In addition, pits were added only where SLEUTH model simulations did not predict urban development in 2040. Some areas, particularly near urban areas, were left open for future urban development or aggregate mining beyond 2040. Because the potential extent of aggregate mining in 2040 is not based on mining and reclamation plans, the actual extent of aggregate mining in 2040 could be substantially different than that shown in figure 19B. As with the SLEUTH model simulations, error associated with the potential extent of aggregate mining in both 2020 and 2040 is difficult to quantify and was not estimated as part of this study.

Wetland Mapping

Wetlands in the study area were mapped to verify areas designated as wetlands on existing USGS land-use/land-cover maps (U.S. Geological Survey, 1999, 2001a, b, c). Wetland mapping was completed by the USGS and U.S. Bureau of Reclamation during July–August, 2004. False-color infrared aerial photographs were obtained at 18 locations (fig. 20) in the central and western parts of the study area at a scale of 1:24,000. The aerial photographs are presented in the appendix. The easternmost part of the study area was not covered by

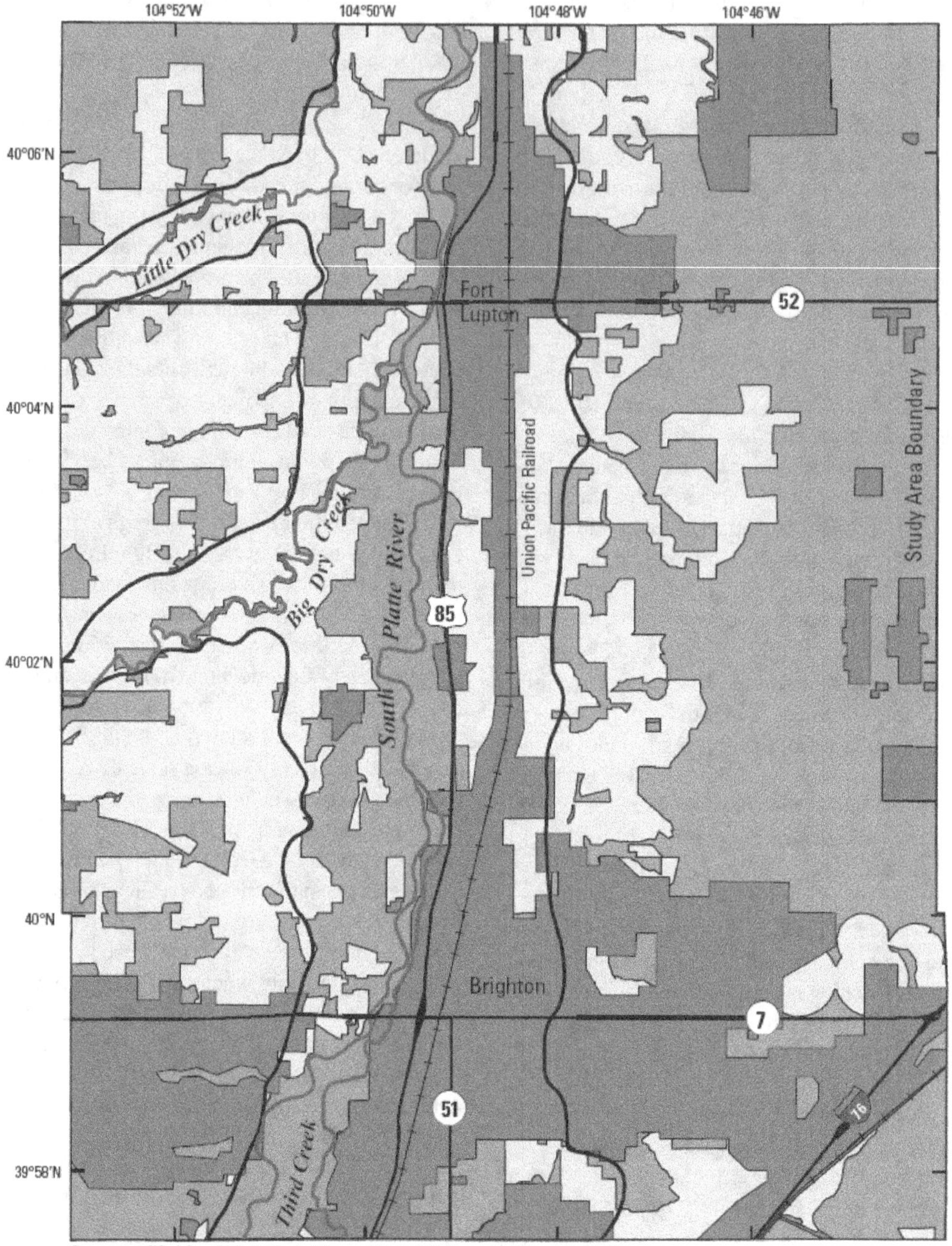

Streams modified from U S Geological Survey National Hydrography Dataset, 1:100,000
Land use modified from U S Geological Survey (1999)
Roads modified from Colorado Department of Transportation
North American Datum of 1983

0 1 2 MILES
0 1 2 KILOMETERS

EXPLANATION

Land Use

Urban

Irrigated agriculture

Non-irrigated

Approximate extent of alluvial aquifer

Figure 18A. Predicted extent of urban land use in 2020 with irrigated and non-irrigated land use shown as unchanged from 2000 except where precluded by changes in urban land use, Brighton to Fort Lupton, Colorado.

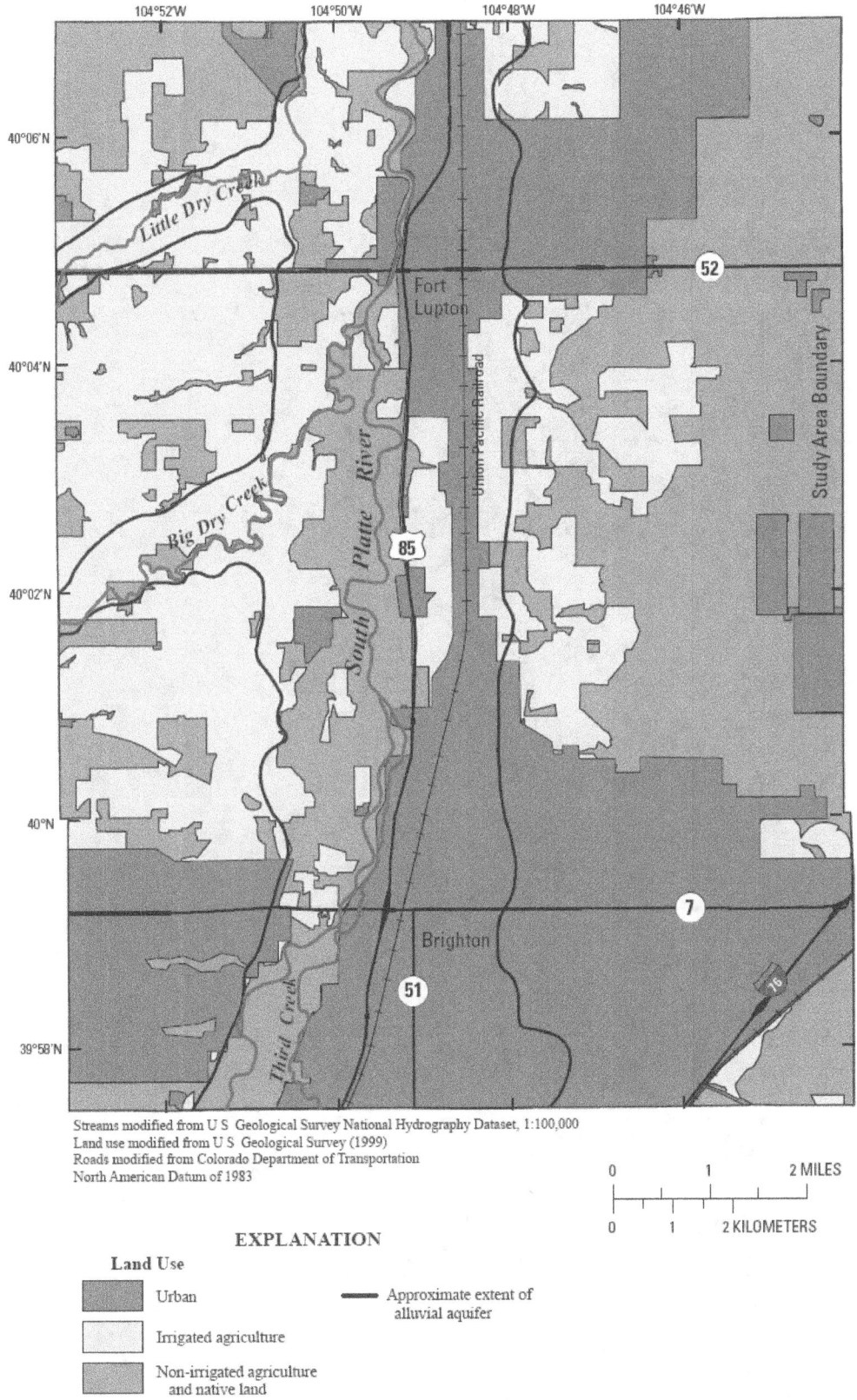

Streams modified from U S Geological Survey National Hydrography Dataset, 1:100,000
Land use modified from U S Geological Survey (1999)
Roads modified from Colorado Department of Transportation
North American Datum of 1983

EXPLANATION

Land Use

Urban

Irrigated agriculture

Non-irrigated agriculture
and native land

—— Approximate extent of
alluvial aquifer

Figure 18B. Predicted extent of urban land use in 2040 with irrigated and non-irrigated land use shown as unchanged from 2000 except where precluded by changes in urban land use, Brighton to Fort Lupton, Colorado.

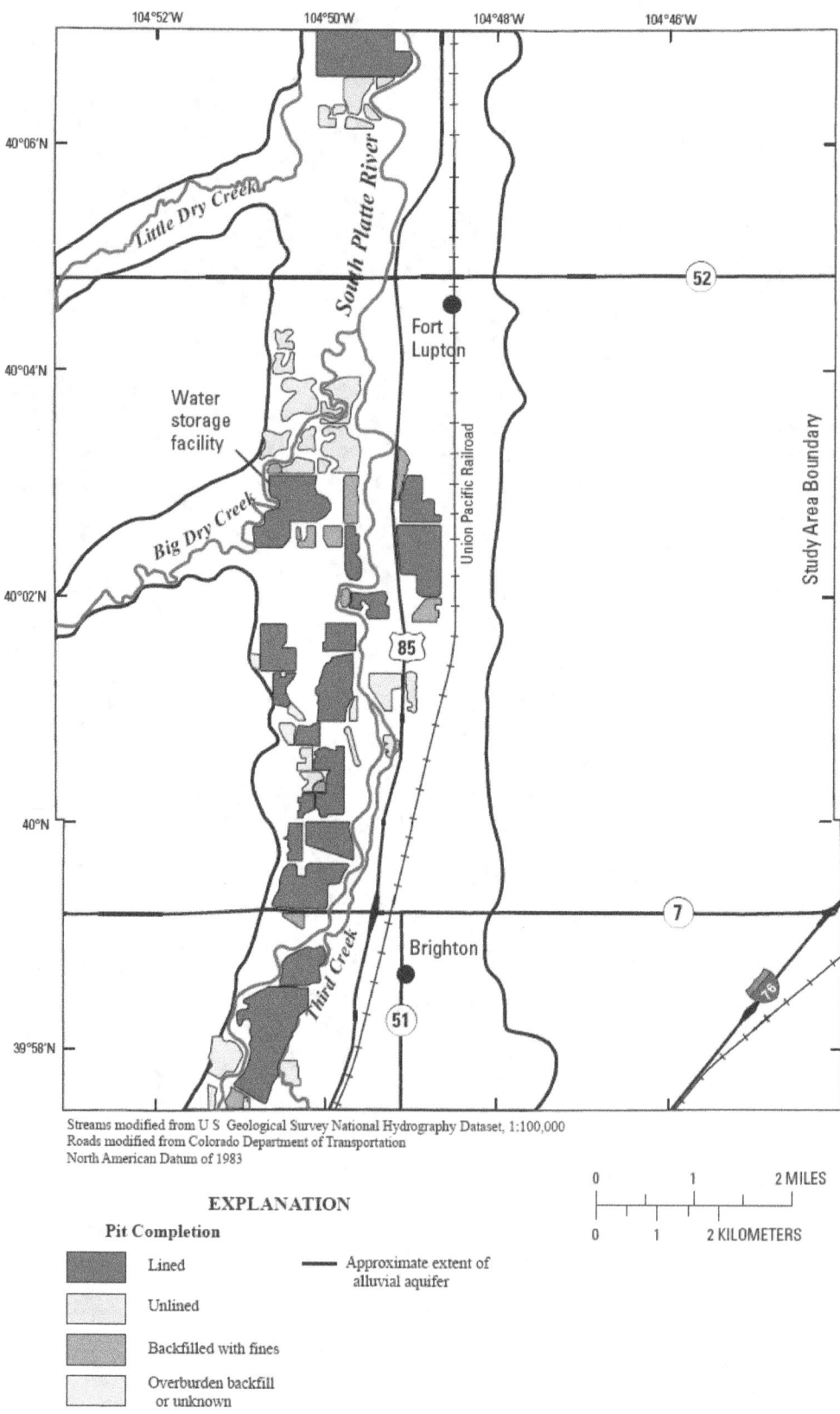

Streams modified from U S Geological Survey National Hydrography Dataset, 1:100,000
Roads modified from Colorado Department of Transportation
North American Datum of 1983

EXPLANATION

Pit Completion

Lined

Unlined

Backfilled with fines

Overburden backfill or unknown

—— Approximate extent of alluvial aquifer

0   1   2 MILES

0   1   2 KILOMETERS

Figure 19A. Predicted extent of aggregate mining in 2020, Brighton to Fort Lupton, Colorado.

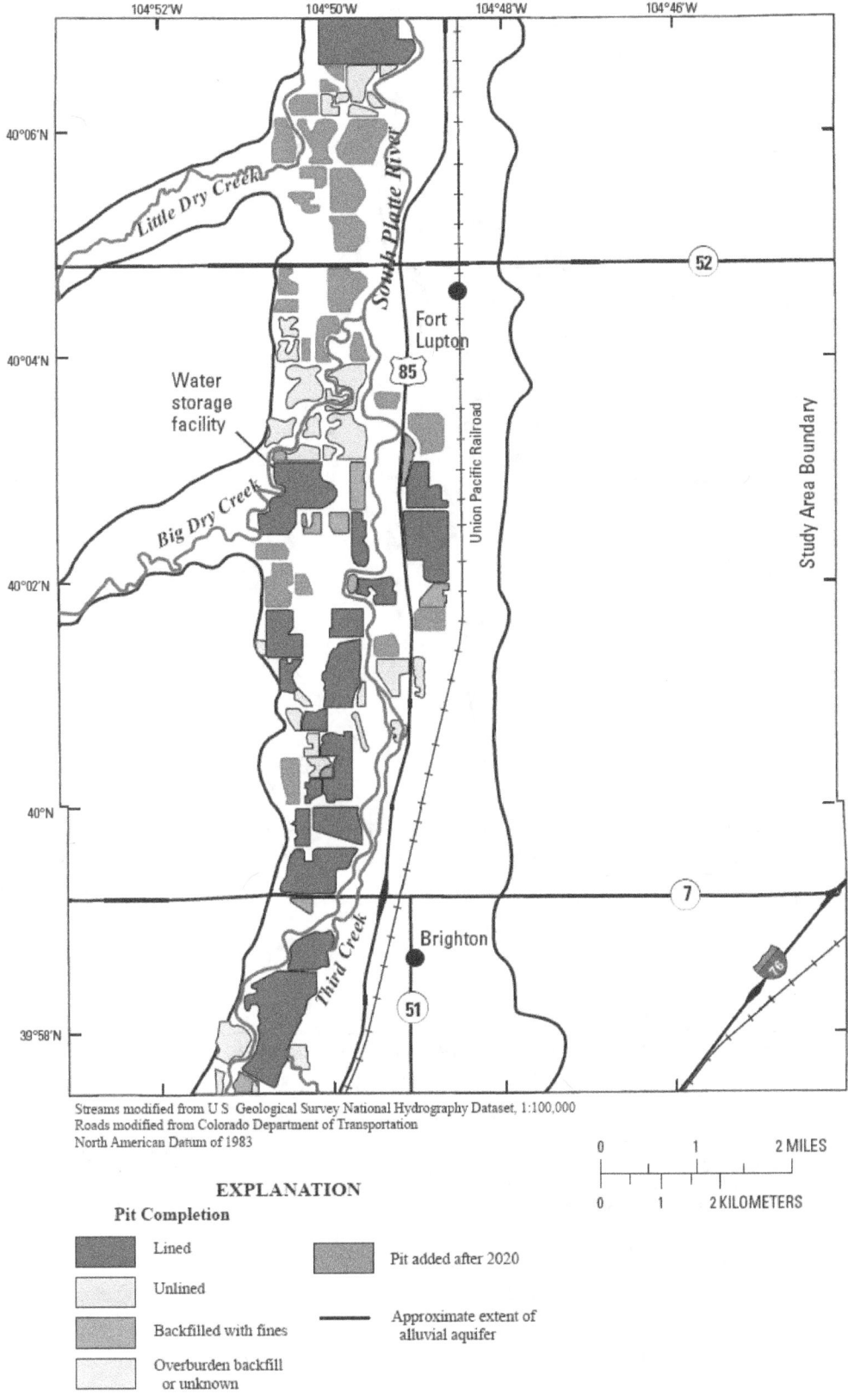

Streams modified from U S Geological Survey National Hydrography Dataset, 1:100,000
Roads modified from Colorado Department of Transportation
North American Datum of 1983

EXPLANATION

Pit Completion

Lined

Unlined

Backfilled with fines

Overburden backfill
or unknown

Pit added after 2020

——— Approximate extent of
alluvial aquifer

0   1   2 MILES

0   1   2 KILOMETERS

Figure 19B.   Predicted extent of aggregate mining in 2040, Brighton to Fort Lupton, Colorado.

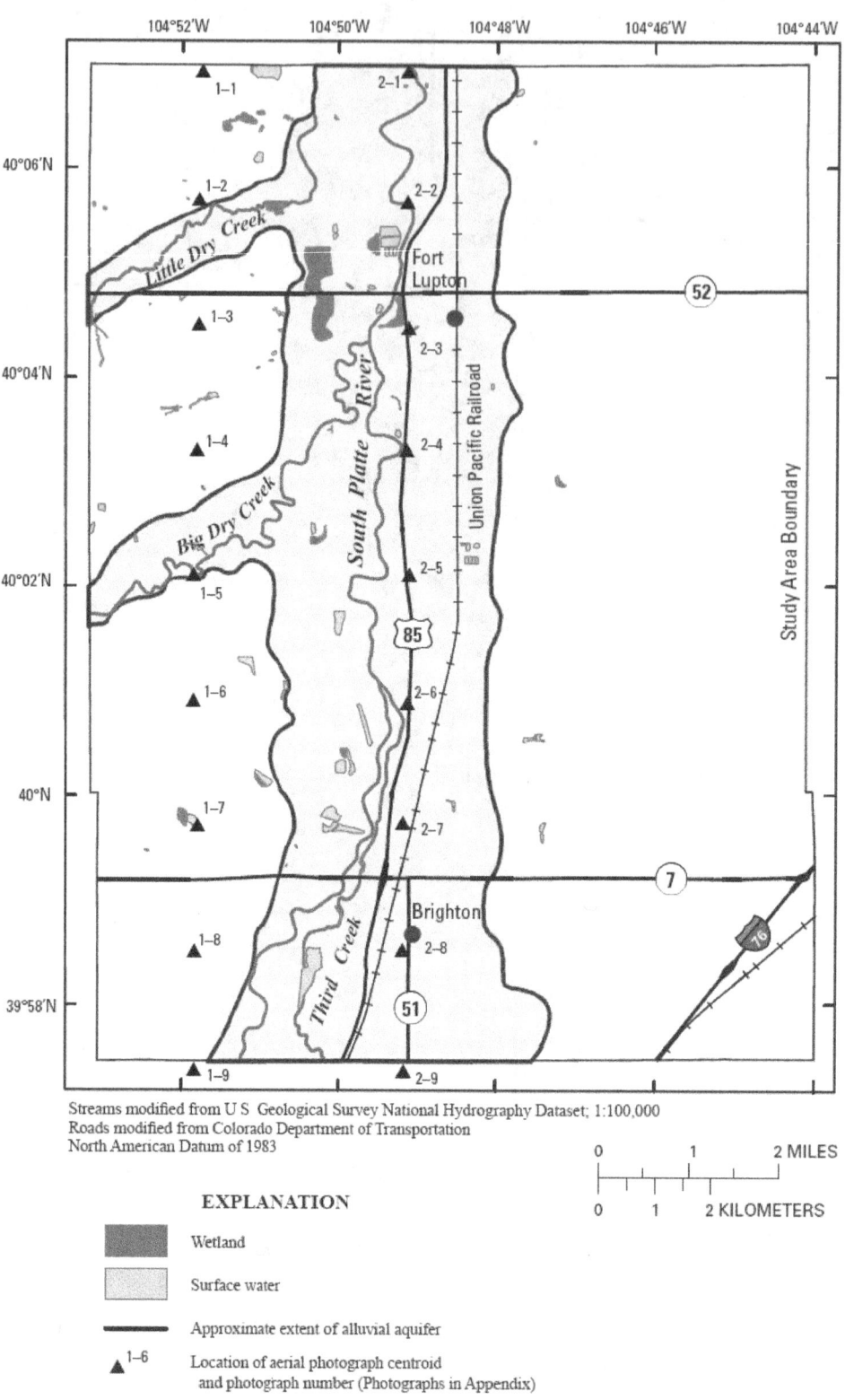

Figure 20.   Location and extent of wetlands and surface water mapped by this study, Brighton to Fort Lupton, Colo., July– August, 2004.

the photography, but depth to water in this area generally precludes the development of groundwater-supported wetlands. Preliminary photo interpretation was performed to identify probable wetland areas, and those areas were subsequently verified by field inspection. In addition to verifying locations of probable wetland areas identified from aerial photographs, specific evaluations were made at less-obvious wetland areas to determine their status. Wetlands on public land or otherwise accessible areas were evaluated by identifying the existence of wetland plant species, the above-ground hydrology, and the existence of reducing soils (necessary for evidence of hydric soils). Several inaccessible sites on private land were visually evaluated from the closest public road. Details of the wetlands mapping effort are presented by Salas (2005).

Wetland types occurring in the study area can be described using the USFWS wetland classification of Shaw and Fredine (1956), as seasonally flooded areas (waterlogged during variable periods, but well drained during much of the growing season), fresh meadows (waterlogged to within about an inch of the land surface), shallow fresh marshes (covered with ≥ 0.5 ft of water), deep fresh marshes (covered with 0.5–3.3 ft of water), and open fresh water (water deeper than 3.3 ft). For ease in mapping and quantifying the wetland areas for the purpose of this study, areas were categorized simply as wetlands or surface water. Areas identified as wetlands included seasonally flooded areas, fresh meadows, shallow marshes, and deep marshes that contained visible wetland vegetation, whereas surface water included all open water areas, including sewage and stock ponds. Small wetlands associated with irrigation ditches in the study area were not mapped because they were too small for the scale of the investigation. Summary statistics for mapped wetlands and surface water in the study area are presented in table 5, and the locations of mapped wetlands and surface water are shown in figure 20.

Wetlands that were easily identified by the existence of surface water (such as along creeks, canals, rivers, and ponds) typically contained the following wetland plants: coyote willow (*Salix exigua*), cottonwood (*Populus Fremontii*), reed canarygrass (*Phalaris arundinacea*), cattail (*Typha spp.*), hardstem bulrush (*Schoenoplectus acutus*), threesquare bulrush (*S. pungens*), algae and/or submersed aquatic vegetation (not identified), and Russian olive (*Elaeagnus angustifolia*). Wetlands that were identified as seasonally flooded or fresh meadows typically contained saltgrass (*Distichlis spicata*), wire rush (*Juncus balticus*), clustered field sedge (*Carex praegracilis*), curly dock (*Rumex crispus*), foxtail (*Alopecurus spp.*), and cattail (*Typha spp.*).

Simulation of Groundwater Flow

The hydrologic effects of land-use change and aggregate mining on groundwater flow and wetlands in the study area were simulated using the USGS modular groundwater modeling program MODFLOW–2000 (Harbaugh and others, 2000). Pre- and post-processing of MODFLOW-2000 files

Table 5. Summary statistics for wetlands and surface water mapped by this study, Brighton to Fort Lupton, Colorado, July–August, 2004.

[Source: Salas (2005)]

Feature	Number	Total area (acres)	Mean size (acres)	Minimum size (acres)	Maximum size (acres)
Wetland	28	262.5	9.37	0.04	132.6
Surface water	75	302.7	4.04	0.05	48.6

primarily were completed using the MODFLOW Graphical User Interface (Winston, 2000) for the Argus ONE geographic information system (Argus Interware, 1997). The model was calibrated to seasonal groundwater-level and flow conditions of the South Platte alluvial aquifer during the irrigation and non-irrigation seasons in 1957, 1977, and 2000 using the Observation, Sensitivity, and Parameter-Estimation processes (Hill and others, 2000) of MODFLOW-2000. The calibrated model then was used to simulate (1) steady-state hydrologic effects of predicted land-use conditions in 2020 and 2040, (2) transient cumulative hydrologic effects of the potential extent of reclaimed aggregate pits in 2020 and 2040, (3) transient hydrologic effects of actively dewatered aggregate pits, and (4) effects of different pit spacings and configurations on groundwater levels.

Nine numerical simulations of the potential hydrologic effects of land-use change, reclaimed pits, and actively dewatered pits are presented as follows:

Simulation 1—The hydrologic effects of reduced aquifer recharge resulting from the conversion of non-irrigated and irrigated land to impervious urban area are simulated for land-use conditions predicted by the SLEUTH urban-growth model for 2020.

Simulation 2—The hydrologic effects of reduced aquifer recharge resulting from the conversion of non-irrigated and irrigated land to impervious urban area are simulated for land-use conditions predicted by the SLEUTH urban-growth model for 2040.

Simulation 3—The cumulative hydrologic effects of multiple reclaimed pits are simulated for the potential extent of aggregate mining in 2020. The simulation includes a combination of lined pits, unlined pits, and pits backfilled with fine sediments.

Simulation 4—The cumulative hydrologic effects of multiple reclaimed pits are simulated for the potential extent of aggregate mining in 2040. Pits excavated after 2020 are simulated as lined.

Simulation 5—The cumulative hydrologic effects of multiple reclaimed pits are simulated for the potential extent of aggregate mining in 2040. Pits excavated after 2020 are simulated as unlined.

Simulation 6—The hydrologic effects of a single dewatered pit added after 2020 are simulated.

Simulation 7—The hydrologic effects of two closely spaced, dewatered pits added after 2020 are simulated.

Simulation 8—The hydrologic effects of two widely spaced, dewatered pits added after 2020 are simulated.

Simulation 9—The hydrologic effects of three closely spaced, dewatered pits added after 2020 are simulated.

In addition, simulations of the hydrologic effects of three hypothetical lined pits are used to assess the effect that pit spacing and configuration (size and location relative to other pits) have on groundwater levels near reclaimed lined pits.

Mathematical Methods

MODFLOW-2000 simulates three-dimensional movement of groundwater of constant density through porous earth material using the following partial differential equation (McDonald and Harbaugh, 1988):

$$\frac{\partial}{\partial x}\left(K_{xx}\frac{\partial h}{\partial x}\right)+\frac{\partial}{\partial y}\left(K_{yy}\frac{\partial h}{\partial y}\right)+\frac{\partial}{\partial z}\left(K_{zz}\frac{\partial h}{\partial z}\right)+W=S_S\frac{\partial h}{\partial t} \quad (5)$$

where

K_{xx}, K_{yy}, and K_{zz} are values of hydraulic conductivity along the x, y, and z coordinate axes, which are assumed parallel to the major axes of hydraulic conductivity in the aquifer (L/T);

h is hydraulic head (L);

W is volumetric flux per unit volume from a hydrologic source or sink as a function of location and time, with $W<0$ for flow out of the aquifer and $W>0$ for flow into the aquifer (T^{-1});

S_S is specific storage of the porous material (L^{-1}); and

t is time (T).

MODFLOW-2000 solves equation (5) using a finite-difference method in which the model domain is discretized into a grid of cells, and hydraulic head is computed at the center of each cell. Flows into or out of the aquifer from hydrologic sources and sinks and head-dependent boundaries also are computed for each simulation. Changes in aquifer storage are computed for transient (time-varying) simulations.

Model Design

Spatial Discretization

The South Platte alluvial aquifer represented by the model (fig. 21) is about 11 mi long, extending from the south end of the study area to the north end, and about 3.6 mi wide at its widest point at the south end of the study area. The simulated area includes saturated alluvium in tributary valleys of Big and Little Dry Creeks within 0.7–0.85 mi of the main stem of the South Platte River valley. The model grid has 116 rows and 38 columns with a uniform cell size of 500 ft by 500 ft. The model simulates groundwater flow by using one layer under unconfined conditions with rewetting capability active. Layer thickness ranges from 12 to 65 ft (fig. 22) as determined by the difference between land-surface altitude estimated from a USGS DEM with 30-m resolution (accessed June 10, 2005 at *http://rockyweb.cr.usgs.gov/elevation*) and bedrock altitude at the base of the alluvium indicated by Char and Arnold (2002).

Boundary Conditions and Hydrologic Stresses

The base and most of the west side of the model are simulated as no-flow boundaries (inactive cells) (fig. 21) to represent relatively low-permeability bedrock in contact with the alluvial aquifer. Although the east side of the model also is underlain by relatively shallow bedrock, unconsolidated sediments on hillslopes east of the aquifer generally are thicker (fig. 8), and the east side of the model is simulated as a specified-flow boundary by using the MODFLOW Well Package to represent subsurface irrigation return flow occurring through the unconsolidated sediments from ditch seepage and infiltration of water beneath irrigated fields located upgradient and outside the model domain to the east. Simulated return flow during the non-irrigation season is one-half of that during the irrigation season to represent less inflow resulting from reduced recharge and lower groundwater levels during the non-irrigation season. The upgradient and downgradient ends of the aquifer, including the upgradient ends of tributary valleys, are simulated as general-head boundaries by using the MODFLOW General-Head Boundary package to allow groundwater flow into and out of the model, while also permitting hydraulic head to change at the boundaries in response to land-use changes and aggregate mining. General-head boundaries are defined using a saturated thickness, hydraulic conductivity, and hydraulic gradient representative of the aquifer at each boundary location. Hydrologic stresses simulated by the model include distributed recharge at the water table, streams and ditches, well pumping, and phreatophyte evapotranspiration. Definition and values of parameters used to represent boundary conditions and hydrologic stresses in the model are presented in the "Parameterization" section of this report.

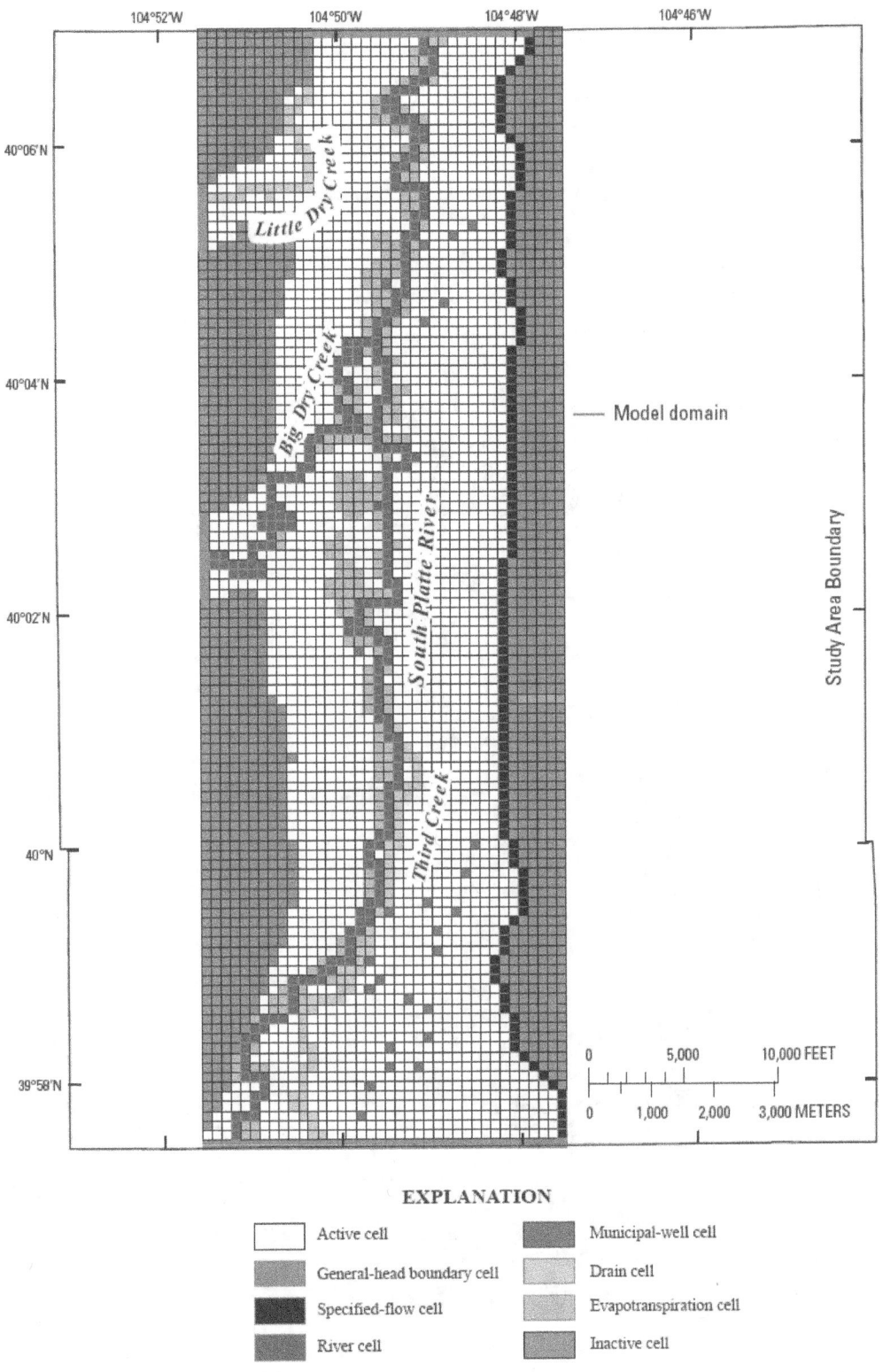

Figure 21. Model grid and boundary conditions of the simulated South Platte alluvial aquifer, Brighton to Fort Lupton, Colorado.

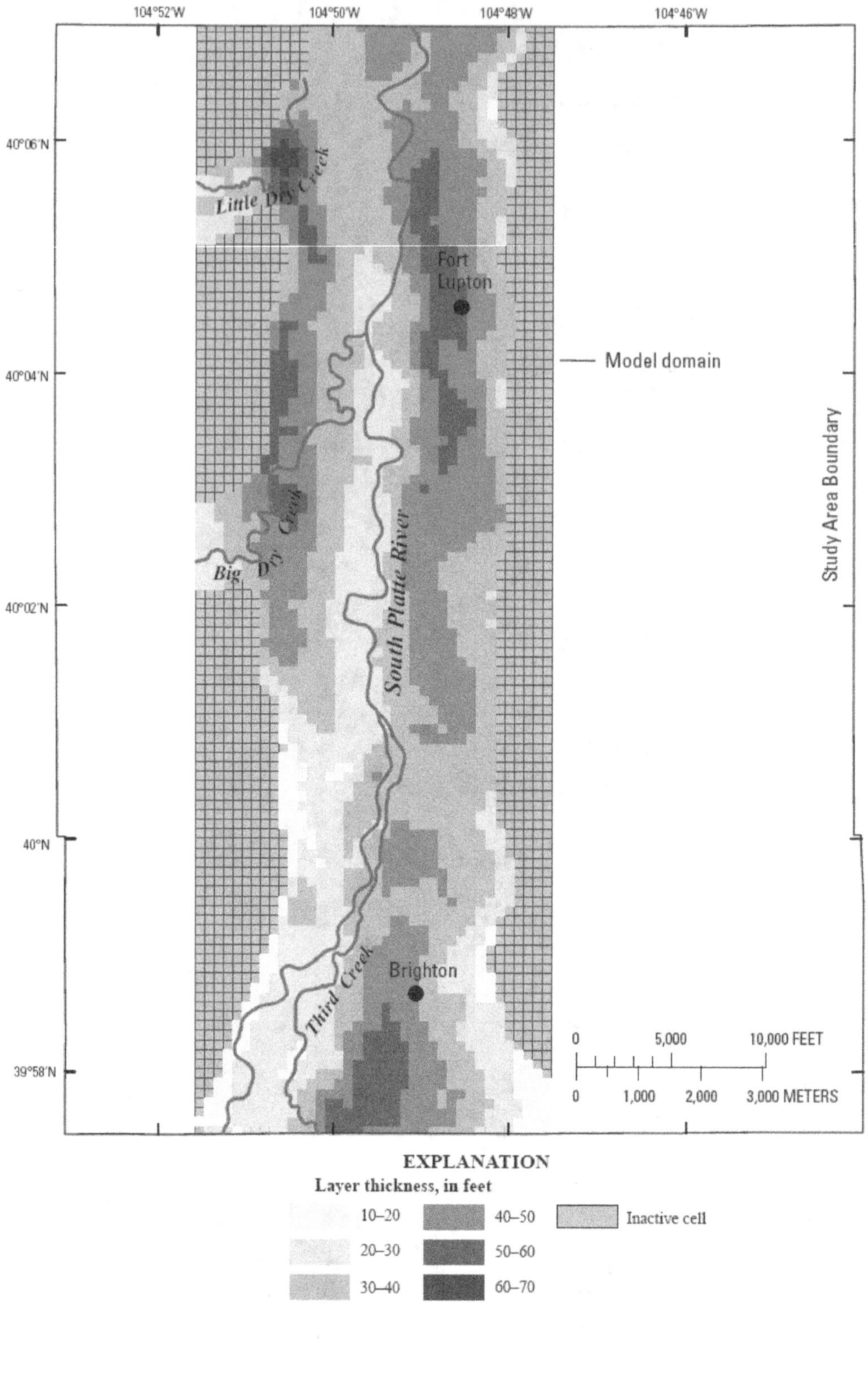

Figure 22.   Layer thickness of the simulated South Platte alluvial aquifer, Brighton to Fort Lupton, Colorado.

Recharge. Recharge from infiltration at the land surface is simulated by using the MODFLOW Recharge package and is distributed in the model based on land-use conditions in 1957, 1977, and 2000 as shown in figures 17A–C. Recharge beneath non-irrigated land and urban areas is simulated as having the same value during both the irrigation and non-irrigation seasons. Recharge beneath irrigated agricultural areas during the irrigation season is simulated as greater than during the non-irrigation season to reflect increased recharge from infiltration of water applied to irrigated fields and seepage losses from irrigation ditches. Recharge beneath irrigated agricultural areas during the non-irrigation season is simulated to be the same as recharge beneath non-irrigated areas.

Streams and ditches. The South Platte River and Big Dry Creek are simulated by the MODFLOW River package, which contributes water to or releases water from the aquifer at river cells as determined by the hydraulic gradient between the aquifer and the river and as a function of streambed conductance. Locations of the South Platte River and Big Dry Creek were determined from USGS 7.5-minute topographic quadrangle maps (1994) at 1:24,000 scale. River stage of the South Platte River and Big Dry Creek is defined 2 ft below land surface to represent the lower altitude of the stream channel relative to the mean altitude of each 500-ft-wide cell. Streambed conductance is defined as a function of the stream-channel width and length, streambed thickness, and hydraulic conductivity of the streambed material. Average stream-channel width was estimated from USGS 7.5-minute topographic quadrangle maps. Stream-channel length within each model cell was calculated by the MODFLOW Graphical User Interface (Winston, 2000) on the basis of stream locations. A streambed thickness of 1 ft and a streambed hydraulic conductivity of 1 ft/d were assumed for initial values.

Little Dry Creek and Third Creek are simulated by the MODFLOW Drain package rather than the River package because flow in the creeks is intermittent and is assumed not to contribute substantially to the alluvial aquifer. However, the creeks can drain water from the aquifer if the water table rises to near land surface. Locations of Little Dry Creek and Third Creek are based on CDWR mapping provided by Schupbach and Lewis (1996). Drain altitude of Little Dry Creek and Third Creek is defined 2 ft below land surface to represent the incised stream-channel altitude. Drain conductance is defined as described for streambed conductance, assuming the stream channels are 10-ft wide with a 1-ft thick streambed having a hydraulic conductivity of 1 ft/d.

Irrigation ditches in the model domain are not explicitly simulated except where Lupton Bottom Ditch intercepts and conveys drainage from Little Dry Creek (fig. 1). In this circumstance, Lupton Bottom Ditch is simulated as a drain in the same manner as Little Dry Creek.

Some areas of the model (fig. 21) appear to have an excessively wide (more than one model cell) simulated stream feature. This is caused by the meandering stream feature flowing across a small part of many adjacent model cells. However, the net hydrologic effect of the stream feature is representative of a stream flowing across a single model cell because streambed and drain conductance are apportioned by the extent of the stream feature within each model cell.

Well pumping. Municipal-well pumping is simulated by using the MODFLOW Well package to specify flow out of the model at municipal-well locations. The location and withdrawal rate for each simulated well is based on data provided by the cities of Brighton and Fort Lupton as described in the "Aquifer Outflows" section of this report. Withdrawals from irrigation wells are not simulated by the model because of large uncertainties in the location and withdrawal rate of irrigation wells during the time periods simulated. However, because irrigation wells generally are collocated with or near irrigated land and generally are fairly evenly distributed within irrigated areas, the steady-state effects of irrigation-well withdrawals are assumed to be approximately accounted for by the term used to represent net recharge beneath irrigated areas.

Evapotranspiration. Evapotranspiration by shallow-rooted vegetation over large areas is not explicitly simulated in the model because such evapotranspiration is considered in the simulation of net recharge for each land-use category. However, phreatophyte evapotranspiration is explicitly simulated in the model by using the MODFLOW Evapotranspiration (EVT) package because phreatophytes commonly withdraw water directly from the water table. The Evapotranspiration package simulates the removal of water from the aquifer in proportion to the depth of the water table below a user-defined altitude. Evapotranspiration occurs at a maximum rate when the water table is at the user-defined altitude, and evapotranspiration decreases linearly to zero at a user-defined extinction depth, below which evapotranspiration does not occur. Phreatophyte evapotranspiration in the model is simulated relative to DEM-derived land-surface altitude and has an extinction depth of 10 ft.

Evapotranspiration cells in the model (fig. 21) are assigned on the basis of phreatophyte extent mapped by the Colorado Division of Wildlife (2007a, b) with small (<2,500 ft^2), isolated phreatophyte areas removed. Because phreatophyte extent within each model cell generally is less than the total cell area, a multiplier array is used to apportion phreatophyte evapotranspiration in each cell based on the ratio of phreatophyte area to total cell area.

Hydraulic Conductivity

The spatial distribution of hydraulic conductivity in the simulated South Platte alluvial aquifer is represented by using four parameter zones as shown in figure 23. Hydraulic conductivity within each zone is uniform, and each zone is associated with a hydraulic-conductivity parameter value estimated by the model. Zone 1 represents areas of least hydraulic conductivity along parts of the aquifer margins and in tributary valleys, zone 2 represents areas of medium hydraulic conductivity along most of the aquifer margins, zone 3 represents areas of greater hydraulic conductivity along the central part of the aquifer, and zone 4 represents a small area of greatest hydraulic conductivity near Brighton. Hydraulic-conductivity zones were assigned to reflect the spatial distribution of hydraulic-conductivity values shown on figure 12.

Parameterization

A parameter represents a hydrologic property of the model such as hydraulic conductivity or recharge. Fifteen parameters are used in the model. Four parameters are used to represent the hydraulic-conductivity distribution (LPF_Par1, LPF_Par2, LPF_Par3, and LPF_Par4) (fig. 23) of the alluvial aquifer. Three parameters are used to represent the distribution of recharge (figs. 17A–C) based on land use. Recharge beneath irrigated agricultural land during the irrigation season is represented by parameter RCH_Irr. Recharge beneath non-irrigated land and recharge beneath irrigated agricultural land during the non-irrigation season are represented by parameter RCH_Nonirr. Recharge beneath urban areas is represented by parameter RCH_Urban. Other properties or aspects of the model that are represented by parameters are (1) hydraulic conductance per unit length of general-head boundaries at the upgradient and downgradient ends of the South Platte River valley (GHB_Splt), (2) hydraulic conductance per unit length of general-head boundaries at the upgradient ends of Big Dry Creek and Little Dry Creek tributary valleys (GHB_Trib), (3) streambed conductance per unit length of the South Platte River (RIV_Splt), (4) streambed conductance per unit length of Big Dry Creek (RIV_Bdry), (5) drain conductance per unit length of Little Dry Creek and Third Creek tributaries (DRN_Trib), (6) subsurface return-flow rate along the east side of the model (Q_ReturnE), (7) municipal-well withdrawal rate (Q_Mwells), and (8) maximum phreatophyte evapotranspiration rate (EVT_Par1). Parameters representing conductance values per unit length (GHB_Splt, GHB_Trib, RIV_Splt, RIV_Bdry, and DRN_Trib) were multiplied by the length of the represented stream feature within each model cell to calculate total conductance values. The parameter Q_Mwells represents the mean withdrawal rate per munici-pal well during the 2000 irrigation season. Multipliers were used to adjust individual well withdrawals to represent flow conditions during the irrigation and non-irrigation seasons of each time period simulated. A sixteenth parameter (specific yield) was added for transient simulations of the effects of aggregate mining but was not included in model calibra-tion because specific yield is not relevant for steady-state calibra-tion. Specific yield was assigned a value of 0.25 in all transient simulations. The initial and final estimated values for each parameter are presented in table 6. Initial parameter values are based on data and estimated hydrologic conditions described under "Groundwater Hydrology." All final estimated param-eter values appear reasonable compared to available data and estimated error associated with the data. The initial value (0.0038 ft/d) of parameter RCH_Irr represents recharge of about 8 in. during the irrigation season, and the final esti-mated value (0.0056 ft/d) represents recharge of about 12 in. during the irrigation season. The initial value (0.00011 ft/d) of

parameters RCH_Nonirr and RCH_Urban represents recharge of about 0.5 in/yr, and final estimated values for RCH_Nonirr (0.000082 ft/d) and RCH_Urban (0 ft/d) represent recharge of about 0.4 in/yr and 0 in/yr, respectively.

Model Calibration

The model was calibrated by using the Observation, Sensitivity, and Parameter-Estimation Processes of MODFLOW-2000 (Hill and others, 2000), which uses inverse modeling methods to minimize the difference between measured values and model-simulated values. MODFLOW-2000 allows individual stress periods in a single simulation to be either steady-state or transient. The model is calibrated to six successive steady-state stress periods in a single simulation that represents hydraulic head and base-flow conditions during the irrigation seasons and the non-irrigation seasons in 1957, 1977, and 2000. Calibration to hydrologic conditions in multiple time periods was used to facilitate estimation of recharge as it relates to land-use change. The years 1957, 1977, and 2000 were selected for model calibration because spatial datasets indicating land-use conditions (U.S. Geological Survey, 1999, 2001b, c) were available for these time periods. The spatial distribution of recharge by land use in the model was changed between 1957 and 1977 and between 1977 and 2000 by using separate MODFLOW-2000 Instances (Harbaugh and others, 2000), which allow a parameter to vary spatially between stress periods. Calibration to seasonal hydrologic conditions was used to simulate the seasonal, dynamic nature of the alluvial aquifer. The model was calibrated to successive steady-state seasonal stress periods, rather than transient stress periods, because the aquifer has high hydraulic conductivity that allows the effects of hydrologic stresses to be rapidly distributed throughout the aquifer. As a general rule, it is reasonable to use successive steady-state solutions to periodic (seasonal) stresses when the dimensionless variable τ is less than 0.1 (Haitjema, 2006). The variable τ is defined by the following relation (Townley, 1995):

$$\tau = SL^2/4KHP \qquad (6)$$

where

S   is storage coefficient of the aquifer (dimensionless),
L   is the average distance between boundary conditions, in feet,
K   is hydraulic conductivity, in feet per day,
H   is saturated thickness, in feet, and
P   is the period of the forcing function (365 days for seasonal fluctuations).

By using a specific yield value of 0.25 for the storage coefficient, an average distance between boundary conditions of 4,000 ft, average hydraulic conductivity of 1,000 ft/d, average saturated thickness of 30 ft, and a forcing period of

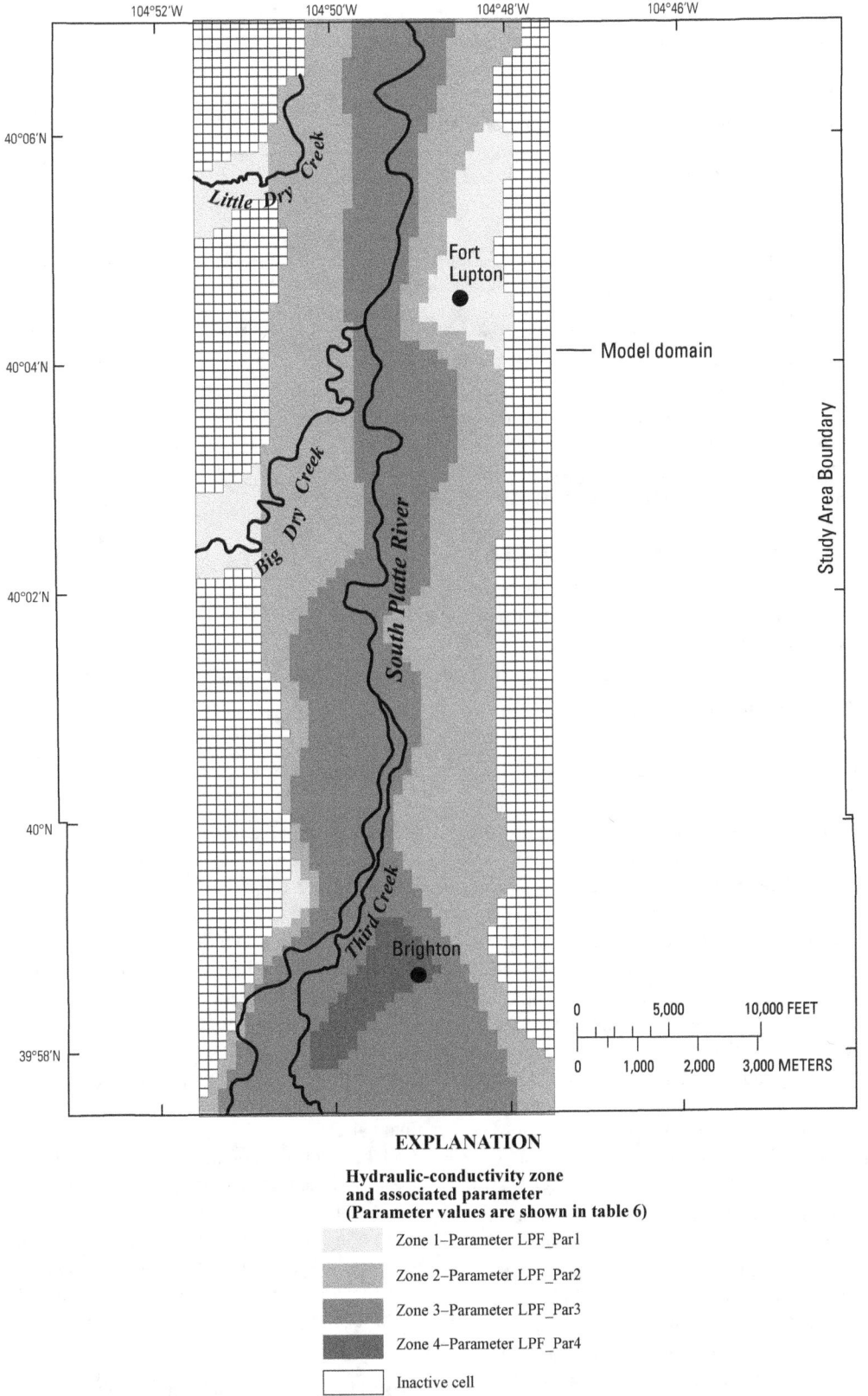

Figure 23. Hydraulic-conductivity zones of the simulated South Platte alluvial aquifer, Brighton to Fort Lupton, Colorado.

Table 6.   Initial and final estimated parameter values for the calibrated steady-state model of the South Platte alluvial aquifer, Brighton to Fort Lupton, Colorado.

[ft/d, feet per day; ft³/d, cubic feet per day]

Parameter name	Model feature represented by parameter	Initial value	Final estimated value	Units
LPF_Par1	Horizontal hydraulic conductivity of zone 1	450	430	ft/d
LPF_Par2	Horizontal hydraulic conductivity of zone 2	740	880	ft/d
LPF_Par3	Horizontal hydraulic conductivity of zone 3	1,200	1,070	ft/d
LPF_Par4	Horizontal hydraulic conductivity of zone 4	2,100	2,110	ft/d
RCH_Urban	Recharge rate beneath urban areas	1.1E-4	0	ft/d
RCH_Irr	Recharge rate beneath irrigated land during irrigation season	3.8E-3	5.6E-3	ft/d
RCH_Nonirr	Recharge rate beneath non-irrigated land and beneath irrigated land during non-irrigation season	1.1E-4	8.2E-5	ft/d
GHB_Splt	Hydraulic conductance per unit length of general-head boundaries at upgradient and downgradient ends of South Platte River valley	1,000	870	ft/d
GHB_Trib	Hydraulic conductance per unit length of general-head boundaries at upgradient ends of Big Dry Creek and Little Dry Creek tributary valleys	10	10	ft/d
RIV_Splt	Streambed conductance per unit length of South Platte River	140	100	ft/d
RIV_Bdry	Streambed conductance per unit length of Big Dry Creek	20	2.2	ft/d
DRN_Trib	Drain conductance per unit length of Third Creek and Little Dry Creek tributaries	10	17	ft/d
Q_ReturnE	Subsurface return-flow rate along east model boundary	10,000	8,490	ft³/d
Q_Mwells	Municipal-well withdrawal rate	−68,000	−95,700	ft³/d
EVT_Par1	Maximum phreatophyte evapotranspiration rate	1.4E-2	1.3E-2	ft/d

365 days, τ for the model is 0.09, which indicates steady-state calibration to seasonal conditions likely provides a reasonable representation of the aquifer system. Because the model is calibrated to multiple steady-state stress periods in a single simulation, individual parameter values estimated during calibration represent the overall best fit between measured values and model-simulated values for all stress periods.

To evaluate the viability of alternative model structures, model calibration was accomplished by beginning with a simple model and adding complexity incrementally based on the contribution of each added feature to improving statistical measures of model fit and related measures. The aquifer hydraulic-conductivity distribution and stage of the South Platte River also were adjusted to evaluate their effect on calibration. Incremental model additions included simulation of (1) return flow along the east and west model boundaries, (2) groundwater drainage to Little Dry Creek and Third Creek, (3) phreatophyte evapotranspiration, (4) irrigation- and municipal-well withdrawals, and (5) flow in irrigation ditches. Inclusion of return flow along the east model boundary, groundwater drainage to Little Dry Creek and Third Creek, phreatophyte evapotranspiration, and municipal-well withdrawals improved model fit. Inclusion of return flow along the east model boundary had the greatest influence on model fit. Addition of phreatophyte evapotranspiration had a small effect on model

fit but reduced parameter correlation in the model. Inclusion of irrigation-well withdrawals caused simulated recharge beneath irrigated lands to be unrealistically large and model residuals to have a less-random spatial distribution. Similarly, explicit simulation of flow in individual irrigation ditches reduced model fit and contributed to unrealistic values for other parameters. During parameter estimation, urban recharge and return flow along the west model boundary consistently became very small (near zero), and the model had very little sensitivity to these parameters (see "Sensitivity Analysis"). Consequently, return flow along the west boundary was not included in the final calibrated model. Urban recharge was retained in the model for comparison to recharge beneath other land uses, but it was assigned a value of zero to promote model stability and to simulate the maximum potential effects of converting irrigated or non-irrigated land to urban areas. Because the model has very little sensitivity to urban recharge, the assumption of zero recharge beneath urban areas had little effect on model calibration.

Observations and Prior Information

An observation represents a measurement of a physical aspect of the hydrologic system, such as hydraulic head or flow, that can be used for comparison to simulated values during model calibration. Field measurements of hydrologic properties that are used to define parameter values are called prior information. To simulate average hydrologic conditions during the irrigation and non-irrigation seasons in each calibration year (1957, 1977, and 2000) and avoid calibrating to short-term drought or wet conditions, head and flow observations for 3 years before and after each calibration year are included in the calibration data set for each stress period. Therefore, hydraulic head and flow during the irrigation and non-irrigation seasons in 1957 represent average seasonal (irrigation or non-irrigation) conditions for the period 1954–60, hydraulic head and flow during 1977 represent average seasonal conditions for 1974–80, and hydraulic head and flow during 2000 represent average seasonal conditions for 1997–2003. If multiple head or flow observations were available at a single location for a given time period, the average of the observations was used to represent hydrologic conditions at that location.

Hydraulic head observations. Hydraulic-head observations consist of 159 groundwater-level measurements (fig. 24; table 7) distributed throughout the aquifer during the six seasonal calibration stress periods. Forty-one groundwater-level measurements represent the 1957 irrigation season, 11 measurements represent the 1957 non-irrigation season, 6 measurements represent the 1977 irrigation season, 48 measurements represent the 1977 non-irrigation season, 30 measurements represent the 2000 irrigation season, and 23 measurements represent the 2000 non-irrigation season. If hydraulic-head observations for a location were available for different calibration stress periods, the change in groundwater level between periods was used as the observation rather than hydraulic head to provide for greater observation accuracy at a specific location. Of the 159 groundwater-level measurements, 40 represent temporal changes in groundwater levels (table 7).

Flow observations. Flow observations consist of six gain-loss determinations (fig. 24; table 8) based on monthly mass-balance analysis of all substantial inflows and outflows to the South Platte River between stream gages located near Henderson (station number 06720500) and Fort Lupton (station number 06721000). One flow observation was used to represent average base-flow conditions during each of the irrigation and non-irrigation seasons in 1957, 1977, and 2000. Because the gage near Henderson is south of the study area, gain-loss between the south end of the model domain and the gage near Fort Lupton was estimated by linear interpolation as 78 percent of gain-loss between the two gages. No major inflows or outflows occur between the Henderson gage and the south end of the model domain. Because all flow observations are positive, flow observations represent average seasonal gain to the South Platte River during each seasonal stress period.

Observation weights. Hydraulic-head and flow observation weights were assigned based on estimated measurement accuracy by using statistical methods described by Hill (1998, p. 45–49). Three different standard-deviation values were used to represent measurement error for hydraulic-head observations. The standard deviation of measurement error for most

hydraulic-head observations is estimated to be about 3 ft based on errors in land-surface datum and measurement method. However, the standard deviation of measurement error for hydraulic-head observations was considered to be 1.5 ft if the land-surface datum for the groundwater-level measurement was indicated with a precision greater than 1 ft. Because measurements of temporal changes in groundwater levels at a specific location remove errors associated with land-surface datum, observations of temporal hydraulic-head change were estimated to have a standard deviation of measurement error of 1 ft.

Because flow observations are determined from the mass-balance analysis of all inflows and outflows to the South Platte River between stream gages at the upstream and downstream ends of the observation reach, flow-observation weights include measurement errors associated with each inflow and outflow measurement. The standard deviation of measurement error for each flow observation was calculated by summing the variances of measurement error associated with each inflow or outflow and taking the square root of the total variance. The accuracy rating of streamflow measurements was assumed to be good, in which 95 percent of the measured flows are within 10 percent of their true values (Rantz and others, 1982).

Prior information. Use of prior information allows direct measurements of model input values to be included in the calibration regression (Hill, 1998). Prior information was used to constrain estimates of parameters LPF_Par1, LPF_Par2, LPF_Par3, LPF_Par4, RCH_Irr, RCH_Nonirr, GHB_Splt, GHB_Trib, DRN_Trib, Q_Mwells, and EVT_Par1. Prior-information values were assigned on the basis of initial parameter values (table 6), and weights for prior-information values generally were assigned on the basis of the standard deviation of estimated prior-information measurement error as described by Hill (1998, p. 45–49).

Calibration Assessment

Statistical Measures of Overall Model Fit

The difference between an observation and a simulated value or between a prior-information value and a parameter estimate is called a residual. Overall model fit was evaluated by using the standard error of the model regression and the mean absolute error (MAE) of unweighted residuals. The standard error of the regression is an indicator of the overall magnitude of weighted residuals and is expressed as (Hill, 1998):

$$s = \sqrt{\frac{S(\underline{b})}{(ND + NPR - NP)}} \qquad (7)$$

where

s is the standard error of the regression,
$S(\underline{b})$ is the value of the weighted least-squares objective function, calculated as

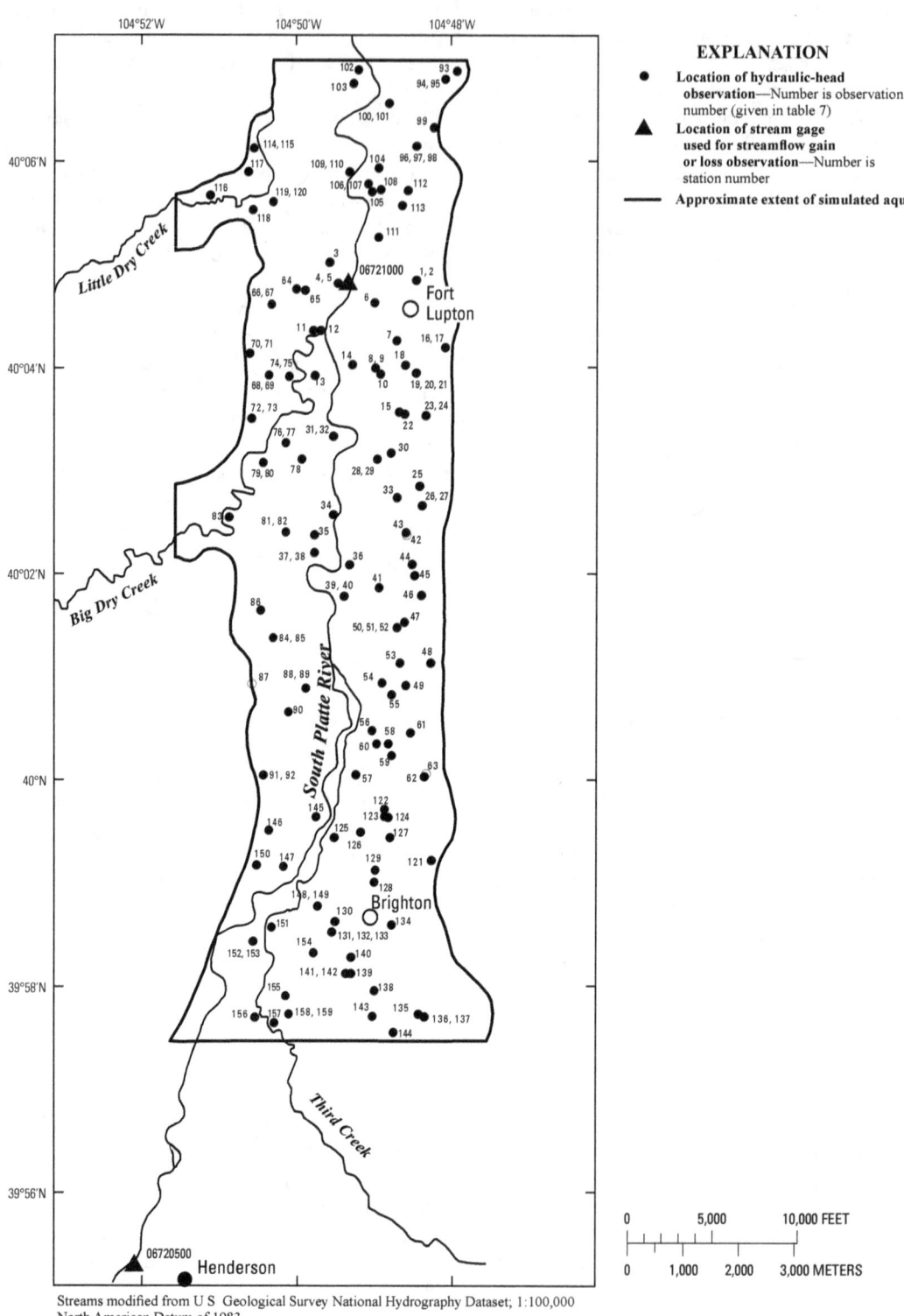

Figure 24.   Location of hydraulic-head observations and stream gages used to estimate streamflow gain-loss observations for the simulated South Platte alluvial aquifer, Brighton to Fort Lupton, Colorado.

Table 7.   Hydraulic-head observations used to calibrate the steady-state model of the South Platte alluvial aquifer, Brighton to Fort Lupton, Colorado.

[Hydraulic head in feet above National Geodetic Vertical Datum of 1929; Observation date(s) in mm/dd/yyyy; --, no data; CDWR, Colorado Division of Water Resources; USGS NWIS, U.S. Geological Survey National Water Information System; CDMRS, Colorado Division of Mining, Reclamation, and Safety]

Observation number	Observation name	Hydraulic head[1]	Observation date(s)	Well identifier[2]	Source
1	B16605BCD_1	4893.8	10/25/1956, 11/04/1957	SB00106605BCD	USGS NWIS
2	B16605BCD_2	**4893.8**	03/14/1974	SB00106605BCD	USGS NWIS
3	B16606BB	4885	03/08/2002	239289A	CDWR
4	B16606BDC_1	4888	11/--/1957	--	Smith and others (1964)
5	B16606BDC_2	**4888.8**	03/17/1974, 01/05/1975	SB00106606BDC	USGS NWIS
6	B16606DBD	4887.2	03/17/1974	SB00106606DBD	USGS NWIS
7	B16607AA	4889	04/16/1957	SB00106607AA	CDWR
8	B16607ACD_1	4898.6	11/04/1957	SB00106607ACD1	USGS NWIS
9	B16607ACD_2	**4895.2**	03/14/1974, 01/05/1975	SB00106607ACD	USGS NWIS
10	B16607AD	4899	09/19/1977	93440A	CDWR
11	B16607BBB	4892.8	03/17/1974, 01/05/1975	SB00106607BBB	USGS NWIS
12	B16607BBB1	4894.5	08/30/1956	SB00106607BBB1	USGS NWIS
13	B16607BC	4899	04/30/1997	13697R	CDWR
14	B16607BD	4897	10/03/1997	197906	CDWR
15	B16607DD	4908	04/21/1977	19791RF	CDWR
16	B16608BAD_1	4914.3	11/04/1957	SB00106608BAD1	USGS NWIS
17	B16608BAD_2	**4906.6**	03/17/1974, 01/05/1975	SB00106608BAD2	USGS NWIS
18	B16608BC	4901	09/04/1998	123510A	CDWR
19	B16608BCD_1	4906.8	04/04/1955, 04/17/1956, 05/07/1957, 04/15/1958, 04/01/1959, 04/05/1960	SB00106608BCD	USGS NWIS
20	B16608BCD_2	**4910.6**	11/08/1955, 11/13/1956, 11/--/1957, 11/13/1958, 11/11/1959, 11/02/1960	SB00106608BCD	USGS NWIS; Smith and others (1964)
21	B16608BCD_3	**4907.6**	03/01/1977	SB00106608BCD1	Schneider and Hillier (1978)
22	B16608CC	4906	08/25/1978	99795A	CDWR
23	B16608CCD_1	4924	11/04/1957	SB00106608CCD1	USGS NWIS
24	B16608CCD_2	**4914.3**	03/14/1974, 01/05/1975	SB00106608CCD	USGS NWIS
25	B16617CB	4917	11/19/1999	11384R	CDWR
26	B16617CCD_1	4930.5	11/04/1957	SB00106617CCD1	USGS NWIS
27	B16617CCD_2	**4920.5**	03/14/1974, 01/05/1975	SB00106617CCD2	USGS NWIS
28	B16618ACD_1	4915.6	11/04/1957	SB00106618ACD1	USGS NWIS
29	B16618ACD_2	**4911.8**	03/14/1974	SB00106618ACD	USGS NWIS
30	B16618AD	4909	11/29/1999	11383R	CDWR
31	B16618BB_1	4904.9	02/07/2003	250147	CDWR
32	B16618BB_2	**4908.7**	07/02/2003	M2000-016 CH03-MW03	CDMRS
33	B16618DD	4918	05/27/1978	99034A	CDWR
34	B16619BAB	4915.5	11/04/1957	SB00106619BAB1	USGS NWIS

Table 7.   Hydraulic-head observations used to calibrate the steady-state model of the South Platte alluvial aquifer, Brighton to Fort Lupton, Colorado.—Contiued

[Hydraulic head in feet above National Geodetic Vertical Datum of 1929; Observation date(s) in mm/dd/yyyy; --, no data; CDWR, Colorado Division of Water Resources; USGS NWIS, U.S. Geological Survey National Water Information System; CDMRS, Colorado Division of Mining, Reclamation, and Safety]

Observation number	Observation name	Hydraulic head[1]	Observation date(s)	Well identifier[2]	Source
35	B16619BCB	4915.2	03/14/1974, 01/05/1975	SB00106619BCB	USGS NWIS
36	B16619CA	4920	03/16/1979	13699F	CDWR
37	B16619CB_1	4918.2	02/12/2002, 03/27/2003	M2000-016 RI01-MW08	CDMRS
38	B16619CB_2	**4920**	07/12/2002, 07/02/2003	M2000-016 RI01-MW08	CDMRS
39	B16619CD_1	4923.9	04/09/2002, 03/27/2003	M2000-016 RI01-MW02	CDMRS
40	B16619CD_2	**4925.6**	07/12/2002, 07/02/2003	M2000-016 RI01-MW02	CDMRS
41	B16619DCD	4926.2	08/08/1956	SB00106619DCD1 USGS 4001	USGS NWIS
42	B16620BC1	4922	04/22/1976	83526A	CDWR
43	B16620BC2	4921	07/10/1998	46066A	CDWR
44	B16620CB	4927	10/16/1997	20138R	CDWR
45	B16620CBD	4925	03/14/1974	SB00106620CBD	USGS NWIS
46	B16620CCD	4936.2	11/04/1957	SB00106620CCD1	USGS NWIS
47	B16629BC	4930	02/18/2002	232950A	CDWR
48	B16629CA	4935	04/07/1998	205941A	CDWR
49	B16629CCC	4944	11/04/1957	SB00106629CCC1 USGS 4000	USGS NWIS
50	B16630ADA_1	4933.8	04/05/1955, 04/17/1956, 05/07/1957, 04/07/1958, 04/01/1959, 04/12/1960	SB00106630ADA	USGS NWIS
51	B16630ADA_2	**4936.9**	11/11/1954, 11/08/1955, 11/13/1956, 11/12/1957, 11/13/1958, 11/11/1959, 11/02/1960	SB00106630ADA	USGS NWIS
52	B16630ADA_3	**4932.2**	03/01/1977	SB00106630ADA1	Schneider and Hillier (1978)
53	B16630DA	4930	04/13/2002	57300F	CDWR
54	B16630DD	4935	10/16/1997	17900A	CDWR
55	B16631AA	4932	03/27/1998	181391A	CDWR
56	B16631AC	4952	09/18/1998	214916A	CDWR
57	B16631CDD	4947.2	11/04/1957	SB00106631CDD1 USGS 4000	USGS NWIS
58	B16631DA1	4944	05/15/1975	79073	CDWR
59	B16631DA2	4945.5	05/01/1997	212525	CDWR
60	B16631DB	4945	10/07/1977	81358	CDWR
61	B16632BC	4940	11/25/2000	22531A	CDWR
62	B16632CCD	4955.3	11/04/1957	SB00106632CCD1	USGS NWIS
63	B16632CDC	4950.6	03/14/1974, 01/05/1975	SB00106632CDC	USGS NWIS

Table 7.   Hydraulic-head observations used to calibrate the steady-state model of the South Platte alluvial aquifer, Brighton to Fort Lupton, Colorado.—Continued

[Hydraulic head in feet above National Geodetic Vertical Datum of 1929; Observation date(s) in mm/dd/yyyy; --, no data; CDWR, Colorado Division of Water Resources; USGS NWIS, U.S. Geological Survey National Water Information System; CDMRS, Colorado Division of Mining, Reclamation, and Safety]

Observation number	Observation name	Hydraulic head[1]	Observation date(s)	Well identifier[2]	Source
64	B16701DA	4885	03/05/2002	236955	CDWR
65	B16701DAA	4888.8	03/17/1974, 01/05/1975	SB00106701DAA2	USGS NWIS
66	B16701DBC_1	4893	02/04/2003	250149	CDWR
67	B16701DBC_2	**4898.4**	07/02/2003	M2000-016 DS03-MW01	CDMRS
68	B16712ACC_1	4901.6	11/04/1957	SB00106712ACC1	USGS NWIS
69	B16712ACC_2	**4899.1**	03/17/1974, 01/05/1975	SB00106712ACC	USGS NWIS
70	B16712BD_1	4901.8	03/27/2003	M2000-016 DS03-MW03	CDMRS
71	B16712BD_2	**4905.7**	08/14/2003	M2000-016 DS03-MW03	CDMRS
72	B16712CD_1	4910	01/29/2003	250142	CDWR
73	B16712CD_2	**4914.3**	08/18/2003	M2000-016 MY03-MW01	CDMRS
74	B16712DB_1	4903.1	02/05/2003	250139	CDWR
75	B16712DB_2	**4904.8**	07/02/2003	M2000-016 MF03-MW02	CDMRS
76	B16713AC_1	4907.2	02/07/2003	250146	CDWR
77	B16713AC_2	**4912.6**	07/02/2003	M2000-016 CH03-MW01	CDMRS
78	B16713ADD	4911.7	03/01/1977	SB00106713ADD1	Schneider and Hillier (1978)
79	B16713BDD_1	4916	11/--/1957	--	Smith and others (1964)
80	B16713BDD_2	**4914.1**	03/17/1974, 01/05/1975	SB00106713BDD	USGS NWIS
81	B16724AB_1	4919.6	02/14/2003	250144	CDWR
82	B16724AB_2	**4922**	07/02/2003	M2000-016 NO03-MW02	CDMRS
83	B16724BBB	4929.2	04/19/1977	SB00106724BBB1	Schneider and Hillier (1978)
84	B16725ACC_1	4930.9	11/04/1957	SB00106725ACC1	USGS NWIS
85	B16725ACC_2	**4929.9**	03/17/1974, 01/05/1975	SB00106725ACC	USGS NWIS
86	B16725BA	4929	07/12/1979	13320RF	CDWR
87	B16725CD	4930	03/21/1997	202399A	CDWR
88	B16725DD_1	4930.9	03/14/2002, 03/04/2003	M2004051 MW-5	CDMRS
89	B16725DD_2	**4932.2**	10/3/02, 7/9/03	M2004051 MW-5	CDMRS
90	B16736ACA	4936.7	03/17/1974, 01/05/1975	SB00106736ACA	USGS NWIS
91	B16736CDD_1	4948	11/--/1957	--	Smith and others (1964)
92	B16736CDD_2	**4948.1**	03/01/1977	SB00106736CDD1	Schneider and Hillier (1978)
93	B26629AB	4873	07/15/1977	17749R	CDWR
94	B26629ABC_1	4872.7	11/08/1957	SB00206629ABC2 USGS 4006	USGS NWIS
95	B26629ABC_2	**4868.3**	03/14/1974, 01/05/1975	SB00206629ABC2 USGS 4006	USGS NWIS

Table 7.   Hydraulic-head observations used to calibrate the steady-state model of the South Platte alluvial aquifer, Brighton to Fort Lupton, Colorado.—Continued

[Hydraulic head in feet above National Geodetic Vertical Datum of 1929; Observation date(s) in mm/dd/yyyy; --, no data; CDWR, Colorado Division of Water Resources; USGS NWIS, U.S. Geological Survey National Water Information System; CDMRS, Colorado Division of Mining, Reclamation, and Safety]

Observation number	Observation name	Hydraulic head[1]	Observation date(s)	Well identifier[2]	Source
96	B26629CCD_1	4873.7	04/04/1955, 04/17/1956, 05/06/1957, 04/02/1958, 04/01/1959, 04/05/1960	SB00206629CCD	USGS NWIS
97	B26629CCD_2	**4875.5**	11/10/1954, 11/08/1955, 11/13/1956, 11/12/1957, 11/12/1958, 11/11/1959, 11/02/1960	SB00206629CCD	USGS NWIS
98	B26629CCD_3	**4875.5**	03/01/1977	SB00206629CCD1	Schneider and Hillier (1978)
99	B26629CDB	4877.1	11/08/1957	SB00206629CDB1	USGS NWIS
100	B26630ADD_1	4870.3	11/08/1957	SB00206630ADD1	USGS NWIS
101	B26630ADD_2	**4871.3**	03/14/1974, 01/05/1975	SB00206630ADD	USGS NWIS
102	B26630BA	4863	08/01/1997	202995	CDWR
103	B26630BD	4863	08/14/1975	80437A	CDWR
104	B26631AB	4872	10/19/2000	226861	CDWR
105	B26631AC	4880	03/19/1976	20306RF	CDWR
106	B26631ACD_1	4874.3	04/14/1997, 04/29/1998, 03/24/1999, 04/11/2000, 03/08/2001, 04/02/2002, 04/28/2003	6818R	CDWR
107	B26631ACD_2	**4874.6**	10/15/1997, 10/01/1998, 11/01/2001	6818R	CDWR
108	B26631AD	4876	11/30/1999	6818RR	CDWR
109	B26631BDA_1	4876.8	11/04/1957	SB00206631BDA1	USGS NWIS
110	B26631BDA_2	**4876.7**	03/17/1974, 01/05/1975	SB00206631BDA	USGS NWIS
111	B26631DCD	4886.2	11/27/1957	SB00206631DCD1	USGS NWIS
112	B26632BCC	4883.9	11/04/1957	SB00206632BCC1	USGS NWIS
113	B26632CB	4883	02/20/1979	103272	CDWR
114	B26725CDC_1	4877.2	11/04/1957	SB00206725CDC1	USGS NWIS
115	B26725CDC_2	**4874.8**	03/17/1974, 01/05/1975	SB00206725CDC	USGS NWIS
116	B26735DAA	4898	3/--/1974	65643	CDWR
117	B26736BDB	4881.1	11/04/1957	SB00206736BDB1	USGS NWIS
118	B26736CAC	4885.1	04/19/1977	SB00206736CAC1	Schneider and Hillier (1978)
119	B26736DBB_1	4880.8	11/04/1957	SB00206736CBB1	USGS NWIS
120	B26736DBB_2	**4879.4**	03/01/1977	SB00206736DBB1	Schneider and Hillier (1978)
121	C16605CC	4964.2	05/09/2002	40808MH	CDWR
122	C16606AC	4945	02/28/2001	227721A	CDWR
123	C16606ACD	4954.9	03/17/1974, 02/28/1976	SC00106606ACD	USGS NWIS
124	C16606ADC	4956.6	11/04/1957	SC00106606ADC1 USGS 3955	USGS NWIS
125	C16606CBD	4950.6	11/04/1957	SC00106606CBD1	USGS NWIS

Table 7. Hydraulic-head observations used to calibrate the steady-state model of the South Platte alluvial aquifer, Brighton to Fort Lupton, Colorado.—Continued

[Hydraulic head in feet above National Geodetic Vertical Datum of 1929; Observation date(s) in mm/dd/yyyy; --, no data; CDWR, Colorado Division of Water Resources; USGS NWIS, U.S. Geological Survey National Water Information System; CDMRS, Colorado Division of Mining, Reclamation, and Safety]

Observation number	Observation name	Hydraulic head[1]	Observation date(s)	Well identifier[2]	Source
126	C16606CDB2	4946.8	03/15/1955	SC00106606CDB2	USGS NWIS
127	C16606DA	4947	11/10/2000	227512A	CDWR
128	C16607AB	4956	09/30/1999	47474A	CDWR
129	C16607ABB	4964	04/20/1959	SC00106607ABB1	USGS NWIS
130	C16607CB	4957	08/17/2000	21337A	CDWR
131	C16607CCB_1	4966.3	04/05/1955, 04/17/1956, 05/07/1957, 04/08/1958, 04/01/1959, 04/05/1960	SC00106607CCB	USGS NWIS
132	C16607CCB_2	**4967.5**	11/11/1954, 11/08/1955, 11/13/1956, 11/12/1957, 11/13/1958, 11/11/1959, 11/02/1960	SC00106607CCB	USGS NWIS
133	C16607CCB_3	**4966.6**	03/03/1977	SC00106607CCB1	Hillier and others (1979)
134	C16607DAC	4971.8	11/04/1957	SC00106607DAC1 USGS 3958	USGS NWIS
135	C16617CBC1	5004	03/08/1955	SC00106617CBC1	USGS NWIS
136	C16617CBD_1	5007.5	11/04/1957	SC00106617CBD1	USGS NWIS
137	C16617CBD_2	**5005.4**	03/14/1974, 02/28/1976	SC00106617CBD	USGS NWIS
138	C16618AC	4979	10/07/1999	220074	CDWR
139	C16618BA	4970	07/28/2000	13744R	CDWR
140	C16618BAB1	4967	03/05/1956	SC00106618BAB1	USGS NWIS
141	C16618BAC_1	4978.4	11/04/1957	SC00106618BAC1	USGS NWIS
142	C16618BAC_2	**4977.1**	03/14/1974, 02/28/1976	SC00106618BAC	USGS NWIS
143	C16618DBC1	4986.8	09/29/1955	SC00106618DBC1	USGS NWIS
144	C16618DD	5002	05/08/1997	24161A	CDWR
145	C16701AD	4944	04/24/1975	49687F	CDWR
146	C16701CA	4950	04/16/1960	SC00106701CA	CDWR
147	C16712AB	4950	09/24/1997	202569A	CDWR
148	C16712ADD_1	4961	11/05/1957	SC00106712ADD	USGS NWIS
149	C16712ADD_2	**4957**	03/11/1976	SC00106712ADD2	USGS NWIS
150	C16712BB	4955	03/23/1980	101310	CDWR
151	C16712CA	4957	07/20/1998	M1998-036 TH-15	CDMRS
152	C16712CCD_1	4965	11/--/1957	--	Smith and others (1964)
153	C16712CCD_2	**4962.6**	03/17/1974, 03/11/1976	SC00106712CCD USGS 39582	USGS NWIS
154	C16713AA	4972	08/09/2002	242942A	CDWR
155	C16713AC	4978.5	01/15/1997	M1987049 Well4	CDMRS

Table 7. Hydraulic-head observations used to calibrate the steady-state model of the South Platte alluvial aquifer, Brighton to Fort Lupton, Colorado.—Continued

[Hydraulic head in feet above National Geodetic Vertical Datum of 1929; Observation date(s) in mm/dd/yyyy; --, no data; CDWR, Colorado Division of Water Resources; USGS NWIS, U.S. Geological Survey National Water Information System; CDMRS, Colorado Division of Mining, Reclamation, and Safety]

Observation number	Observation name	Hydraulic head[1]	Observation date(s)	Well identifier[2]	Source
156	C16713CB	4965	05/15/1975	78907A	CDWR
157	C16713CDA1	4980	05/11/1956	SC00106713CDA1	USGS NWIS
158	C16713DBD_1	4976.6	10/04/1956	SC00106713DBD1	USGS NWIS
159	C16713DBD_2	**4979.5**	03/03/1977	SC00106713DBD1	Hillier and others (1979)

[1]Hydraulic head is the average of observations on the dates indicated. Hydraulic-head values in bold were used to compute observations as the temporal change in hydraulic head from the previous observation at the same location.

[2]Identifier for USGS NWIS wells, Schneider and Hillier (1978), and Hillier and others (1979) is the local well number. Identifier for CDWR wells is the well permit number. Identifier for CDMRS wells is the pit permit number followed by local well number.

Table 8. Flow observations used to calibrate the steady-state model of the South Platte alluvial aquifer, Brighton to Fort Lupton, Colorado.

[ft³/d, cubic feet per day]

Observation name	Years included in observation	Months included in observation	Average gain to South Platte River[1] (ft³/d)
Splt_57dry	1954–60	November–April	449,000
Splt_57wet	1954–60	May–October	3,797,000
Splt_77dry	1974–80	November–April	710,000
Splt_77wet	1974–80	May–October	6,622,000
Splt_00dry	1997–2003	November–April	985,000
Splt_00wet	1997–2003	May–October	10,623,000

[1]Gain is average of mean monthly gains for years and months indicated.

$$\sum_{i=1}^{ND} \omega_i \left[y_i - y'_i(\underline{b}) \right]^2 + \sum_{p=1}^{NPR} \omega_p \left[P_P - P'_P(\underline{b}) \right]^2$$

ND is the number of observations,
NPR is the number of prior-information values,
NP is the number of estimated parameters.
y_i is the ith observation being matched by the regression,
$y'_i(\underline{b})$ is the simulated value that corresponds to the ith observation (a function of $\underline{b}$),
P_p is the pth prior estimate included in the regression,
$P'_p(\underline{b})$ is the pth simulated value,
ω_i is the weight for the ith observation, and
ω_p is the weight for the pth prior estmate.

Smaller values of standard error indicate better fit of simulated values to observations. The value of standard error should be close to 1.0 if weighting used on observations and prior information represents true data accuracy. In practice, standard error commonly is greater than 1.0 because of model error or greater-than-expected measurement error. The standard error of regression (table 9) for the calibrated model is 1.7.

The MAE (Anderson and Woesner, 1992) is another general measure of model fit. The MAE is calculated as the mean of the absolute value of residuals in the model. Therefore, the MAE indicates average deviation of the simulated values from the observed values, whether the deviation is positive or negative. The MAE of unweighted hydraulic-head residuals in the calibrated model is 3.3 ft (table 9), which is about 2 percent of the 145-ft range of observed hydraulic-head values across the model domain. The MAE of unweighted flow residuals in the calibrated model is 2,550,000 ft³/d, which is about 25 percent of the 10,170,000 ft³/d range of observed base-flow values. Although the MAE of unweighted residuals provides a general measure of model fit, it does not consider observation measurement error. Similarly, the standard error of the

Table 9.   Statistics used to assess calibration of the steady-state model of the South Platte alluvial aquifer, Brighton to Fort Lupton, Colorado.

[Unweighted hydraulic-head residuals in feet; unweighted flow residuals in cubic feet per day; all other values dimensionless]

Statistic	Value
Minimum unweighted hydraulic-head residual	−12.1
Maximum unweighted hydraulic-head residual	10.7
Mean absolute error of unweighted hydraulic-head residuals	3.3
Minimum unweighted flow residual	−8,170,000
Maximum unweighted flow residual	1,230,000
Mean absolute error of unweighted flow residuals	2,550,000
Standard error of regression, s	1.7
Minimum weighted residual	−4.1
Maximum weighted residual	4.4
Mean weighted residual	−0.39
Correlation coefficient, R^2N	0.988
Critical value of R^2N at the 5 percent significance level	0.985
Modified Beale's measure[1]	4.2

[1]Cooley and Naff (1990).

model regression and the MAE of unweighted residuals do not indicate the spatial distribution of error or the validity of the model regression.

Randomness, Independence, and Normality of Residuals

A valid regression requires observation and prior-information errors used in the regression to be random and weighted errors to be uncorrelated (Draper and Smith, 1981). In addition, observation errors need to be normally distributed for use in calculating inferential statistics (Helsel and Hirsch, 1992) such as confidence intervals on parameters and predictions. If the model reasonably represents the groundwater system and the foregoing error conditions are met, weighted residuals should either be random, independent, and normal or have predictable correlations (Hill, 1998).

Weighted residuals relative to weighted simulated values and unweighted residuals relative to unweighted hydraulic-head observations. To evaluate the randomness and independence of weighted residuals, weighted residuals are plotted relative to weighted simulated values (figs. 25A and 25B). For a valid regression, weighted residuals are randomly distributed above and below the zero line for all weighted simulated values (Draper and Smith, 1981). A nonrandom distribution or systematic trend in weighted residuals might indicate weighted residuals are not random or independent (Hill, 1994). Hydraulic-head residuals in figure 25A plot in three distinct bands because three different weights were used to calculate simulated equivalents for hydraulic head based on estimated accuracy of hydraulic-head observations, and the range of hydraulic-head observations is small relative to

the range of all observation data (hydraulic head and flow) and prior information. The distribution of weighted residuals relative to weighted simulated hydraulic head for values between 1,620 and 1,670 is provided in figure 25B to show the distribution of weighted residuals relative to weighted simulated values over a smaller range of values. For comparison, the distribution of unweighted head residuals relative to unweighted hydraulic-head observations is shown in figure 26. The slight negative bias in residuals in figures 25B and 26 might indicate that simulated heads near the lower and upper limits of the head range in the model generally are higher than observed head values. Because the hydraulic-head gradient of the water table in the aquifer generally is from south to north (fig. 9), the lower limit of the head range represents conditions near the north end of the simulated aquifer, and the upper limit of the head range represents conditions near the south end of the simulated aquifer. Although figures 25B and 26 display a slight negative bias, figure 25A indicates weighted residuals likely are random and independent when all calibration data are considered. A summary of the minimum, maximum, and mean weighted and unweighted residuals for the final calibrated model are presented in table 9.

Normal probability of weighted residuals and correlation coefficient R^2_N. To evaluate normality of weighted residuals and further test for their independence, a normal probability graph of weighted residuals (fig. 27) is used. Because weighted residuals fall approximately on a straight line in the graph, weighted residuals can be considered independent and normally distributed. The correlation coefficient R^2_N provides another statistical measure of residual independence and normality by determining the correlation

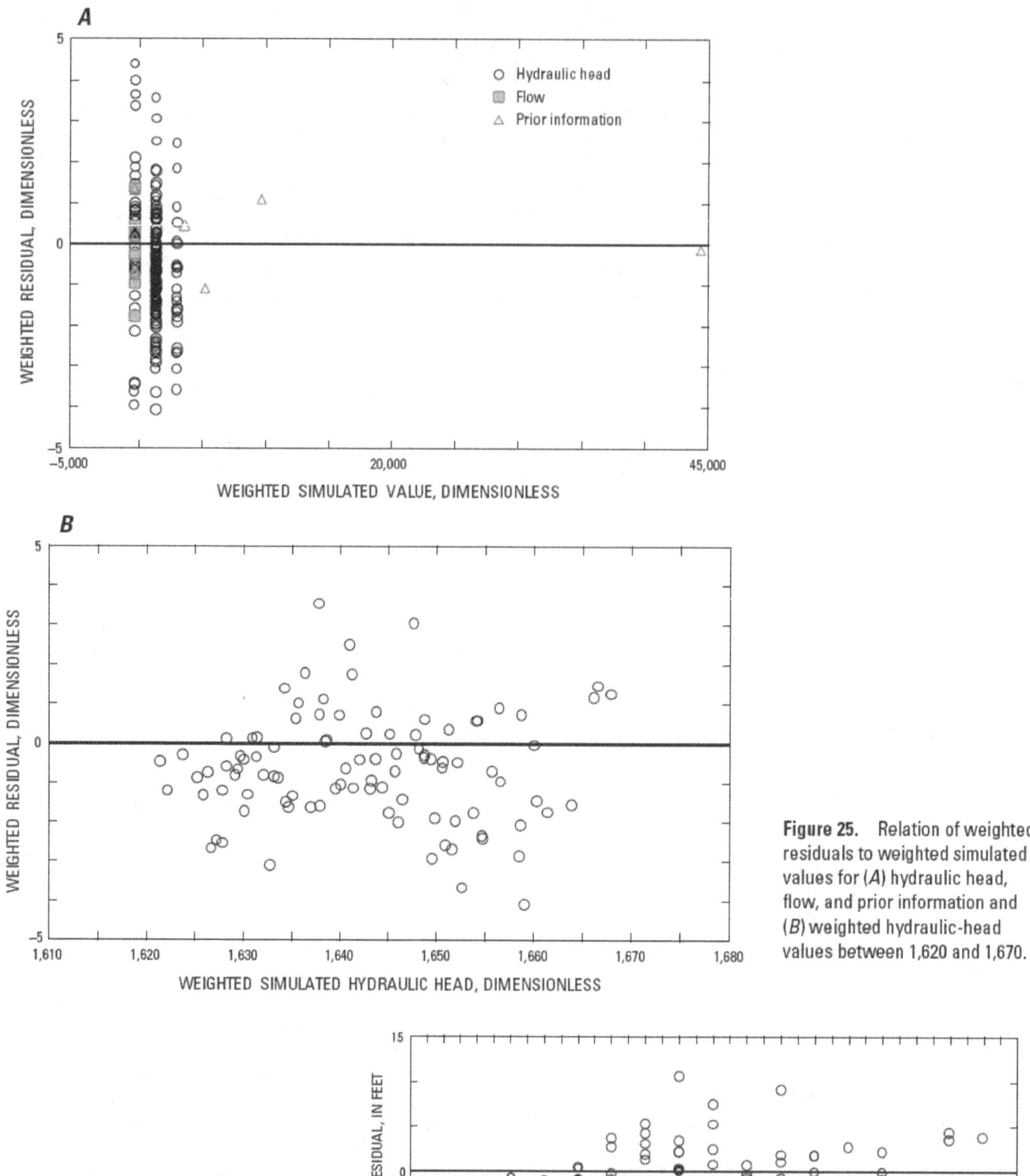

Figure 25.   Relation of weighted residuals to weighted simulated values for (*A*) hydraulic head, flow, and prior information and (*B*) weighted hydraulic-head values between 1,620 and 1,670.

Figure 26.   Relation of unweighted residuals to unweighted hydraulic-head observations.

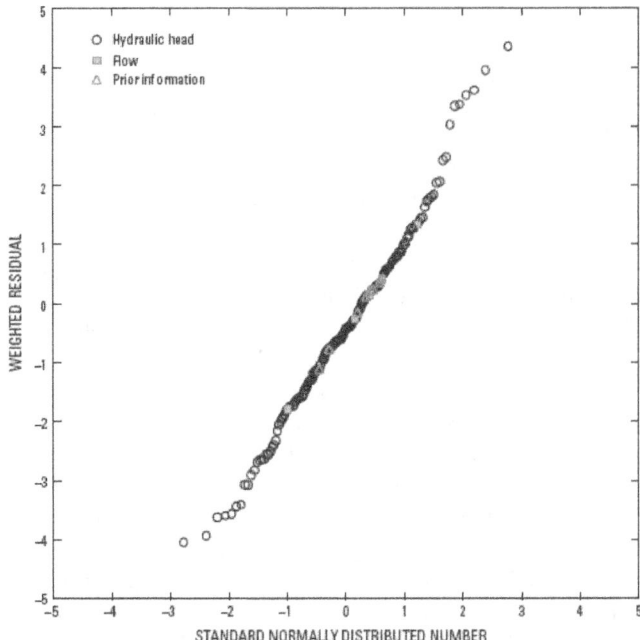

Figure 27. Normal probability of weighted residuals.

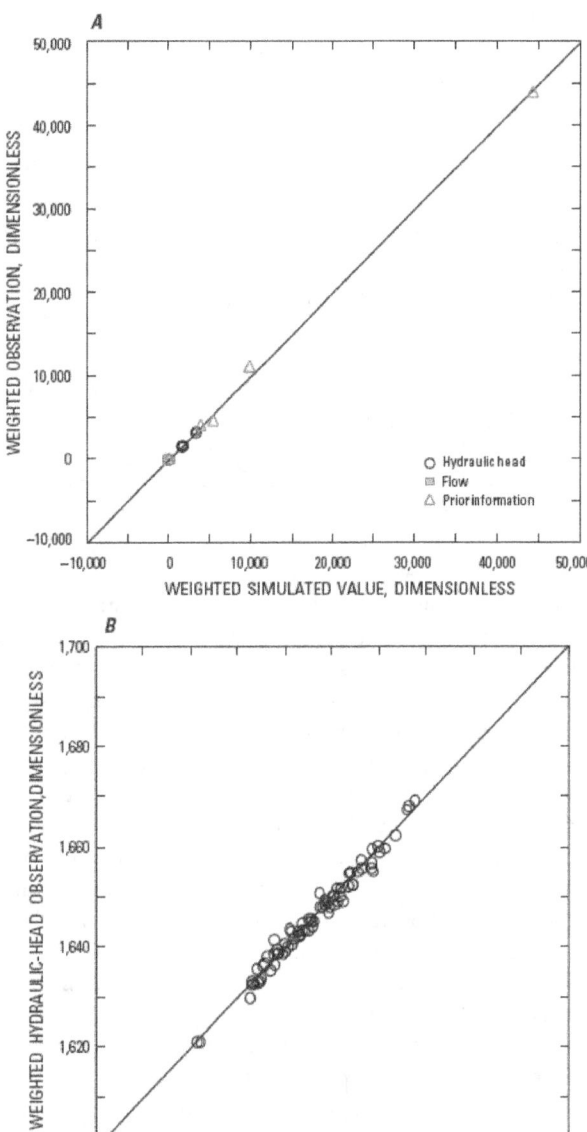

Figure 28. Relation of weighted observations to weighted simulated values for (*A*) hydraulic head, flow, and prior information and (*B*) weighted hydraulic-head values between 1,620 and 1,670.

between ordered weighted residuals and order statistics from a probability distribution function (Hill, 1998). If the value of R^2_N is significantly less than 1.0, weighted residuals are not likely to be independent and normally distributed. The value of R^2_N is calculated by MODFLOW-2000 and presented along with critical values for R^2_N representing significance levels of 0.05 and 0.10. The value of R^2_N for the final calibrated model is 0.988 (table 9), which is greater than the 0.05 significance level of 0.985 and indicates the probability that weighted residuals are independent and normally distributed is greater than 95 percent.

Correlation between weighted observations and weighted simulated values. Correlation between weighted observations and weighted simulated values is evaluated by plotting weighted observations relative to weighted simulated values (fig. 28*A*). If weighted simulated values are similar to weighted observations, points should fall on a straight line with an intercept of zero (Hill, 1998). Because the range of all weighted values in figure 28*A* is much larger than for weighted hydraulic head and flow alone, hydraulic head and flow values appear as only a few points on the graph. To better show the correlation between weighted observations and weighted simulated values over a smaller range of values, the distribution of weighted hydraulic head observations relative to weighted simulated values is shown in figure 28*B* for weighted values between 1,620 and 1,670. Because the plots shown in figures 28*A* and 28*B* are approximately linear, weighted simulated values (and consequently, unweighted simulated values)

can be considered to reasonably approximate weighted (and unweighted) observations.

Runs statistic and parameter correlation coefficients. The runs statistic (Draper and Smith, 1981, p. 157–162) evaluates the spatial and temporal randomness of weighted residuals. A run consists of an unbroken sequence of positive or negative residuals. Too few or too many runs might indicate significant model error that could affect simulated predictions (Hill, 1998). MODFLOW-2000 uses the order of observations listed in the observation input file to determine the runs statistic. The number of runs in the final calibrated model is

85 in 176 observations (including prior information), which equals the number of runs expected for randomly distributed weighted residuals. Because observations are distributed spatially and temporally in the model, the runs statistic indicates that residuals likely are random in both space and time.

Parameter correlation coefficients indicate whether estimated parameter values are likely to be unique (Hill, 1998). Parameter correlation coefficients for all estimated parameters in the final model were less than 0.95, indicating that final parameter values likely are unique.

Simulated Steady-State Groundwater Flow in the Alluvial Aquifer

The simulated steady-state distributions of aquifer hydraulic head representing water-table conditions during the 2000 irrigation and non-irrigation seasons are shown in figure 29, and the water budget for each simulation is provided in table 10. The simulated water table during the irrigation season is higher than during the non-irrigation season in most of the model domain. The simulated water table during the irrigation season is lower than during the non-irrigation season only in a small area near Brighton where heavy municipal-well pumping, which is greater in the irrigation season than the non-irrigation season, occurs. The difference between simulated seasonal groundwater levels generally is larger near aquifer margins than near the South Platte River because of the stabilizing influence of the river, and differences in simulated seasonal groundwater levels are similar in magnitude to those indicated by observations. Simulated saturated thickness within the model area ranges from 10 to 50 ft, except near model edges where saturated thickness is less than 10 ft in some places. Simulated saturated thickness generally is 20–40 ft throughout most of the model domain.

Wetland locations mapped as part of this study are shown in figure 30 relative to areas where simulated depth to water is less than 5 ft below land surface during the 2000 irrigation season. Areas of riparian herbaceous vegetation (including cattails, sedges, rushes, and mesic grasses) with moist to waterlogged soils or permanent standing water mapped by CDOW (2007a, b) also are presented in figure 30 for comparison to areas where the simulated depth to water is less than 5 ft. Most wetlands and riparian herbaceous vegetation are located in areas where the simulated water table is less than 5 ft below ground surface, indicating that most wetlands and riparian herbaceous vegetation in the study area might be affected by changes in groundwater levels. However, determination of the specific effects of groundwater-level changes on wetlands and riparian herbaceous vegetation in the study area would require site-specific investigations beyond the scope of this report.

All components of the simulated groundwater budgets for the calibrated steady-state model during the irrigation and non-irrigation seasons represent reasonable values compared to available data. General-head boundaries at the upgradient ends of the simulated South Platte River valley and tributaries provide the largest source of inflow to the model area during both the irrigation season (28.2 percent) and non-irrigation season (43.5 percent). During the irrigation season, inflow along the east model boundary and recharge distributed at the land surface account for 25.5 percent and 25.2 percent, respectively, of inflow to the model area. During the non-irrigation season, inflow along the east model boundary and recharge distributed at the land surface are a smaller component of the groundwater budget (18.4 percent and 1.0 percent, respectively), consistent with the conceptual understanding of groundwater flow. Groundwater discharge to the South Platte River and Big Dry Creek constitutes the largest outflow from the simulated aquifer during the irrigation season (54.6 percent) and non-irrigation season (55.9 percent) with most outflow occurring to the South Platte River. Discharge to the South Platte River and Big Dry Creek during the irrigation season is greater than that during the non-irrigation season because of increased recharge and steeper water-table gradients toward the South Platte River during the irrigation season. During the non-irrigation season, outflow at the general-head boundary at the downgradient end of the model exceeds net discharge (outflow minus inflow) to the river and represents 24.9 percent of the total outflow. Phreatophyte evapotranspiration and groundwater discharge to tributaries simulated as drains (Little Dry Creek and Third Creek) during the irrigation season represent small (3.1 percent and 1.8 percent, respectively) components of the total aquifer outflow. Phreatophyte evapotranspiration during the non-irrigation season is assumed zero in the model input. Groundwater discharge to tributary drains is slightly greater during the non-irrigation season (3.7 percent) than during the irrigation season likely because greater municipal-well withdrawals during the irrigation season reduce groundwater flow to Third Creek. Municipal-well withdrawals during the irrigation season are about twice as large as municipal-well withdrawals during the non-irrigation season. Municipal-well withdrawals represent 21.2 percent of total aquifer outflow during the irrigation season and 15.5 percent of outflow during the non-irrigation season.

Sensitivity Analysis

Composite scaled sensitivities were calculated for each parameter using the Sensitivity Process (Hill and others, 2000) of MODFLOW-2000. Composite scaled sensitivities are dimensionless quantities that indicate the total amount of information provided by all observations for estimation of a parameter (Hill, 1998). When parameter correlation is not a problem, parameters with high sensitivity generally can be more precisely estimated from available observations than parameters with low sensitivity. Parameters with high sensitivity also have greater influence on quantities (head and flow) simulated by the model and can be more important to accurately define for model simulations than parameters with low sensitivity. Parameters with very low sensitivity have little effect on simulated values and accurate definition of these

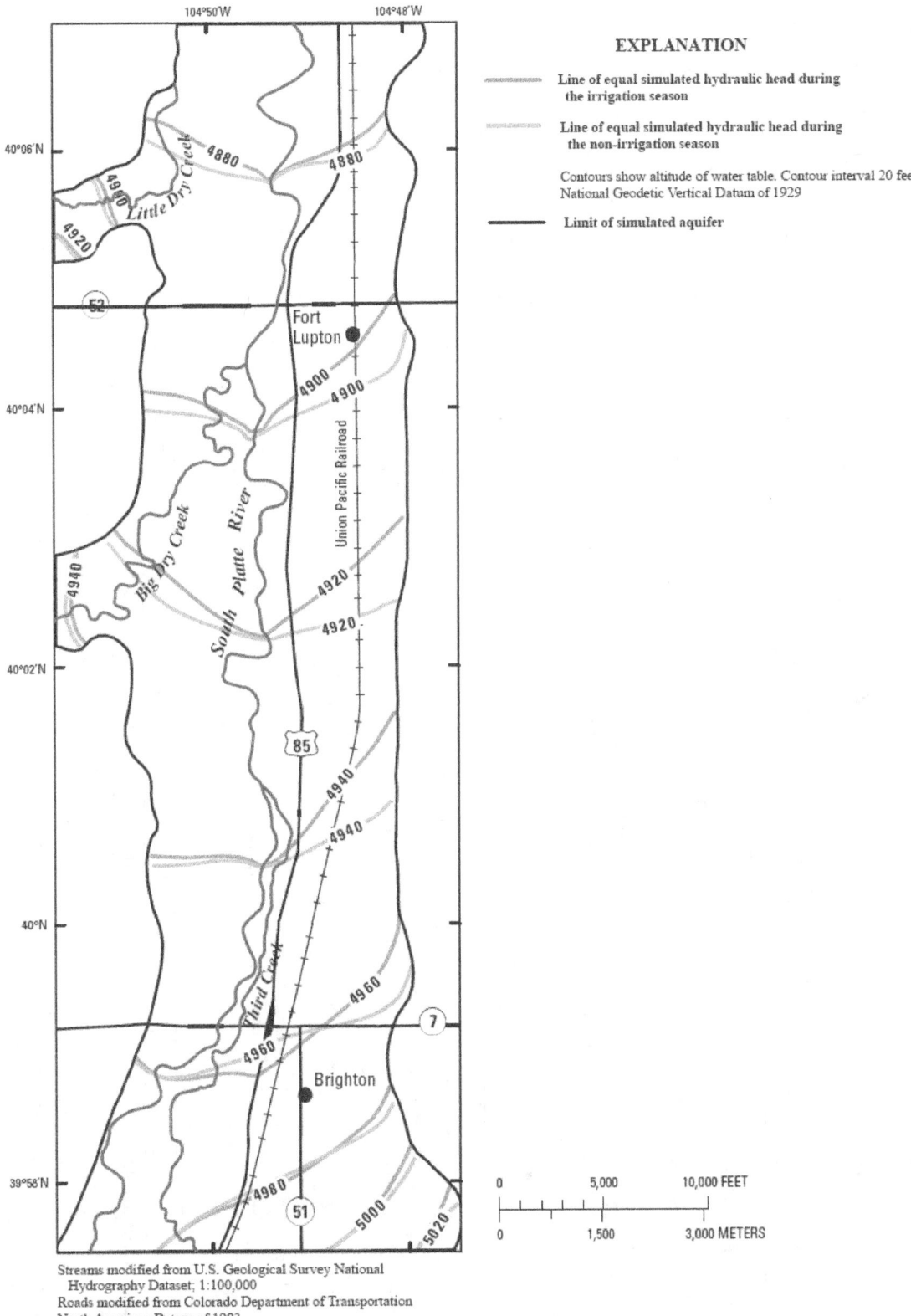

Figure 29. Simulated steady-state distributions of hydraulic head in the South Platte alluvial aquifer during the irrigation and non-irrigation seasons in 2000, Brighton to Fort Lupton, Colorado.

Table 10. Groundwater budgets for the calibrated model and simulations of the hydrologic effects of predicted land-use change and reclaimed pits in 2020 and 2040, Brighton to Fort Lupton, Colorado.

[All values are in cubic feet per day; totals reflect sum of all rounded components; --, not applicable]

Budget component	Calibrated model 2000 irrigation season	Calibrated model 2000 non-irrigation season	Simulation 1[1]	Simulation 2[2]	Simulation 3[3]	Simulation 4[4]	Simulation 5[5]
Aquifer inflows							
Groundwater inflow from general-head boundaries at upgradient end of South Platte River valley and tributaries	1,969,000	2,103,000	2,022,000	2,051,000	2,057,000	2,042,000	2,057,000
Subsurface irrigation return flow along east model boundary	1,782,000	891,000	1,782,000	1,782,000	1,782,000	1,782,000	1,782,000
Distributed recharge at the land surface	1,763,000	50,000	1,448,000	1,206,000	1,467,000	1,253,000	1,253,000
Leakage to aquifer from South Platte River and Big Dry Creek	1,469,000	1,789,000	1,526,000	1,574,000	1,748,000	1,752,000	2,016,000
Leakage to aquifer from unlined pits	--	--	--	--	3,719,000	2,868,000	11,317,000
Groundwater released from storage	--	--	--	--	107,000	108,000	110,000
Total	6,983,000	4,833,000	6,778,000	6,613,000	10,880,000	9,805,000	18,535,000
Aquifer outflows							
Groundwater outflow to general-head boundary at downgradient end of South Platte River valley	1,345,000	1,205,000	1,323,000	1,301,000	1,157,000	1,152,000	1,168,000
Groundwater discharge to South Platte River and Big Dry Creek	3,810,000	2,702,000	3,632,000	3,495,000	3,644,000	3,388,000	3,787,000
Groundwater discharge to Little Dry Creek and Third Creek	127,000	178,000	122,000	116,000	144,000	155,000	141,000
Groundwater discharge to unlined pits	--	--	--	--	3,757,000	2,955,000	11,527,000
Phreatophyte evapotranspiration	219,000	0	218,000	217,000	191,000	191,000	186,000
Municipal-well withdrawals	1,483,000	748,000	1,483,000	1,483,000	1,421,000	1,421,000	1,421,000
Groundwater entering storage	--	--	--	--	570,000	545,000	425,000
Total	6,984,000	4,833,000	6,778,000	6,612,000	10,884,000	9,807,000	18,655,000
Percent discrepancy (Recharge–Discharge)	-0.01	0.00	0.00	0.02	-0.04	-0.02	-0.65

[1] Land-use conditions in 2020.
[2] Land-use conditions in 2040.
[3] Reclaimed pits in 2020.
[4] Reclaimed lined pits in 2040.
[5] Reclaimed unlined pits in 2040.

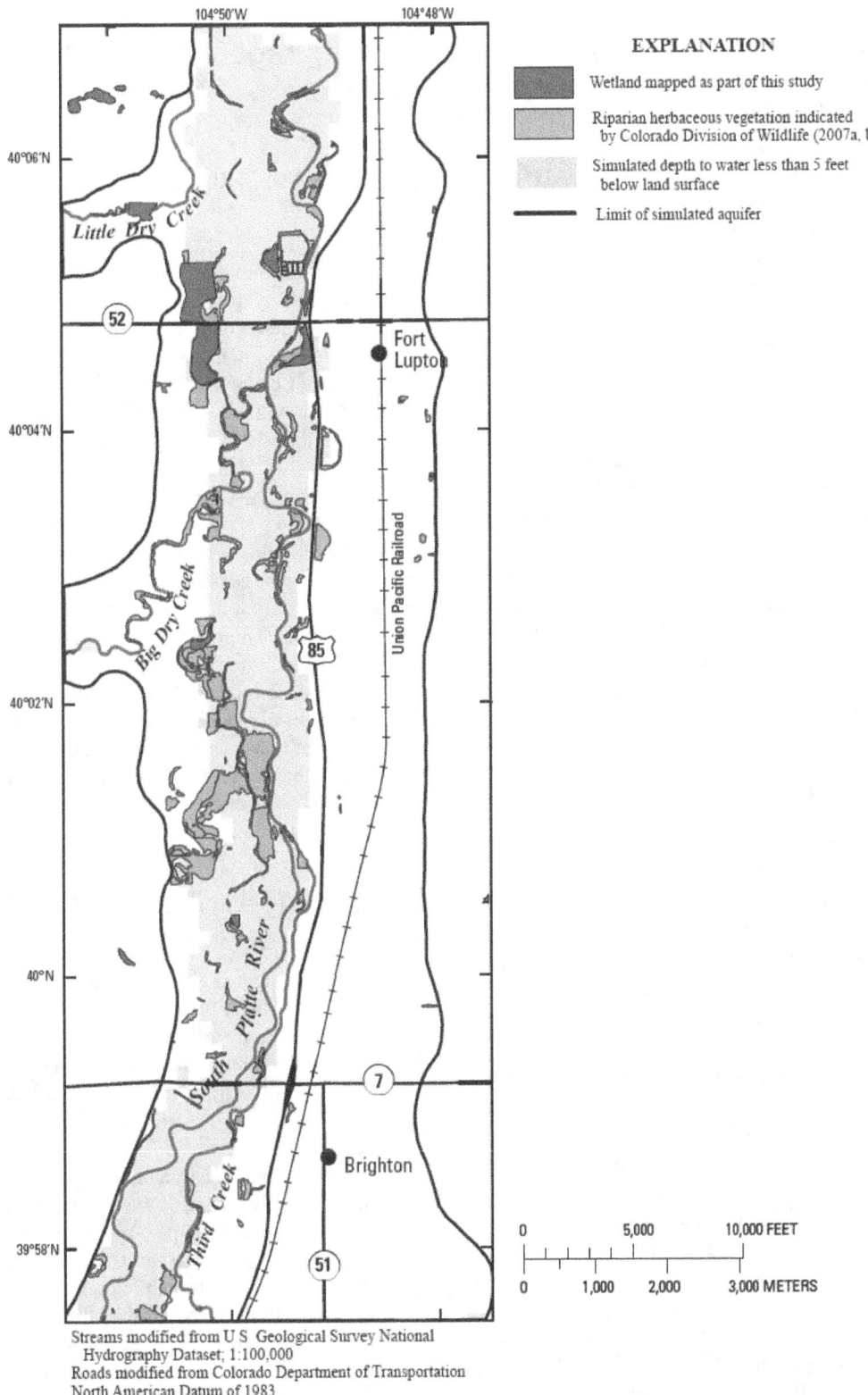

Figure 30. Location of largest wetlands mapped as part of this study and riparian herbaceous flora indicated by Colorado Division of Wildlife relative to areas where simulated depth to water is less than 5 feet below land surface in the South Platte River valley, Brighton to Fort Lupton, Colorado.

parameters is less important to model calibration. However, parameters with low sensitivity could be important to predictions if predictions are distant from observation locations or occur under conditions substantially different than those used to calibrate the model. Because composite scaled sensitivities depend on model structure and the number and location of observations, the absolute magnitude of composite scaled sensitivity for a parameter is less meaningful than its magnitude relative to that of other parameters. Composite scaled sensitivity of each parameter in the calibrated steady-state model is presented in figure 31. The parameter representing recharge beneath irrigated areas (RCH_Irr) has the highest composite scaled sensitivity in the model. Other parameters with relatively high composite scaled sensitivities represent (1) inflow along the east side of the model (Q_ReturnE), (2) hydraulic conductivity of zones 2 (LPF_Par2) and 3 (LPF_Par3), and (3) municipal well pumping (Q_Mwells). Parameters with relatively low composite sensitivity represent (1) phreatophyte evapotranspiration (EVT_Par1), (2) drain conductance of Little Dry Creek and Third Creek (DRN_Trib), (3) recharge beneath non-irrigated areas (RCH_Nonirr), (4) hydraulic conductance of general-head boundaries at upgradient and downgradient ends of the South Platte River valley (GHB_Splt), and (5) recharge beneath urban areas (RCH_Urban). Other model parameters (LPF_Par1, LPF_Par4, GHB_Trib, RIV_Splt, and RIV_Bdry) have moderate sensitivity.

Model Nonlinearity

The post-processing program BEALE-2000 (Hill and others, 2000) provided with MODFLOW-2000 was used to evaluate model nonlinearity. BEALE-2000 uses the modified Beale's measure (Cooley and Naff, 1990) to test model nonlinearity near the optimized parameter values. The model needs to be approximately linear near optimized parameter values for linear confidence intervals on parameters and predictions to be valid (Hill, 1994). Interpretation of the modified Beale's measure is different for each model and is provided as output from BEALE-2000. For the current study, the model is considered effectively linear near optimized parameter values if the Beale's measure is less than 0.051. The model is considered nonlinear if the Beale's measure is between 0.051 and 0.56, and highly nonlinear if the Beale's measure is greater than 0.56. Because the Beale's measure for the calibrated model is 4.2 (table 9), the model is considered highly nonlinear, and linear confidence intervals on predictions of the effects of land-use change and aggregate mining likely would not accurately represent prediction uncertainty. The model is most nonlinear with respect to (1) non-irrigation recharge (RCH_nonirr), (2) streambed conductance of the South Platte River (RIV_Splt), and (3) irrigation recharge (RCH_irr). Because the model is highly nonlinear, linear confidence intervals are not presented for parameters or predictions concerning the effects of land-use change and aggregate mining on groundwater flow.

Simulated Effects of Land-Use Change and Aggregate Mining on Groundwater Flow

Simulated Hydrologic Effects of Land-Use Change

Land-use conditions in 2020 and 2040 (figs. 18A and 18B) predicted by the SLEUTH urban-growth model are used to simulate the hydrologic effects of converting non-irrigated and irrigated land to impervious urban area. Two numerical simulations of the potential hydrologic effects of land-use change are presented as follows:

Simulation 1—The hydrologic effects of predicted land-use conditions in 2020.

Simulation 2—The hydrologic effects of predicted land use conditions in 2040.

All hydrologic stresses in the simulations, except the distribution of recharge based on land use, are the same as in the calibrated model for 2000 in order to determine the individual effect land-use change might have on the aquifer. Hydraulic head simulated by the calibrated model for the 2000 irrigation season is used to represent initial hydraulic-head conditions for predictions of the effects of land-use change. Because conversion of non-irrigated and irrigated land to urban areas are likely to be relatively permanent, the long-term hydrologic effects of land-use change are of interest and are predicted using steady-state simulations.

Simulation 1—Land-Use Conditions in 2020

Simulation 1 represents the potential hydrologic effects of converting irrigated and non-irrigated land to impervious urban area using land-use conditions predicted for 2020. The simulated hydrologic effects of land-use conditions in 2020 relative to water-table conditions during the 2000 irrigation season are shown in figure 32, and the simulated groundwater budget for simulation 1 is provided in table 10. Groundwater-level declines relative to the 2000 irrigation-season water table are as much as 1.2 ft in areas converted to urban land use. Declines are greatest where irrigated land is converted to urban areas because of the large difference (about 12 in. during the irrigation season) in recharge between the two land uses. Because recharge beneath non-irrigated areas (about 0.4 in.) is only slightly greater than the zero recharge value assigned to impervious urban areas and because the aquifer has relatively high hydraulic conductivity, the conversion of non-irrigated areas to urban areas in the model has little effect on the simulated aquifer. Groundwater-level declines relative to the 2000 non-irrigation season water table (which does not receive recharge from irrigation) are less than 0.04 ft at all locations in 2020 and are not presented graphically. Because simulated groundwater-level declines are small and wetlands

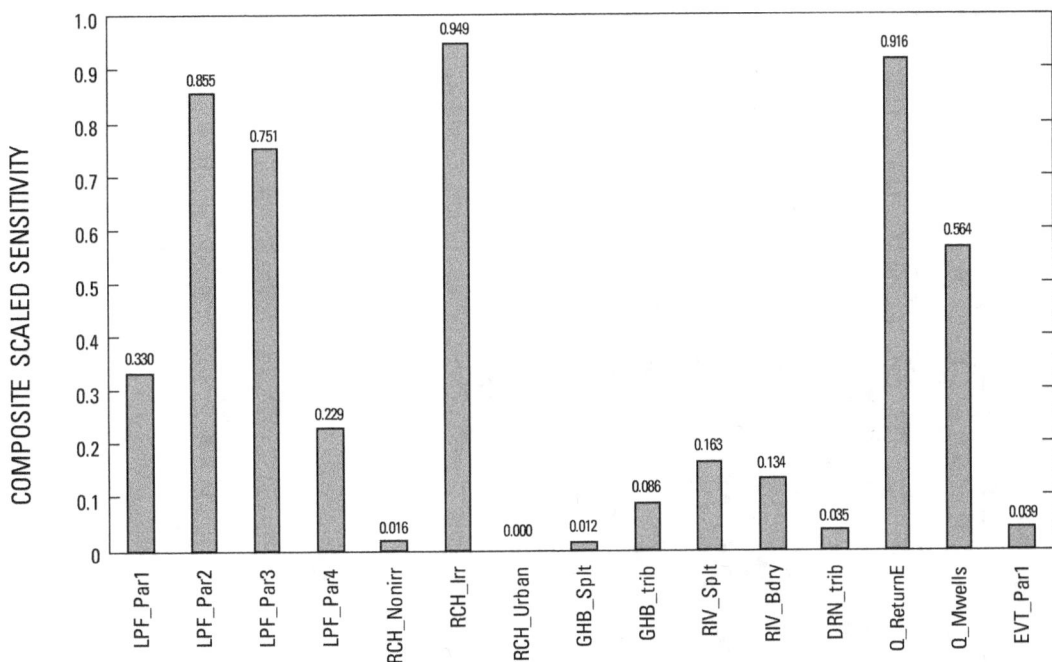

EXPLANATION

LPF_Par1	Horizontal hydraulic conductivity of zone 1
LPF_Par2	Horizontal hydraulic conductivity of zone 2
LPF_Par3	Horizontal hydraulic conductivity of zone 3
LPF_Par4	Horizontal hydraulic conductivity of zone 4
RCH_Nonirr	Recharge rate beneath non-irrigated land
RCH_Irr	Recharge rate beneath irrigated land
RCH_Urban	Recharge rate beneath urban areas
GHB_Splt	General-head boundary conductance at upgradient and downgradient ends of South Platte River valley
GHB_trib	General-head boundary conductance at upgradient ends of tributary valleys
RIV_Splt	Riverbed conductance of the South Platte River
RIV_Bdry	Riverbed conductance of Big Dry Creek
DRN_trib	Drain conductance of Third Creek and Little Dry Creek
Q_ReturnE	Inflow rate along east model boundary
Q_Mwells	Municipal-well withdrawal rate
EVT_Par1	Maximum phreatophyte evapotranspiration rate

Figure 31.   Composite scaled sensitivities of parameters for the calibrated steady-state model of the South Platte alluvial aquifer, Brighton to Fort Lupton, Colorado.

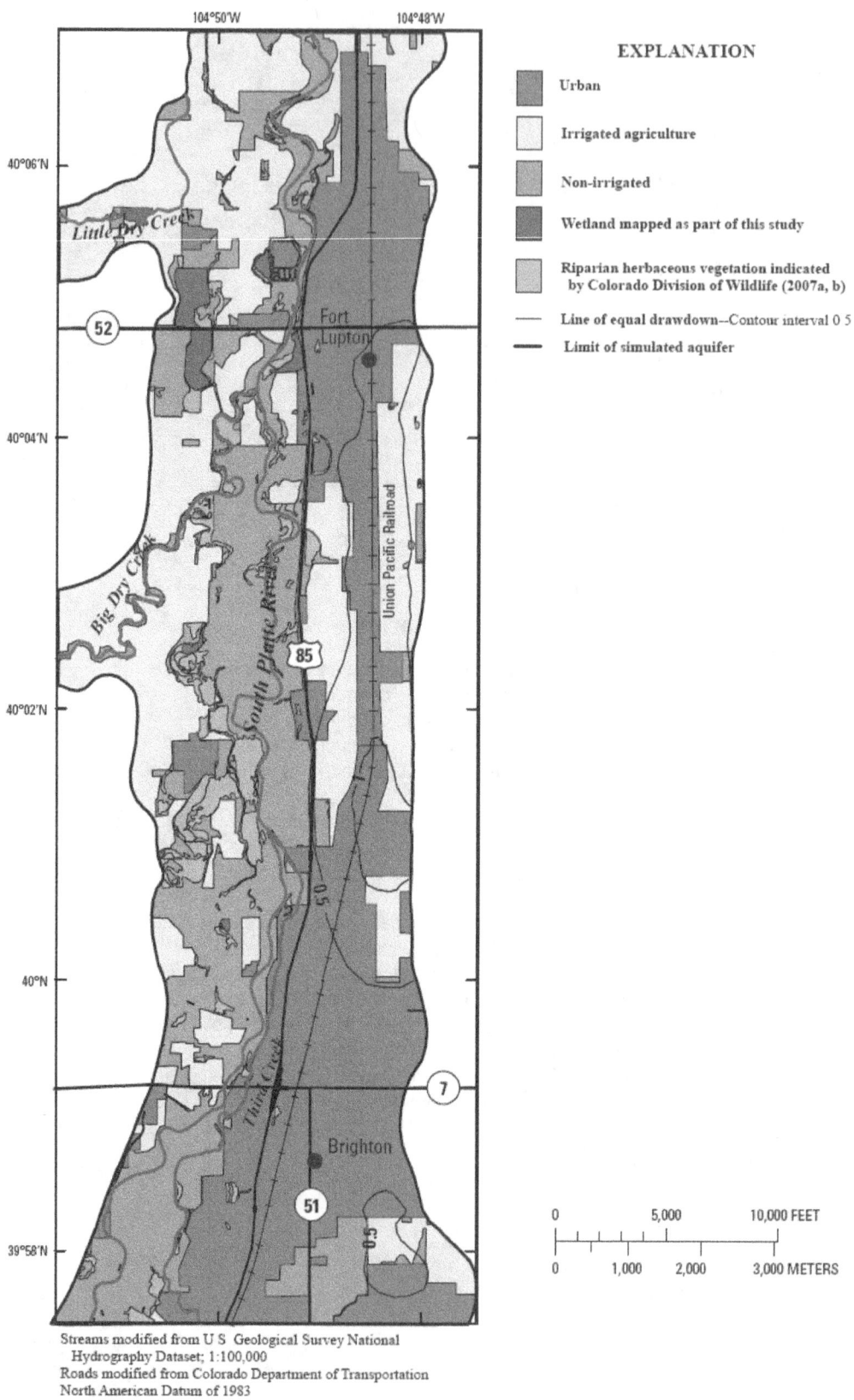

EXPLANATION

Urban

Irrigated agriculture

Non-irrigated

Wetland mapped as part of this study

Riparian herbaceous vegetation indicated by Colorado Division of Wildlife (2007a, b)

—— Line of equal drawdown—Contour interval 0 5 feet

—— Limit of simulated aquifer

0   5,000   10,000 FEET

0   1,000   2,000   3,000 METERS

Streams modified from U S Geological Survey National
  Hydrography Dataset; 1:100,000
Roads modified from Colorado Department of Transportation
North American Datum of 1983

Figure 32. Simulation 1—Steady-state drawdown resulting from predicted land-use conditions in 2020, Brighton to Fort Lupton, Colorado.

mapped by this study and areas of riparian herbaceous vegetation mapped by CDOW (2007a, b) generally are located where little or no decline occurs (fig. 32), wetlands and riparian herbaceous vegetation in the study area likely would not be substantially affected by declines resulting from the predicted land-use conditions in 2020.

Distributed recharge at the land surface in simulation 1 (table 10) is 17.9 percent less than in the 2000 irrigation season because of the larger urban extent in simulation 1, which is assumed not to contribute recharge to the aquifer. Groundwater inflow at the upgradient ends of South Platte River valley and its tributaries is 2.7 percent greater than in the 2000 irrigation season, and leakage from the South Platte River and Big Dry Creek is 3.9 percent greater. Similarly, discharge to the South Platte River and Big Dry Creek is 4.7 percent less, discharge to Little Dry Creek and Third Creek is 3.9 percent less, and outflow at the downgradient end of the South Platte valley is 1.6 percent less. Phreatophyte evapotranspiration and irrigation return flow along the east model boundary are not substantially affected by the lower water table beneath urban areas in simulation 1.

Simulation 2—Land-Use Conditions in 2040

Simulation 2 represents the potential hydrologic effects of converting irrigated and non-irrigated land to impervious urban area using land-use conditions predicted for 2040. The hydrologic effects of land-use conditions in 2040 relative to water-table conditions during the 2000 irrigation season are shown in figure 33, and the simulated groundwater budget for simulation 2 is provided in table 10. Groundwater-level declines relative to the 2000 irrigation-season water table are as much as 1.9 ft in areas converted to urban land use. Declines in 2040 are greater than in 2020 because a larger part of the model has been converted to impervious urban area. As with declines in 2020, declines in 2040 are greatest where irrigated land is converted to urban area and near the east model boundary. Groundwater-level declines relative to the 2000 non-irrigation season water table are less than 0.05 ft at all locations and are not presented graphically. As with declines resulting from land-use conditions in 2020, simulated declines resulting from land-use conditions in 2040 appear to have little effect on mapped wetlands and areas of riparian herbaceous vegetation because they are mostly located where little or no decline occurs (fig. 33).

The effects of land-use change on the groundwater budget (table 10) in simulation 2 are similar but greater than the effects indicated by simulation 1 because a larger urban area is simulated, which reduces recharge to a greater extent. Distributed recharge at the land surface in simulation 2 is 31.6 percent less than in the 2000 irrigation season. Groundwater inflow at the upgradient ends of South Platte River valley and its tributaries is 4.2 percent greater than in the 2000 irrigation season, and leakage from the South Platte

River and Big Dry Creek is 7.1 percent greater. Similarly, discharge to the South Platte River and Big Dry Creek is 8.3 percent less, discharge to Little Dry Creek and Third Creek is 8.7 percent less, and outflow at the downgradient end of the South Platte valley is 3.3 percent less in 2040 relative to the 2000 irrigation season. As in simulation 1, phreatophyte evapotranspiration and irrigation return flow along the east model boundary are not substantially affected by the lower water table beneath urban areas in simulation 2.

Summary of Land-Use Change Simulations

Steady-state simulations of the hydrologic effects of land-use conditions in 2020 and 2040 indicate groundwater-level declines resulting from conversion of irrigated and non-irrigated land to urban areas are less than 2 ft relative to the irrigation-season water table in 2000. Groundwater-level declines are largest where irrigated agricultural land is converted to urban area because of the large difference in recharge between the two land uses. Groundwater levels change little where non-irrigated land is converted to urban area because estimated recharge beneath non-irrigated land is only slightly greater than that assumed for urban areas. Groundwater-level declines resulting from land-use conditions in 2020 and 2040 are predicted to not substantially affect wetlands and riparian herbaceous vegetation in the study area because the declines are small and mapped wetlands and areas of riparian herbaceous vegetation generally are located where little or no simulated decline occurs. The larger urban extent in simulations of land-use change in 2020 and 2040 decreases recharge to the simulated aquifer by 17.9–31.6 percent, and the resulting lower water table increases groundwater inflow from the upgradient ends of South Platte River valley and its tributaries by 2.7–4.2 percent and leakage from the South Platte River and Big Dry Creek by 3.9–7.1 percent. Similarly, discharge to the South Platte River and Big Dry Creek decreases by 4.7–8.3 percent, discharge to Little Dry Creek and Third Creek decreases by 3.9–8.7 percent, and groundwater outflow at the downgradient end of the South Platte valley decreases by 1.6–3.3 percent.

Simulated Hydrologic Effects of Aggregate Mining

Simulated Cumulative Hydrologic Effects of Reclaimed Aggregate Pits

Cumulative effects of reclaimed aggregate pits on groundwater flow in the study area are simulated for the potential extent of mining shown in figures 19*A* and 19*B* for 2020 and 2040, respectively. Three numerical simulations of the

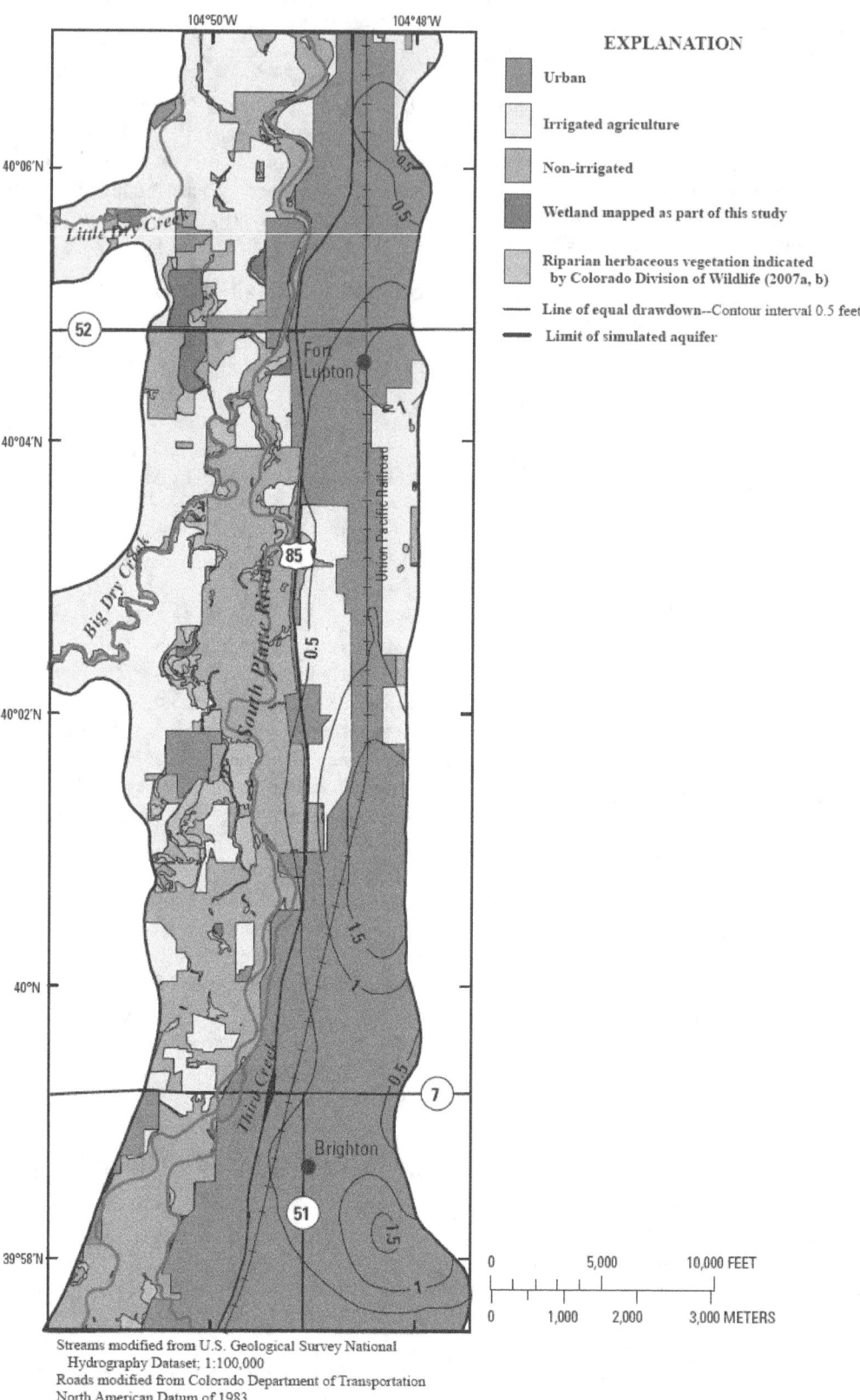

Figure 33. Simulation 2—Steady-state drawdown resulting from predicted land-use conditions in 2040, Brighton to Fort Lupton, Colorado.

potential cumulative hydrologic effects of reclaimed pits are presented as follows:

Simulation 3 – The cumulative hydrologic effects of multiple reclaimed pits representing the potential extent of aggregate mining in 2020.

Simulation 4 – The cumulative hydrologic effects of multiple reclaimed pits representing the potential extent of aggregate mining in 2040. All pits added after 2020 are simulated as lined.

Simulation 5 – The cumulative hydrologic effects of multiple reclaimed pits representing the potential extent of aggregate mining in 2040. All pits added after 2020 are simulated as unlined.

Simulation Design

All reclaimed pits are simulated either as (1) lined, (2) unlined, or (3) backfilled with fine-grained sediments based on review of reclamation plans on file with CDMRS. Pits indicated as backfilled with unspecified overburden in CDMRS records are assumed to have hydraulic conductivity similar to the surrounding aquifer and are not explicitly simulated. Pits for which reclamation information was not found are assumed backfilled with unspecified overburden and also are not explicitly simulated. Lined pits are simulated by using inactive model cells at pit locations, thereby simulating no-flow barriers at pit edges where slurry walls or clay liners would be present. Unlined pits are simulated using the Lake package (Merritt and Konikow, 2000) of MODFLOW-2000. The Lake package simulates water exchange between a surface-water body and the aquifer based on lakebed leakance (hydraulic conductivity divided by lakebed thickness) and the relative difference between lake stage and adjacent groundwater levels. Unlined pits in the model have lakebed leakance defined using the value of aquifer hydraulic conductivity at the pit location and a lakebed thickness of 1 ft to simulate the open hydraulic connection between the pit and the aquifer. Simulation of lake stage in unlined pits considers the effects of seasonal direct precipitation and evaporation at the lake surface based on long-term climate records (see "Physiography and Climate" section). Simulated precipitation is about 9 in. during the irrigation season and 4 in. during the non-irrigation season. Simulated evaporation is about 41 in. during the irrigation season and 7 in. during the non-irrigation season. Pits backfilled with fine-grained sediments are simulated by using model cells with a hydraulic conductivity value of 10 ft/d at backfilled pit locations. In some locations, reclaimed pits overlap Third Creek and phreatophyte areas. Drain cells used to simulate Third Creek and evapotranspiration cells used to simulate phreatophyte evapotranspiration at areas overlapped by pits are deactivated.

Because reclaimed pits commonly are spaced less than 500 ft apart, the cell size (500 ft by 500 ft) of the calibrated model is too large to simulate groundwater flow between pits in some places. To enable simulation of groundwater flow between closely spaced pits and more accurately simulate the effects of reclaimed pits on groundwater flow and wetlands, a revised model grid with 289 rows, 96 columns, and a uniform cell size of 200 ft by 200 ft is used for simulations 3–5. Initial hydraulic head for simulations of reclaimed pits was determined by rerunning the steady-state calibrated model using the revised model grid to avoid attributing groundwater-level changes caused by the finer grid to the effects of pits. Hydraulic head simulated using the revised model grid generally differed from that simulated by the original grid by less than 1 ft throughout the model domain for conditions representing the 2000 irrigation season. Hydraulic-head differences between simulations using the two model grids generally are less than 0.5 ft in the vicinity of simulated pits for conditions representing the 2000 irrigation season. All hydrologic stresses (including recharge distributed by land use) in simulations of reclaimed pits are the same as in the calibrated model except for the addition of pits.

Considerations for Transient Simulations

Because of uncertainties concerning the order and extent to which individual pits will be developed and because the cumulative effects of multiple reclaimed pits are of interest, the hydrologic effects of reclaimed pits are simulated as though pits are added simultaneously to the aquifer in either 2020 or 2040. Because wetlands may be able to adapt to slowly changing water-table conditions, transient simulations are used to indicate how quickly the aquifer responds to the addition of reclaimed pits. The transient aquifer response is simulated for 15 years after the pits are added by using 30 seasonal stress periods that represent hydrologic conditions during the irrigation and non-irrigation seasons. The aquifer response to pit development in 2020 therefore is simulated for the period 2020–2035, and the aquifer response to pit development in 2040 is simulated for the period 2040–2055. The irrigation season is simulated as 183 days, and the non-irrigation season is simulated as 182 days. The first stress period (non-irrigation season) is divided into six time steps of about 30 days each. The second stress period (irrigation season) is divided into two time steps of 91.5 days each. All subsequent stress periods have a single time step equal to the stress-period length.

Groundwater-level declines and rises resulting from the addition of reclaimed pits are calculated relative to simulated water-table conditions for the 2000 irrigation season for all simulations. Groundwater-level declines and rises are calculated relative to the water table during the irrigation season because groundwater levels during the irrigation season generally are higher and are therefore more likely to support wetlands at the land surface. Groundwater-level declines relative to the 2000 non-irrigation season would be less than that indicated for the irrigation season because groundwater levels generally are lower during the non-irrigation season. Conversely, groundwater-level rises resulting from pits would be greater relative to the 2000 non-irrigation season. For the purposes of this report, areas where simulated groundwater levels change more than 2 ft indicate locations where groundwater-supported wetlands might be vulnerable to the cumulative hydrologic effects of reclaimed pits. Groundwater-level declines and rises resulting from a single pit would be different than that shown for the multiple pits simulated.

Simulation 3—Reclaimed Pits in 2020

Simulation 3 indicates the potential cumulative hydrologic effects of pit development in 2020. Simulated groundwater-level changes in 2035 resulting from the potential extent of pit development in 2020 are shown on figure 34 relative to locations of wetlands and riparian herbaceous vegetation, and the simulated groundwater budget for simulation 3 is provided in table 10. Positive values of groundwater-level change in figure 34 indicate areas of groundwater-level rise, whereas negative values indicate areas of groundwater-level decline. Groundwater-level changes represent potential hydrologic conditions 15 years after pits are reclaimed.

The results of simulation 3 show that groundwater levels rise on the upgradient side of lined pits (fig. 34) and decline on the downgradient side of lined pits. Groundwater levels rise upgradient from lined pits because the low-permeability pit lining creates a barrier to groundwater flow, which causes groundwater to mound against the upgradient pit wall. Groundwater levels decline downgradient from lined pits because groundwater is diverted around the pit, creating a hydrologic shadow behind the pit. Unlined pits have an opposite but generally lesser effect on groundwater levels in simulation 3. Unlined pits cause groundwater levels to decline on the upgradient side of pits (fig. 34) and rise on the downgradient side because the lake inside the pit creates an area where the water level is flat within the sloping water table. Because the water level in the unlined pit reaches equilibrium somewhere between the groundwater-table altitude at the upgradient and downgradient ends of the pit, the water table at the upgradient end slopes toward the pit, whereas the water table at the downgradient end slopes away from the pit. Pits backfilled with fine-grained material are simulated as having lower hydraulic conductivity than the surrounding aquifer and result in hydrologic effects similar to those for lined pits, but the effects are less because the backfilled pits are less of a barrier to groundwater flow than lined pits. The hydrologic effects of lined, unlined, and fines-backfilled pits interact to increase the magnitude of groundwater-level changes at some locations and decrease it at others, depending on the relative position of the pits.

The area of greatest groundwater-level decline that occurs near Big Dry Creek (fig. 34) results from the combined effects of the lined water-storage facility and unlined pits downgradient from the facility. Maximum simulated groundwater-level decline at this location is about 9 ft. The areas of greatest groundwater-level rise (fig. 34) occur on the upgradient side of

lined pits on the west side of the South Platte River, where the maximum simulated rise is about 6 ft, and near location B on the east side of the river, where the maximum simulated rise is about 5 ft. Groundwater-level changes near the South Platte River generally are less than 2 ft because the river lessens the hydrologic effects of pits by contributing or receiving water as groundwater levels change.

Wetlands mapped in the study area generally are located where simulated groundwater levels change less than 2 ft (fig. 34) and might not be substantially affected by groundwater-level declines or rises resulting from the potential extent of reclaimed pits in 2020. However, substantial areas of riparian herbaceous vegetation (primarily to the south of Big Dry Creek) mapped by CDOW (2007a, b) are located where groundwater levels change more than 2 ft (fig. 34), indicating that riparian herbaceous vegetation in these areas might be affected by groundwater-level declines or rises resulting from the potential extent of reclaimed pits in 2020. Because most areas where groundwater levels are simulated to rise more than 2 ft on the east side of the South Platte River occur where the simulated premining depth to water is more than 5 ft (fig. 30), higher groundwater levels resulting from reclaimed pits in 2020 are not likely to create conditions favorable to the formation of new wetlands on the east side of the river. However, most areas where groundwater levels were simulated to rise more than 2 ft on the west side of the South Platte River (except near Big Dry Creek upgradient from the lined water-storage facility) occur where the simulated premining depth to water is less than 5 ft, and groundwater-level rises in these areas could create conditions favorable to the formation of new wetlands.

The transient response of groundwater-level declines and rises in the simulated aquifer varies by location depending on the proximity of reclaimed pits, aquifer properties, hydrologic boundaries, and seasonal water-table fluctuations. Because the aquifer is highly transmissive, groundwater levels change most during the first year, and groundwater levels generally change by successively smaller amounts in subsequent years. Examples of transient groundwater-level decline and rise are provided in figures 35A and 35B for two locations in the simulated aquifer. The groundwater-level decline at location A (fig. 34) occurs smoothly over time (fig. 35A) because seasonal water-table fluctuations at this location are small (about 1.5 ft), and groundwater levels are controlled primarily by the combined hydrologic effects of the surrounding pits. The groundwater-level decline at location A occurs rapidly during the first half of the year because of declining groundwater levels throughout the simulated aquifer during the non-irrigation season in the first stress period. Groundwater levels continue to decline during the second half of the first year, but the rate of decline decreases because of increased recharge during the irrigation season. By contrast, the groundwater-level rise at location B (fig. 34) oscillates about 2.5 ft between the irrigation and non-irrigation seasons (fig. 35B) because seasonal fluctuations of the water table at this location are relatively large (about 5 ft). The

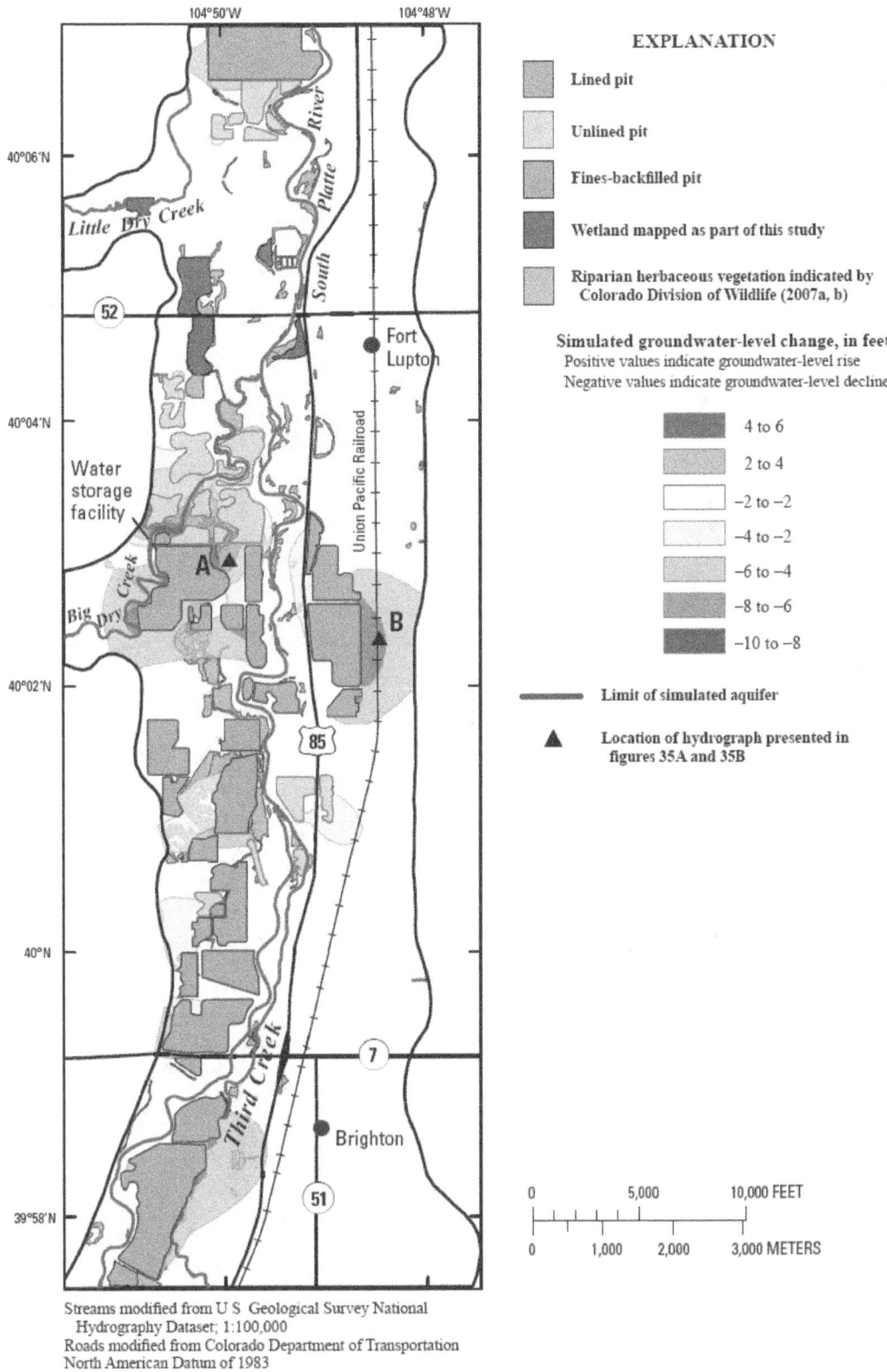

Figure 34.   Simulation 3—Groundwater-level changes in 2035 resulting from the potential extent of reclaimed aggregate pits in 2020, Brighton to Fort Lupton, Colorado.

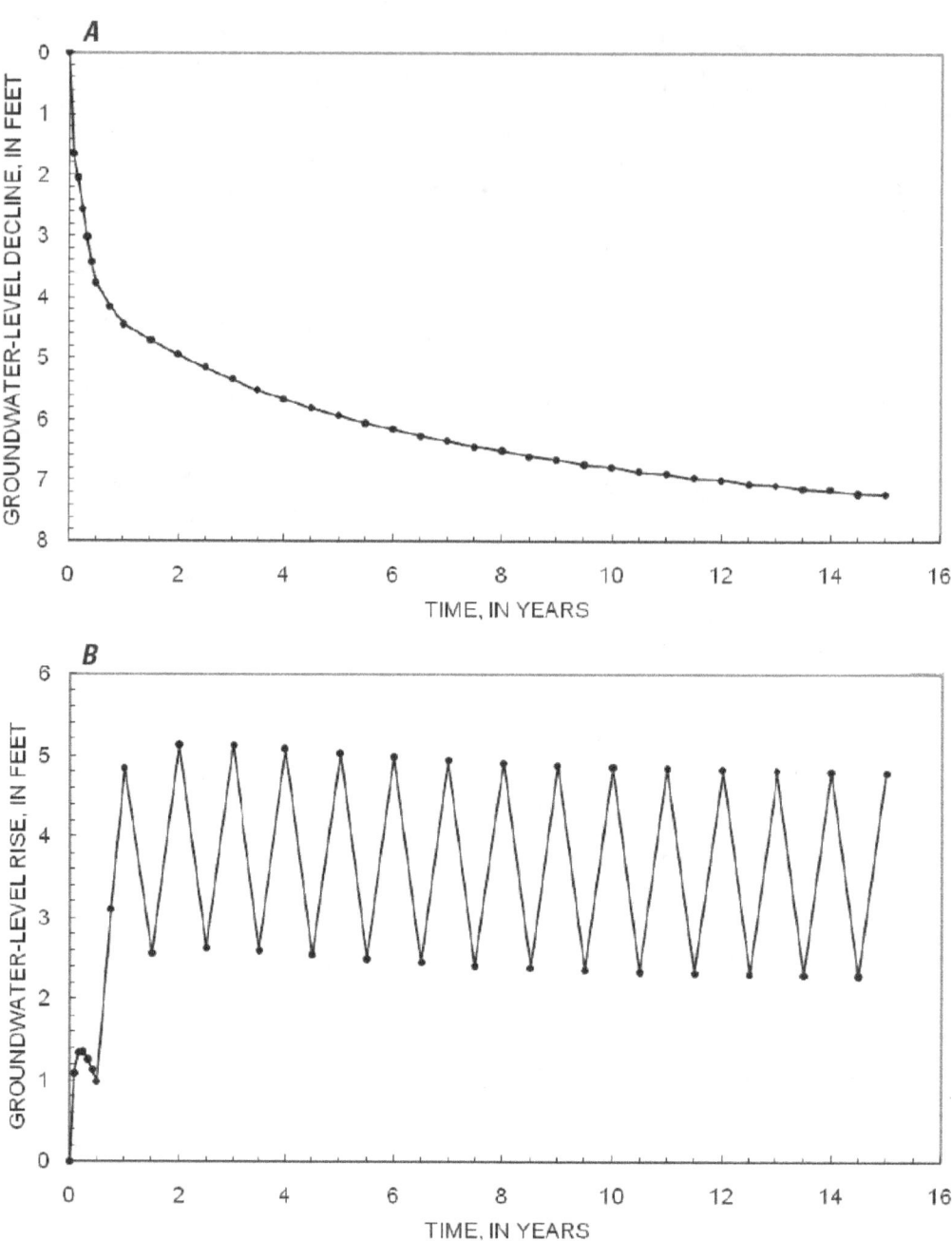

Figure 35. *A.* Simulated transient groundwater-level decline at location resulting from the potential extent of reclaimed pits in 2020, Brighton to Fort Lupton, Colorado. *B.* Simulated transient groundwater-level rise at location resulting from the potential extent of reclaimed pits in 2020, Brighton to Fort Lupton, Colorado. The time period represents 15 years after pit reclamation. Location of groundwater-level decline is shown in figure 34.

groundwater-level rise during the first half year at location B is reduced by declining groundwater levels throughout the simulated aquifer during the non-irrigation season. The groundwater level then rises substantially throughout the second half of the first year because of increased recharge during the subsequent irrigation season. Groundwater levels during subsequent years continue to oscillate with the seasons but remain relatively stable within each season from year to year after the initial rise in groundwater levels. Groundwater-level rise on the upgradient side of lined pits generally is largest within 1–3 years (fig. 35B) after reclaiming the pits and then decreases slightly as groundwater flows around the pit and reaches new equilibrium conditions.

Simulated seasonal groundwater-level changes resulting from reclaimed pits cease to change substantially in most areas of the aquifer within about 10 years (figs. 35A and 35B). Groundwater-level declines and rises (15 years after pits are reclaimed) shown in figure 34, therefore, generally represent the approximate maximum predicted magnitude and extent of groundwater-level changes resulting from reclaimed pits over time. Because reclaimed pits can result in long-term changes in groundwater levels, groundwater-supported riparian herbaceous vegetation located where groundwater-level decline exceeds 2 ft might be permanently altered by lower groundwater levels. Because a large proportion of groundwater-level rise resulting from reclaimed pits occurs rapidly within the first year, groundwater-supported riparian herbaceous vegetation located in areas affected by higher groundwater levels might be susceptible to flooding.

Total aquifer inflow and outflow in simulation 3 (table 10) is larger than in the 2000 irrigation season and in simulations 1 and 2 because the groundwater budget is accounting for inflow and outflow at unlined pits in simulation 3, and the simulation is transient, which considers aquifer storage in computing the groundwater budget. Although groundwater inflow and outflow at unlined pits are the largest components of the groundwater budget, net groundwater discharge to unlined pits (groundwater discharge to pits minus pit leakage) represents only about 0.3 percent of the total groundwater budget of simulation 3. Therefore, the larger groundwater budget of simulation 3 does not represent a large increase in available water in the study area. Other than leakage to the aquifer from unlined pits, distributed recharge at the land surface and leakage from the South Platte River and Big Dry Creek represent the greatest changes to aquifer inflow in simulation 3 relative to the 2000 irrigation season. Distributed recharge at the land surface decreased by 16.8 percent relative to the 2000 irrigation season because substantial land areas contributing recharge to the model are converted to pits, which do not contribute to distributed recharge. Leakage from the South Platte River and Big Dry Creek increased by 19.0 percent relative to the 2000 irrigation season because of groundwater-level declines near streams in some areas. Groundwater declines also caused groundwater inflow at the upgradient end of the South Platte River valley to increase slightly (4.5 percent) in simulation 3 relative to the 2000 irrigation season.

Other than groundwater discharge to unlined pits, groundwater outflow at the downgradient end of the South Platte River valley and discharge to the South Platte River and Big Dry Creek represent the greatest changes to aquifer outflow in simulation 3. Groundwater outflow at the downgradient end of the South Platte River valley decreased by 14.0 percent relative to the 2000 irrigation season likely because the large lined pit simulated at the north (downgradient) end of the aquifer obstructs groundwater outflow from the simulated aquifer. Although discharge to the South Platte River and Big Dry Creek decreased by only 4.4 percent relative to the 2000 irrigation season, the decrease (166,000 ft³/d) represents the second largest absolute change to the outflow water budget. The decreased discharge likely is caused primarily by lined pits obstructing groundwater flow to the streams. The other components of the outflow water budget in simulation 3 also change relative to the 2000 irrigation season. Groundwater discharge to Little Dry Creek and Third Creek increased by 13.4 percent, phreatophyte evapotranspiration decreased by 12.8 percent, and municipal-well withdrawals decreased by 4.2 percent. The increase in groundwater discharge to Little Dry Creek and Third Creek in simulation 3 likely is the result of higher groundwater levels near Third Creek, whereas the decrease in phreatophyte evapotranspiration likely is the result of lower groundwater levels in areas of phreatophyte vegetation. The decrease in municipal-well withdrawals is the result of one well (located near the center of the simulated aquifer) (fig. 21) being removed from the simulation because a lined pit was added at that location.

Simulation 4—Reclaimed Lined Pits in 2040

Simulation 4 indicates the potential cumulative hydrologic effects of pit development in 2040, when mining in the study area has been approximately fully developed and all pits excavated after 2020 are lined with slurry walls or clay. All hydrologic conditions in simulation 4 are the same as in simulation 3 except for the addition of lined pits after 2020. Simulated groundwater-level changes in 2055 resulting from the potential extent of pit development in 2040 are shown in figure 36 relative to locations of wetlands and riparian herbaceous vegetation, and the simulated groundwater budget for simulation 4 is provided in table 10. Groundwater-level changes represent potential hydrologic conditions 15 years after the pits are reclaimed. As with simulation 3, most groundwater-level change occurs during the first year because of the aquifer's high transmissivity, and groundwater levels cease to change substantially in most areas of the simulated aquifer within about 10 years.

The general pattern of simulated groundwater-level decline and rise resulting from the addition of lined pits in 2040 is similar to that resulting from pits in 2020. Simulated groundwater levels rise on the upgradient side of lined pits and decline on the downgradient side of lined pits. However, the extent and magnitude of rise on the upgradient side of lined pits is greater in 2040 than in 2020 because groundwater flow is obstructed over a larger part of the simulated aquifer.

Maximum groundwater-level rise is about 9 ft upgradient from lined pits near Little Dry Creek. The addition of lined pits in 2040 results in greater groundwater-level declines than in 2020 in some areas of the simulated aquifer and lesser declines in other areas. Areas of greater decline occur downgradient from added pits. Areas of lesser decline occur where groundwater-level rises resulting from additional lined pits offset declines resulting from unlined pits. Maximum groundwater-level declines resulting from lined pits in 2040 is about 9 ft near Big Dry Creek downgradient from the lined water-storage facility.

Wetlands mapped in the study area generally are not located where simulated groundwater levels decline more than 2 ft (fig. 36), but substantial wetland areas are located where groundwater levels rise more than 2 ft between Big Dry Creek and Little Dry Creek on the west side of the South Platte River. Wetlands located where the depth to water is less than 5 ft (fig. 30) in this area might be flooded by the higher groundwater levels, or additional wetlands might form. As in simulation 3, substantial areas of riparian herbaceous vegetation are located where groundwater levels decline or rise more than 2 ft, indicating that riparian herbaceous vegetation in these areas might be affected by groundwater changes resulting from the extent of reclaimed lined pits in 2040.

Total aquifer inflow and outflow in simulation 4 is less than in simulation 3 because the additional lined pits obstruct groundwater inflow and outflow in the model. Leakage from unlined pits and distributed recharge at the land surface represent the largest changes to aquifer inflow in simulation 4 relative to simulation 3. Leakage from unlined pits decreased 22.9 percent relative to simulation 3 because groundwater flow from unlined pits is obstructed to a greater extent by the addition of lined pits. Distributed recharge at the land surface in simulation 4 decreased by 14.6 percent relative to simulation 3 because a larger land area contributing recharge to the model is converted to aggregate pits. Groundwater discharge to unlined pits and to the South Platte River and Big Dry Creek represent the largest changes to aquifer outflow in simulation 4. Groundwater discharge to unlined pits decreased 21.3 percent relative to simulation 3, and groundwater discharge to the South Platte River and Big Dry Creek decreased by 7.0 percent.

Simulation 5—Reclaimed Unlined Pits in 2040

Simulation 5 indicates the potential cumulative hydrologic effects of pit development in 2040, when mining in the study area has been approximately fully developed and all pits excavated after 2020 are unlined. All hydrologic conditions in simulation 5 are the same as in simulation 3 except for the addition of unlined pits after 2020. Simulated groundwater-level changes in 2055 resulting from the potential extent of pit development in 2040 are shown on figure 37 relative to locations of wetlands and riparian herbaceous vegetation, and the simulated groundwater budget for simulation 5 is provided in table 10. Comparison of simulation 5 to simulation 4 (lined

pits added after 2020) allows for assessment of which reclamation method would likely minimize the hydrologic effects of reclaimed pits. Groundwater-level changes represent potential hydrologic conditions 15 years after pits are reclaimed. As with simulation 3, most groundwater-level change occurs during the first year because of the aquifer's high transmissivity, and groundwater levels cease to change substantially in most areas of the simulated aquifer within about 10 years.

Groundwater-level declines in simulation 5 generally are greater than in simulations 3 and 4 because the addition of unlined pits creates larger areas where groundwater levels decline to newly imposed pit-lake levels. The magnitude and extent of groundwater-level rise in simulation 5 generally is less than in simulations 3 and 4 because the presence of additional unlined pits lessens groundwater-level rises resulting from nearby lined pits. The maximum groundwater-level decline in simulation 5 is about 11 ft near Big Dry Creek downgradient from the lined water-storage facility and is about 2 ft greater than the maximum decline in simulations 3 and 4. The maximum groundwater-level rise is about 5 ft in small areas along the upgradient walls of lined pits near the south end of the simulated aquifer. Large groundwater-level rises resulting from pits on the west side of the South Platte River in simulations 3 and 4 are greatly reduced by the addition of unlined pits adjacent to the lined pits in simulation 5. Comparison of simulation 5 to simulation 4 indicates the overall effect of adding lined pits to the simulated aquifer is to increase the magnitude and extent of groundwater-level rise, whereas the effect of adding unlined pits is to increase the magnitude and extent of groundwater-level decline.

Wetlands mapped in the study area are located where simulated groundwater levels decline more than 2 ft (fig. 37) between Little Dry Creek and the South Platte River. Because the simulated depth to water (fig. 30) in this area generally is less than 5 ft, wetlands in this area might be affected by lower groundwater levels resulting from the extent of reclaimed unlined pits in 2040. As in simulations 3 and 4, substantial areas of riparian herbaceous vegetation are located where groundwater levels decline or rise more than 2 ft, indicating that riparian herbaceous vegetation in these areas also might be affected by groundwater-level changes resulting from the extent of reclaimed unlined pits in 2040.

Total aquifer inflow and outflow in simulation 5 is much greater than in simulation 3 or any of the other simulations because of groundwater inflow and outflow at additional unlined pits simulated as lakes in simulation 5. Leakage from unlined pits and from the South Platte River and Big Dry Creek represent the largest changes to aquifer inflow in simulation 5 relative to simulation 3. Leakage from unlined pits increased about 204 percent relative to simulation 3, and leakage from the South Platte River and Big Dry Creek increased 15.3 percent. Groundwater discharge to unlined pits, groundwater entering storage, and groundwater discharge to the South Platte River and Big Dry Creek represent the largest changes to aquifer outflow in simulation 5. Groundwater discharge to unlined pits increased about 207 percent relative to

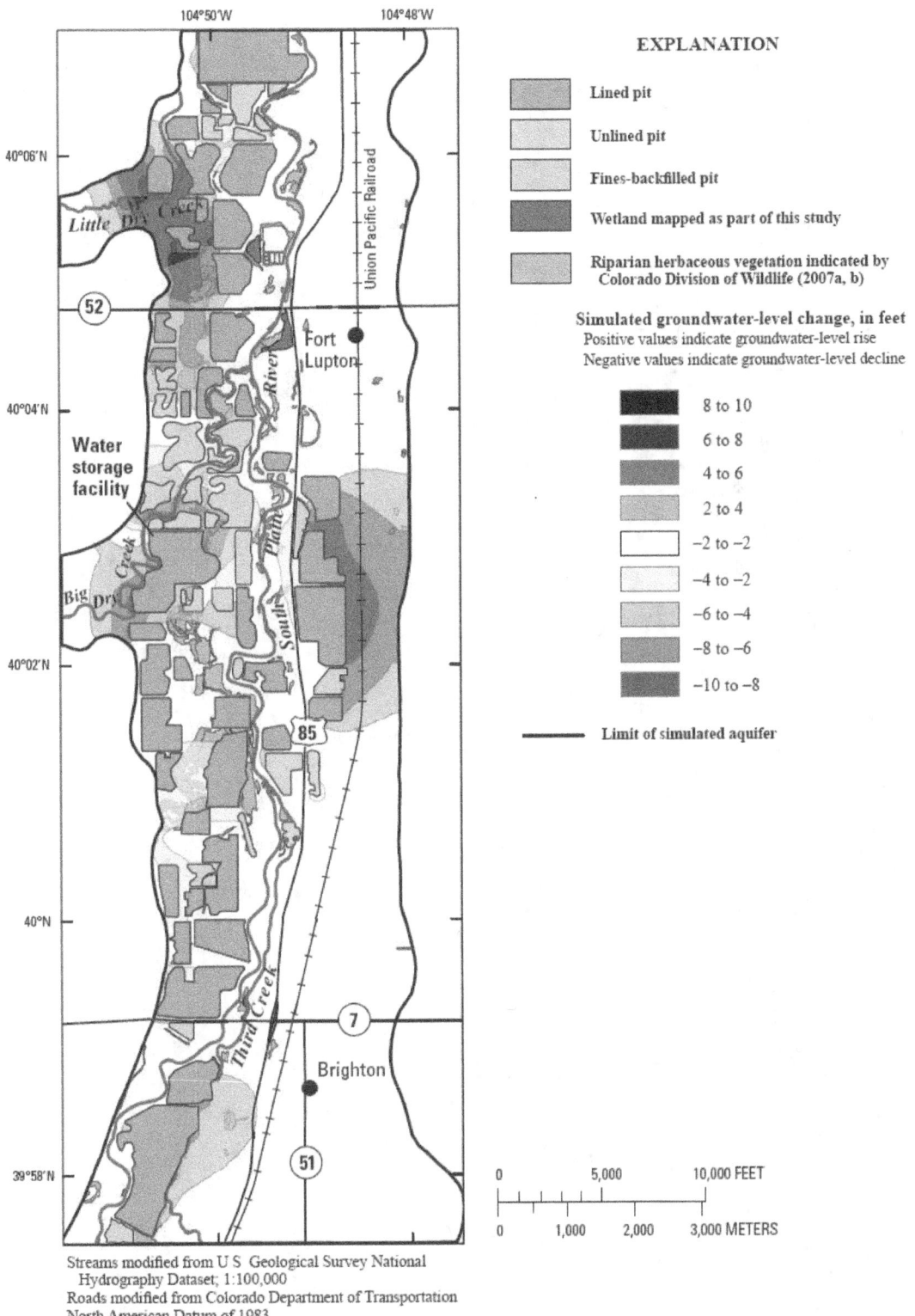

Figure 36. Simulation 4—Groundwater-level changes in 2055 resulting from the potential extent of reclaimed aggregate pits in 2040, Brighton to Fort Lupton, Colorado. Pits added after 2020 are simulated as lined.

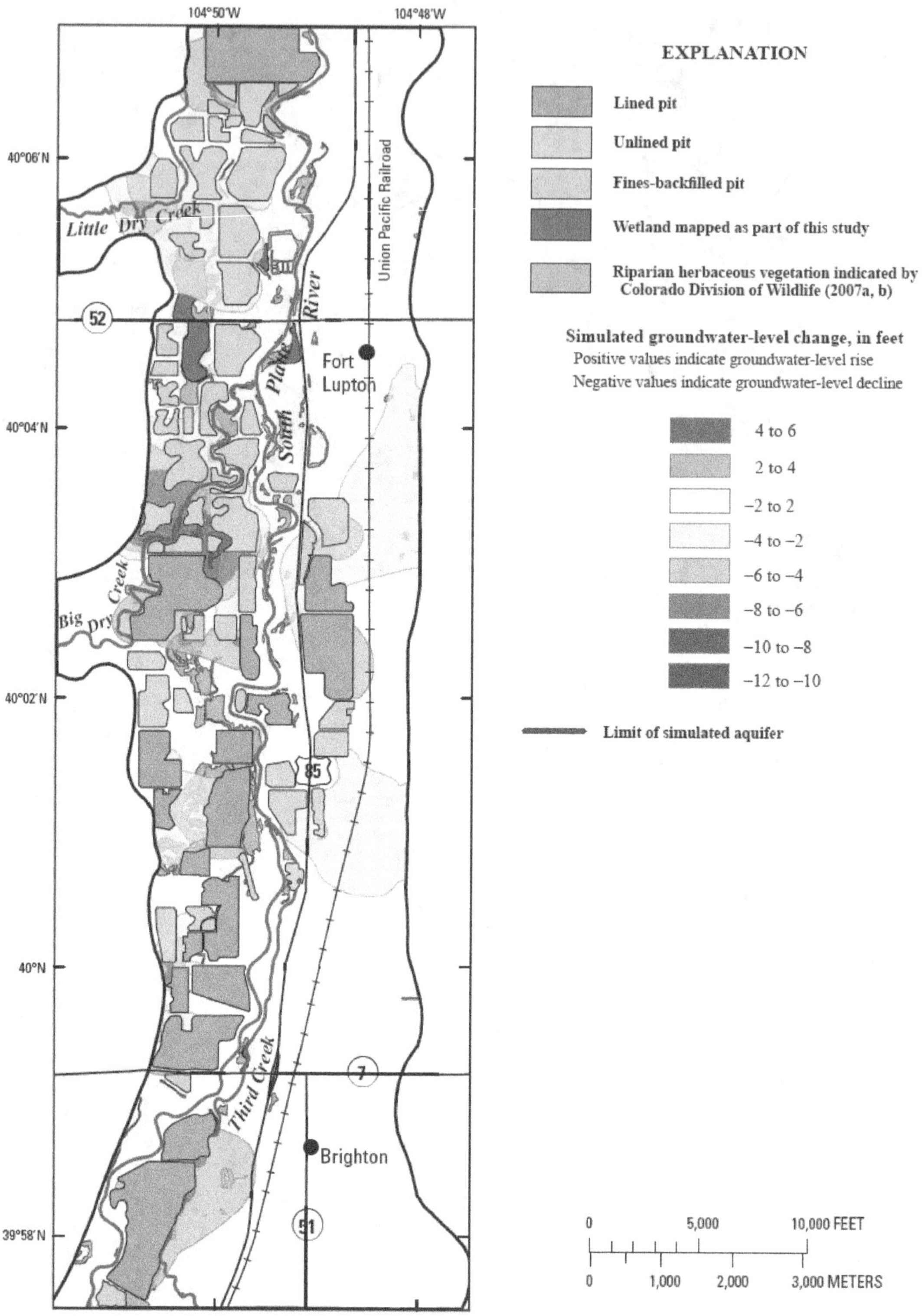

Streams modified from U.S. Geological Survey National Hydrography Dataset; 1:100,000
Roads modified from Colorado Department of Transportation
North American Datum of 1983

Figure 37. Simulation 5—Groundwater-level changes in 2055 resulting from the predicted extent of reclaimed aggregate pits in 2040, Brighton to Fort Lupton, Colorado. Pits added after 2020 are simulated as unlined.

simulation 3, groundwater entering storage decreased by 25.4 percent, and groundwater discharge to the South Platte River and Big Dry Creek increased by 3.9 percent.

Summary of Reclaimed Pit Simulations

Transient simulations of the cumulative hydrologic effects of reclaimed pits in 2020 and 2040 indicate lined pits cause groundwater levels to rise upgradient from pits and decline downgradient from pits, whereas unlined pits have an opposite effect on groundwater levels. The hydrologic effects of pits backfilled with fine-grained sediments are similar to but less than those of lined pits because the pits create less of a barrier to groundwater flow than lined pits. The hydrologic effects of lined, unlined, and fines-backfilled pits interact to increase the magnitude of groundwater-level changes at some locations and decrease it at others, depending on the relative position of the pits. The maximum simulated groundwater-level decline in 2035 (15 years after reclamation) resulting from the extent of reclaimed pits in 2020 is about 9 ft, and the maximum simulated groundwater-level rise is about 6 ft. Groundwater-level changes near the South Platte River generally are less than 2 ft because the river lessens the hydrologic effects of pits by contributing or receiving water as groundwater levels change. Groundwater levels change most during the first year after pits are reclaimed, and groundwater levels cease to change substantially in most areas of the simulated aquifer within about 10 years. The addition of lined pits in 2040 results in a general increase in the magnitude and extent of groundwater-level rise relative to simulated conditions for 2020 because groundwater flow is obstructed over a larger part of the simulated aquifer. The maximum simulated groundwater-level decline and rise resulting from the addition of reclaimed lined pits in 2040 is about 9 ft in 2055, 15 years after reclamation. The addition of unlined pits in 2040 results in a general increase in the magnitude and extent of groundwater-level decline relative to simulated conditions for 2020 because groundwater levels decline to lake levels in unlined pits over a larger area of the simulated aquifer. The maximum groundwater-level decline resulting from the addition of reclaimed unlined pits in 2040 is about 11 ft in 2055, 15 years after reclamation.

Wetlands mapped by this study generally are located where simulated groundwater-level changes resulting from reclaimed pits in 2020 are less than 2 ft, but some areas of riparian herbaceous vegetation mapped by the Colorado Division of Wildlife are located where simulated groundwater-level changes are more than 2 ft. Mapped wetlands and areas of riparian herbaceous vegetation are both located where simulated groundwater-level changes resulting from reclaimed pits in 2040 are more than 2 ft. Wetlands and riparian herbaceous vegetation located where groundwater-level changes are more than 2 ft might be affected by the changes. Some areas where groundwater levels are simulated to rise more than 2 ft at locations where the depth to water is less than 5 ft could create conditions favorable to the formation of new wetlands.

The groundwater budgets for simulations of reclaimed pits in 2020 and 2040 are greater than the budgets for the calibrated model or simulations of the effects of land-use change because of groundwater inflow and outflow at additional unlined pits simulated as lakes in 2020 and 2040. Other than groundwater inflow and outflow at unlined pits, distributed recharge at the land surface and leakage from the South Platte River and Big Dry Creek represent the greatest changes to aquifer inflow in 2020 relative to the 2000 irrigation season, and groundwater outflow at the downgradient end of the South Platte River valley and discharge to the South Platte River and Big Dry Creek (in terms of absolute flow) represent the greatest changes to aquifer outflow. Distributed recharge at the land surface decreases by 16.8 percent because land area that is converted to pits (lined and unlined) no longer contributes to distributed recharge. Leakage from the South Platte River and Big Dry Creek increases by 19.0 percent because of groundwater-level declines resulting from the extent of reclaimed pits in 2020. Groundwater outflow at the downgradient end of the South Platte River valley decreases by 14.0 percent, and discharge to the South Platte River and Big Dry Creek decreases by 4.4 percent, likely because of lined pits in 2020 obstructing groundwater flow in the simulated aquifer. The general effect of adding lined pits in 2040 is to decrease distributed recharge at the land surface by 14.6 percent relative to simulated conditions for 2020 and to obstruct groundwater flow over a larger part of the simulated aquifer, which decreases leakage from unlined pits by 22.9 percent, discharge to unlined pits by 21.3 percent, and discharge to the South Platte River and Big Dry Creek by 7.0 percent. The general effect of adding unlined pits in 2040 (relative to simulated conditions for 2020) is to increase leakage from unlined pits by 204 percent, leakage from the South Platte River and Big Dry Creek by 15.3 percent, discharge to unlined pits by 207 percent, and discharge to the South Platte River and Big Dry Creek by 3.9 percent, and to decrease groundwater entering storage by 25.4 percent.

Simulated Hydrologic Effects of Actively Dewatered Pits

Simulations of the hydrologic effects of actively dewatered pits represent potential drawdown resulting from pits as they are dewatered to allow dry-mining of aggregate. The term drawdown, rather than groundwater-level decline, is used to describe lowering of the water table in simulations of actively dewatered pits because the lowering is the result of withdrawing water from the aquifer rather than obstructing or altering the direction of groundwater flow, such as in the case of lined or unlined reclaimed pits. The dewatered pit locations are hypothetical and were selected to indicate the general effects of dewatered pits and the potential effects that hydrologic boundaries, such as the South Platte River, no-flow boundaries, and reclaimed pits, might have on drawdown near pits being actively dewatered. Four simulations of actively dewatered pits are presented as follows:

Simulation 6—The hydrologic effects of a single
    dewatered pit.

Simulation 7—The hydrologic effects of two closely
    spaced, dewatered pits.

Simulation 8—The hydrologic effects of two widely
    spaced, dewatered pits.

Simulation 9—The hydrologic effects of three closely
    spaced, dewatered pits.

The model grid, time discretization, and all hydrologic
conditions in simulations 6–9 are the same as those in simulation 3 (reclaimed pits in 2020) except for the addition of
actively dewatered pits in 2020. Dewatering of active pits is
simulated by using the Flow and Head Boundary package
(Leake and Lilly, 1997) of MODFLOW-2000. Initial head at
actively dewatered pits is set equal to that of the water table
during the 2000 irrigation season, and final head after dewatering is set 1 ft above bedrock at the base of the simulated aquifer. Lowering of the water level within the pit is simulated to
occur linearly over a period of 90 days as the pit is dewatered
and the final water level is reached.

As with simulations of reclaimed pits (simulations 3–5),
drawdown in all active-pit simulations is determined relative to the 2000 irrigation season rather than the 2000 non-
irrigation season because groundwater-supported wetlands are
more likely affected by groundwater-level changes during the
irrigation season when groundwater levels are highest. Square
pits (1,200 ft by 1,200 ft), representing the average size (about
34 acres) of a mining phase, are used to simulate the general
hydrologic effects of actively dewatered pits. Drawdown
resulting from pits having different size and shape would be
somewhat different than that indicated by the simulations
provided. However, Arnold and others (2003) found pit size
(radius) to have relatively small effect on steady-state drawdown extent compared to other factors, such as horizontal
hydraulic conductivity, recharge, and pit depth below the
water table in hypothetical sand-and-gravel aquifers having
conditions similar to those of the South Platte alluvial aquifer.

Simulation 6—One Actively Dewatered Pit

Simulation 6 represents the potential hydrologic effects of
dewatering a single, average-size pit in the South Platte alluvial aquifer. Simulated drawdown resulting from the pit relative to water-table conditions during the 2000 irrigation season
is shown in figure 38, and the simulated groundwater budget
for simulation 6 is provided in table 11. Although the location
of the pit is hypothetical, locations of wetlands mapped by the
study and locations of riparian herbaceous vegetation mapped
by CDOW (2007a, b) are shown in figure 38 for comparison to
drawdown extent. Drawdown represents hydrologic conditions
1 year and 15 years after the start of pit dewatering. Because
the simulated aquifer has high transmissivity, most drawdown
occurs during the first year, and drawdown extent after 1 year
is almost as large as after 15 years (fig. 38). Drawdown ceases
to increase substantially after 15 years. Maximum drawdown
in simulation 6 is about 37 ft at the pit wall, where dewatering

has lowered groundwater levels to 1 ft above bedrock at the
base of the simulated aquifer. Drawdown decreases rapidly
away from the pit to a value of 20 ft about 100 ft from the
pit wall and decreases more gradually farther from the pit.
Drawdown extent is affected by the presence of hydrologic
boundaries near the pit, such as the South Platte River, the
no-flow west model boundary, and reclaimed pits. Drawdown
between the pit and the South Platte River is less than between
the pit and the west model boundary because the river supplies
water to lessen drawdown, whereas the no-flow west boundary limits the supply of water. Unlined reclaimed pits located
north and south of the dewatered pit also lessen drawdown and
limit drawdown extent. Drawdown of 10 ft occurs about 200
ft from the pit wall in the direction of the South Platte River,
whereas drawdown of 10 ft occurs up to about 1,000 ft from
the pit wall in the direction of the west model boundary. Drawdown of 2 ft occurs at a maximum distance of about 9,500
ft downgradient from the pit center and is affected by the
presence of reclaimed pits. The full drawdown extent defined
by the limit of 2-ft drawdown has a maximum width of about
12,400 ft. Because dewatering typically occurs for multiple
years and most drawdown occurs rapidly during the first year,
groundwater-supported wetlands within the limit of 2-ft drawdown could be affected by lower groundwater levels resulting
from pit dewatering.

Leakage from unlined pits, leakage from the South Platte
River and Big Dry Creek, and groundwater inflow from the
upgradient ends of the South Platte valley and tributaries are
the largest sources of inflow to the aquifer in simulation 6
(table 11). Combined inflow from these sources represents
about 70 percent of total inflow in simulation 6. Groundwater
discharge to unlined pits and groundwater discharge to the
South Platte River and Big Dry Creek are the largest sources
of outflow in simulation 6. Combined outflow from these
sources represents about 60 percent of the total outflow in
simulation 6. Groundwater discharge to the actively dewatered
pit represents about 9 percent of the total simulated outflow.
Relative to baseline conditions represented by the water
budget of simulation 3 (reclaimed pits in 2020 without an
actively dewatered pit), the primary effect of pit dewatering is
to increase leakage from the South Platte River and Big Dry
Creek by 21 percent and to decrease discharge to the South
Platte River and Big Dry Creek by 15 percent.

Simulation 7—Two Closely Spaced, Actively Dewatered Pits

Simulation 7 represents the potential hydrologic effects
of simultaneously dewatering two closely spaced (400 ft apart)
average-size pits or pit phases of a single larger pit in the
South Platte alluvial aquifer. Simulated drawdown resulting
from the pits after 1 year and after 15 years of dewatering is
shown in figure 39 relative to water-table conditions of the
2000 irrigation season, and the simulated groundwater budget
for simulation 7 is provided in table 11. Wetlands and areas
of riparian herbaceous vegetation also are shown in figure 39

Table 11. Groundwater budgets for simulations of the hydrologic effects of actively dewatered pits in the South Platte alluvial aquifer.

[All values are in cubic feet per day; totals reflect sum of all rounded components]

Budget component	Simulation 61	Simulation 72	Simulation 83	Simulation 94
Aquifer inflows				
Groundwater inflow from general-head boundaries at upgradient end of South Platte River valley and tributaries	2,065,000	2,071,000	2,075,000	2,077,000
Subsurface irrigation return flow along east model boundary	1,782,000	1,782,000	1,782,000	1,782,000
Distributed recharge at the land surface	1,457,000	1,449,000	1,447,000	1,438,000
Leakage to aquifer from South Platte River and Big Dry Creek	2,108,000	2,305,000	2,428,000	2,500,000
Leakage to aquifer from unlined pits	3,750,000	3,635,000	3,467,000	3,452,000
Groundwater released from storage	108,000	108,000	108,000	108,000
Total	11,270,000	11,350,000	11,307,000	11,357,000
Aquifer outflows				
Groundwater outflow to general-head boundary at downgradient end of South Platte River valley	1,150,000	1,145,000	1,140,000	1,139,000
Groundwater discharge to South Platte River and Big Dry Creek	3,097,000	2,916,000	2,798,000	2,759,000
Groundwater discharge to Little Dry Creek and Third Creek	144,000	144,000	144,000	144,000
Groundwater discharge to unlined pits	3,690,000	3,541,000	3,360,000	3,332,000
Phreatophyte evapotranspiration	181,000	178,000	177,000	176,000
Municipal-well withdrawals	1,421,000	1,421,000	1,421,000	1,421,000
Groundwater discharge to actively dewatered pits	1,021,000	1,442,000	1,705,000	1,827,000
Groundwater entering storage	570,000	567,000	566,000	563,000
Total	11,274,000	11,354,000	11,311,000	11,361,000
Percent discrepancy (Recharge–Discharge)	−0.04	−0.04	−0.04	−0.04

[1]One actively dewatered pit.

[2]Two closely spaced, actively dewatered pits.

[3]Two widely spaced, actively dewatered pits.

[4]Three closely spaced, actively dewatered pits.

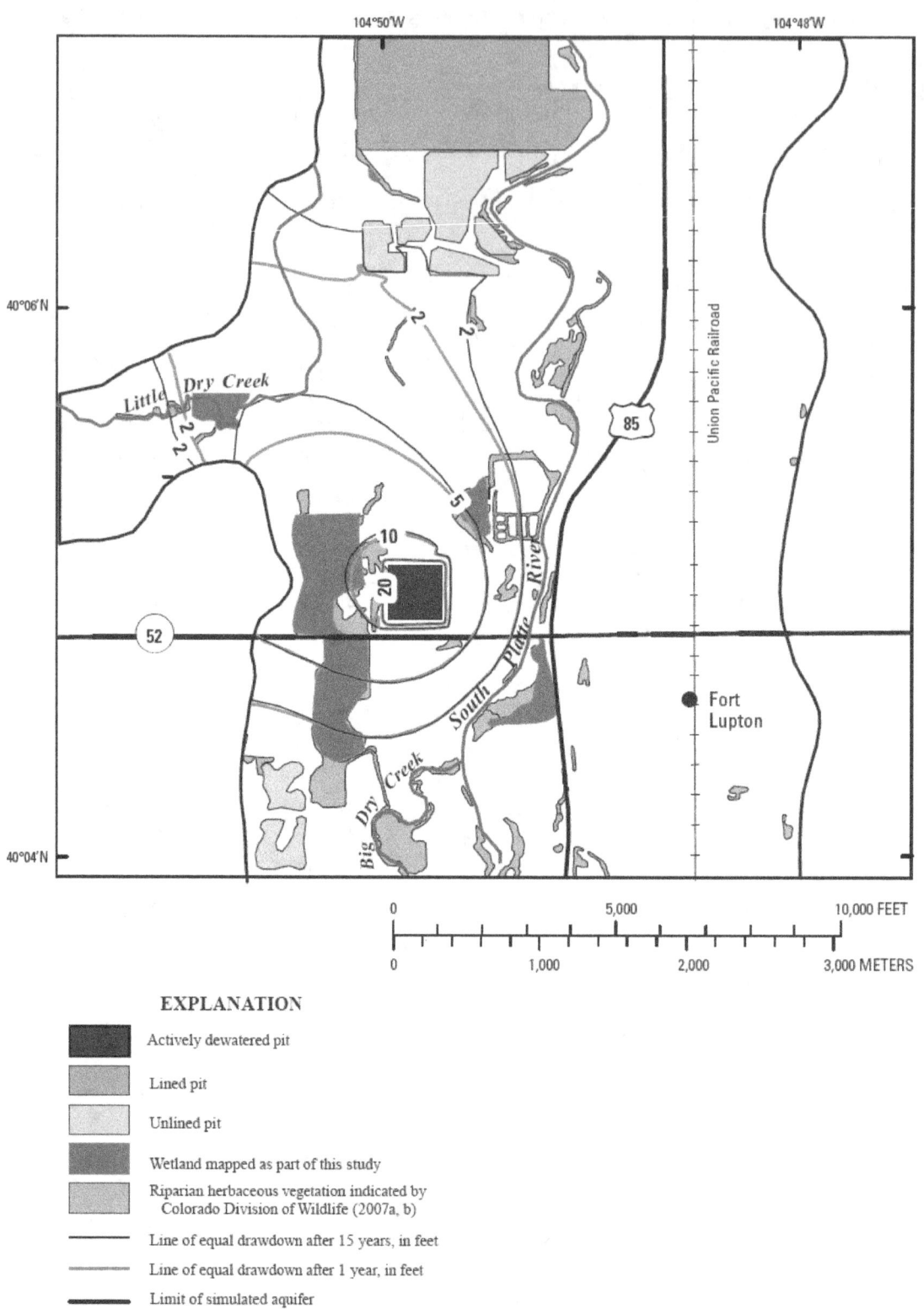

Figure 38. Simulation 6—Drawdown resulting from a single actively dewatered pit in the South Platte alluvial aquifer after 1 year and after 15 years of dewatering.

for comparison to drawdown extent. As in simulation 6, most drawdown occurs during the first year (fig. 39) and increases only slightly after the first year. Maximum drawdown in simulation 7 is the same as in simulation 6 with a value of about 37 ft at the wall of the southern pit. Drawdown in simulation 7 decreases rapidly away from the pits to a value of 20 ft at a distance of 100–200 ft from pit walls and decreases more gradually farther from the pits. Drawdown of 10 ft occurs at a maximum distance of about 200 ft from the pits in the direction of the South Platte River and at a maximum distance of about 3,200 ft from the pits in the direction away from the river. Drawdown near the pits is irregular because of the overlapping effect of each dewatered pit. Farther from the pits, the aquifer responds as though the two pits are a single larger dewatered pit. Drawdown of 2 ft occurs at a maximum distance of about 8,800 ft downgradient from the midpoint of the pits (at the west model boundary) and is affected by the presence of reclaimed pits. The full drawdown extent defined by the limit of 2-ft drawdown has a maximum width of about 12,800 ft.

The overall groundwater budget for simulation 7 is similar to that for simulation 6, but the magnitude of some water-budget components is slightly different (table 11). Combined leakage from unlined pits, leakage from the South Platte River and Big Dry Creek, and groundwater inflow from the upgradient ends of the South Platte valley and tributaries represent about 71 percent of the total inflow in simulation 7. Combined groundwater discharge to unlined pits and groundwater discharge to the South Platte River and Big Dry Creek represent about 57 percent of the total outflow in simulation 7. Groundwater discharge to the actively dewatered pits in simulation 7 represents about 13 percent of the total outflow.

Simulation 8—Two Widely Spaced, Actively Dewatered Pits

Simulation 8 represents the potential hydrologic effects of simultaneously dewatering two widely spaced (2,000 ft apart) average-size pits in the South Platte alluvial aquifer. Simulated drawdown resulting from pits after 1 year and after 15 years of dewatering is shown in figure 40 relative to water-table conditions of the 2000 irrigation season, and the simulated groundwater budget for simulation 8 is provided in table 11. Wetlands and areas of riparian herbaceous vegetation also are shown in figure 40 for comparison to drawdown extent. As in simulation 7, most drawdown occurs during the first year (fig. 40) and increases only slightly after the first year. Maximum drawdown in simulation 8 is the same as in simulation 7 with a value of about 37 ft at the wall of the southern pit. As in simulation 7, drawdown in simulation 8 decreases rapidly away from the pits to a value of 20 ft at a distance of about 100–200 ft from the pits and decreases more gradually farther from the pits. However, the areal extent of drawdown in simulation 8 generally is larger than in simulation 7 because the pits are farther apart and the water table is effectively lowered over a larger area by the combined effects of the separated pits. In addition, the independent drawdown effects of each pit are evident where drawdown is more than about 20 ft. Drawdown of 10 ft occurs at a maximum distance of about 500 ft from the pits in the direction of the South Platte River and about 3,500 ft from the pits in the direction away from the river. The line of 10-ft drawdown is irregular near the pits because of the overlapping effect of each dewatered pit. Farther from the pits, the aquifer responds as though the two pits are a single larger dewatered pit. Drawdown of 2 ft occurs at a maximum distance of about 8,100 ft downgradient from a point midway between the pits (at the west model boundary) and is affected by the presence of reclaimed pits. The full drawdown extent defined by the limit of 2-ft drawdown has a maximum width of about 12,900 ft.

The overall groundwater budget for simulation 8 is similar to those for simulations 6 and 7, but the magnitude of some water-budget components is slightly different (table 11). Combined leakage from unlined pits, leakage from the South Platte River and Big Dry Creek, and groundwater inflow from the upgradient ends of the South Platte valley and tributaries represent about 70 percent of the total inflow in simulation 8. Combined groundwater discharge to unlined pits and groundwater discharge to the South Platte River and Big Dry Creek represent about 54 percent of the total outflow in simulation 8. Groundwater discharge to the actively dewatered pits in simulation 8 represents about 15 percent of the total outflow.

Simulation 9—Three Closely Spaced, Actively Dewatered Pits

Simulation 9 represents the potential hydrologic effects of simultaneously dewatering three closely spaced (400 ft apart) average-size pits or pit phases of a single larger pit in the South Platte alluvial aquifer. Simulated drawdown resulting from the pits after 1 year and after 15 years of dewatering is shown in figure 41 relative to water-table conditions of the 2000 irrigation season, and the simulated groundwater budget for simulation 9 is provided in table 11. Wetlands and areas of riparian herbaceous vegetation also are shown in figure 41 for comparison to drawdown extent. Drawdown extent in simulation 9 (fig. 41) is similar to that of simulation 8, which indicates that the addition of a third pit between two widely spaced pits has relatively little effect on drawdown. The primary difference in drawdown between simulations 8 and 9 is that slightly greater drawdown occurs in the direction of the west model boundary, especially near Little Dry Creek. Drawdown in simulation 9 decreases rapidly away from the pits to a value of 20 ft at a maximum distance of about 100 ft from the pits in the direction of the South Platte River and about 600 ft from the pits in the direction away from the river. Drawdown decreases more gradually farther from the pits. Drawdown of 10 ft occurs at a maximum distance of about 600 ft from pits in the direction of the South Platte River and about 3,900 ft from the pits in the direction away from the river. Drawdown near the pits is irregular because of the overlapping effect of each dewatered pit. Farther from the pits, the aquifer responds

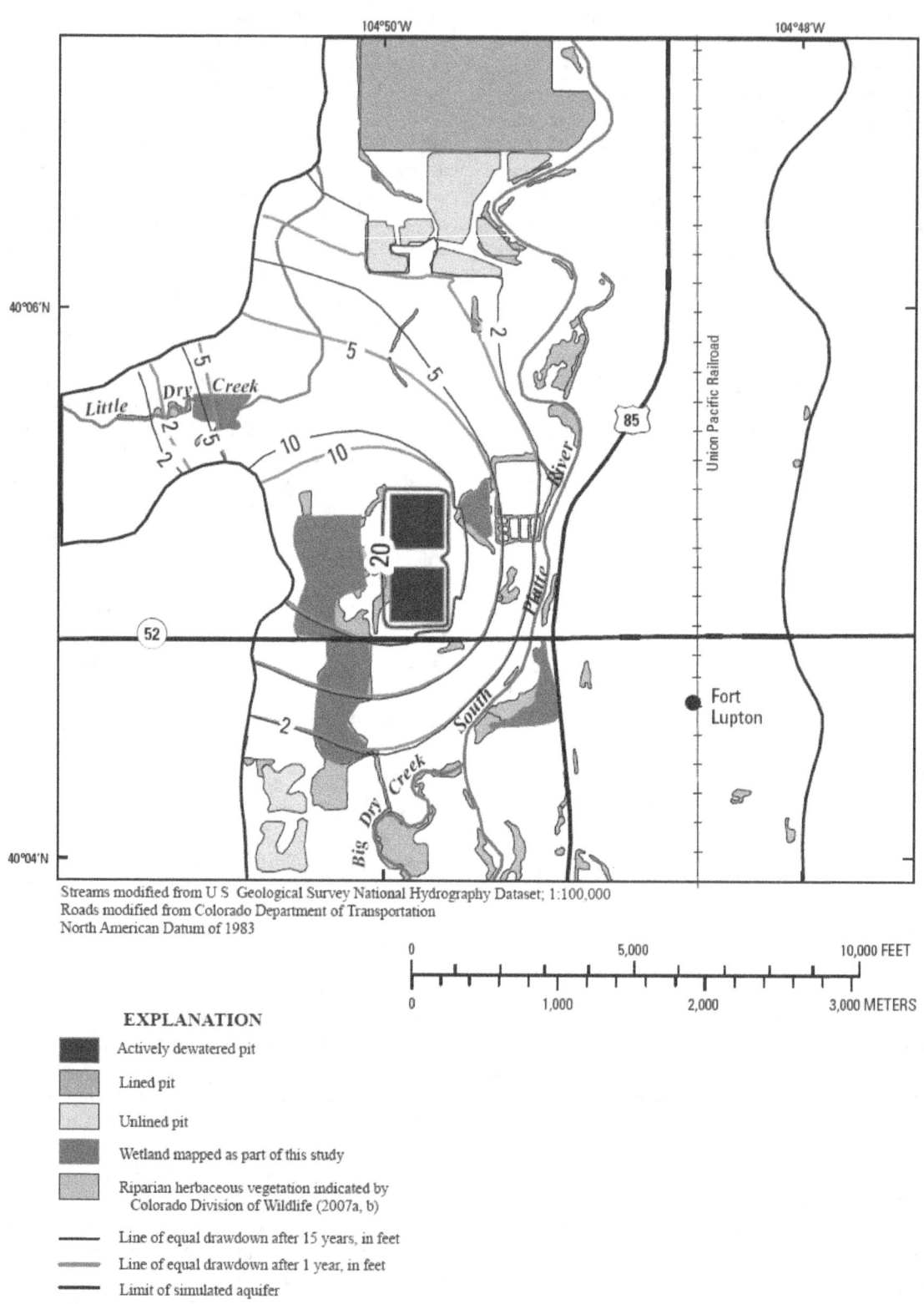

Streams modified from U S Geological Survey National Hydrography Dataset; 1:100,000
Roads modified from Colorado Department of Transportation
North American Datum of 1983

EXPLANATION

Actively dewatered pit

Lined pit

Unlined pit

Wetland mapped as part of this study

Riparian herbaceous vegetation indicated by Colorado Division of Wildlife (2007a, b)

——— Line of equal drawdown after 15 years, in feet

——— Line of equal drawdown after 1 year, in feet

——— Limit of simulated aquifer

Figure 39. Simulation 7—Drawdown resulting from two closely spaced, actively dewatered pits in the South Platte alluvial aquifer after 1 year and after 15 years of dewatering.

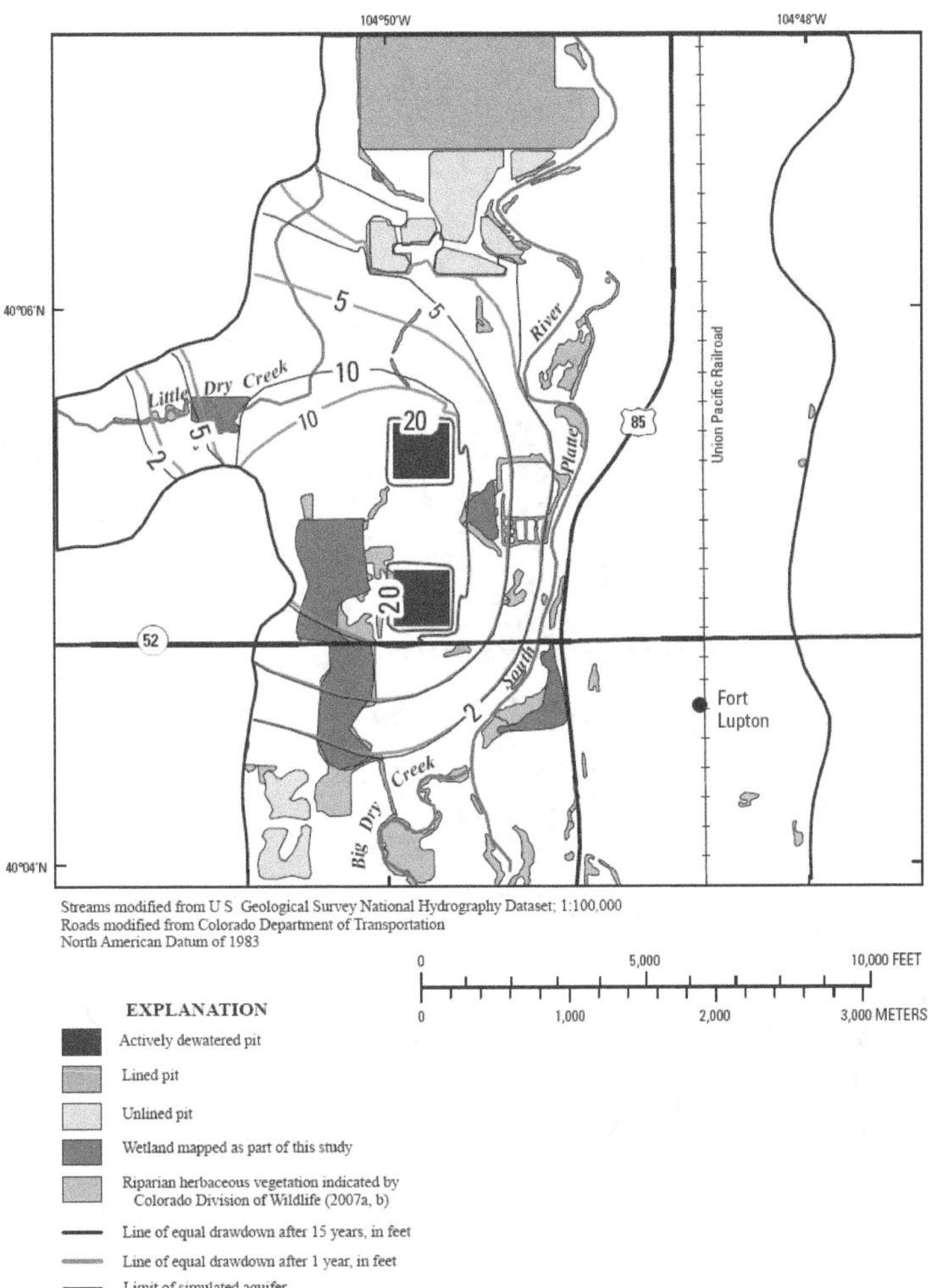

Streams modified from U S Geological Survey National Hydrography Dataset; 1:100,000
Roads modified from Colorado Department of Transportation
North American Datum of 1983

EXPLANATION

- Actively dewatered pit
- Lined pit
- Unlined pit
- Wetland mapped as part of this study
- Riparian herbaceous vegetation indicated by Colorado Division of Wildlife (2007a, b)
- —— Line of equal drawdown after 15 years, in feet
- —— Line of equal drawdown after 1 year, in feet
- —— Limit of simulated aquifer

Figure 40. Simulation 8—Drawdown resulting from two widely spaced, actively dewatered pits in the South Platte alluvial aquifer after 1 year and after 15 years of dewatering.

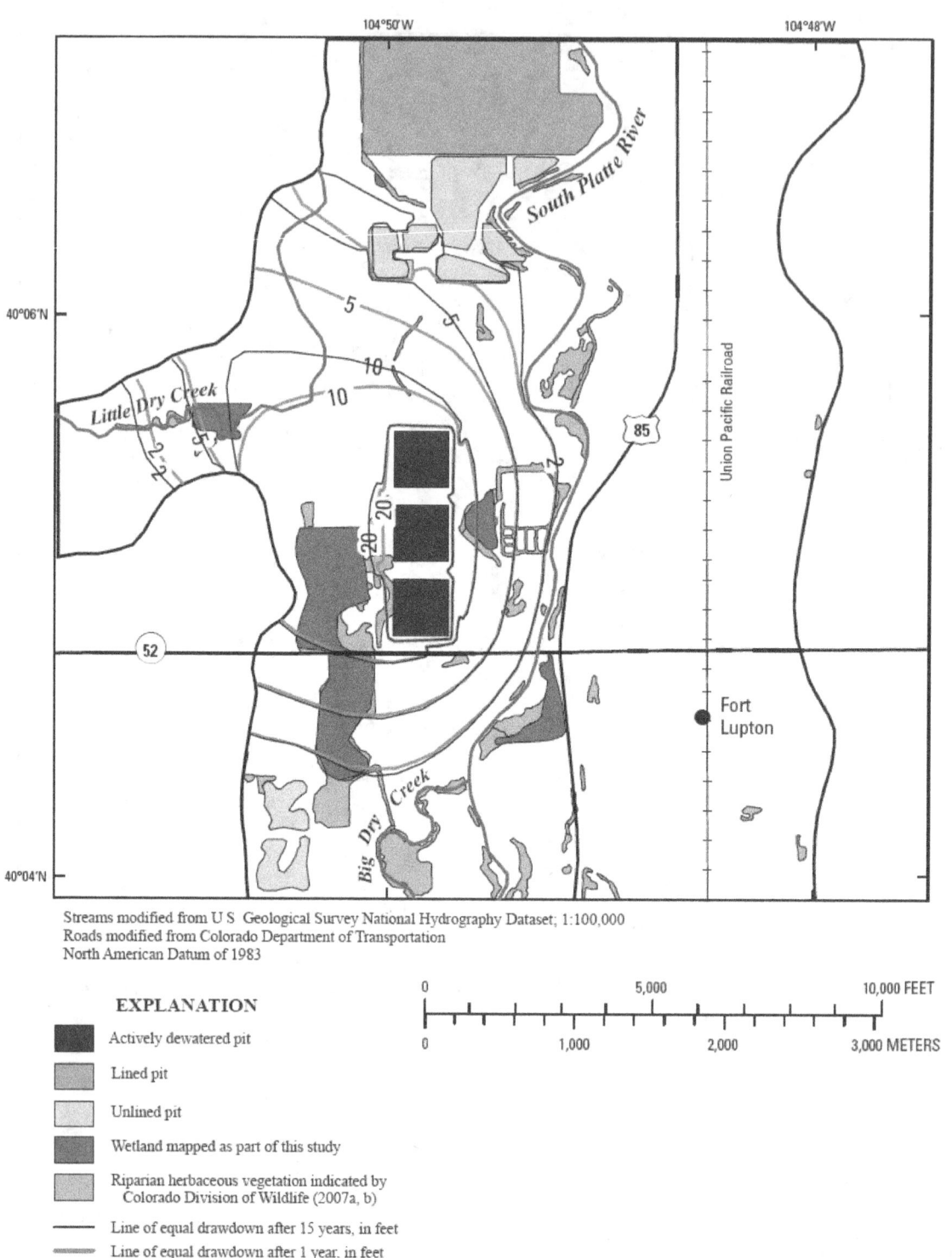

Streams modified from U S Geological Survey National Hydrography Dataset; 1:100,000
Roads modified from Colorado Department of Transportation
North American Datum of 1983

EXPLANATION

Actively dewatered pit

Lined pit

Unlined pit

Wetland mapped as part of this study

Riparian herbaceous vegetation indicated by
Colorado Division of Wildlife (2007a, b)

—— Line of equal drawdown after 15 years, in feet

—— Line of equal drawdown after 1 year, in feet

—— Limit of simulated aquifer

Figure 41.   Simulation 9—Drawdown resulting from three closely spaced, actively dewatered pits in the
South Platte alluvial aquifer after 1 year and after 15 years of dewatering.

as though the three pits are a single larger dewatered pit. Drawdown of 2 ft occurs at a maximum distance of about 8,100 ft downgradient from the center of the middle pit (at the west model boundary) and is affected by the presence of reclaimed pits. The full drawdown extent defined by the limit of 2-ft drawdown has a maximum width of about 13,100 ft.

Combined leakage from unlined pits, leakage from the South Platte River and Big Dry Creek, and groundwater inflow from the upgradient ends of the South Platte valley and tributaries represent about 71 percent of the total inflow in simulation 9 (table 11). Combined groundwater discharge to unlined pits and groundwater discharge to the South Platte River and Big Dry Creek represent about 54 percent of the total outflow in simulation 9. Groundwater discharge to the actively dewatered pits in simulation 9 represents about 16 percent of the total outflow.

Summary of Actively Dewatered Pit Simulations

Comparison of the hydrologic effects of actively dewatered pits in simulations 6–9 indicates that the extent of drawdown increases as the number of pits increases because the drawdown effects of each pit are additive. Increasing the distance between two actively dewatered pits from 400 ft to 2,000 ft increased the areal extent of drawdown, rather than reduced it, because drawdown resulting from each pit combined to create a single larger drawdown extent. Maximum drawdown in all simulations of actively dewatered pits was 37 ft. Drawdown decreased to 20 ft within about 100–600 ft of actively dewatered pits and decreased more gradually farther from pits. The full drawdown extent defined by the limit of 2-ft drawdown has a maximum width of about 12,400 ft for a single dewatered pit, 12,800 ft for two pits spaced 400 ft apart, 12,900 ft for two pits spaced 2,000 ft apart, and 13,100 ft for three pits spaced 400 ft apart. Drawdown was affected by the presence of the simulated South Platte River, the no-flow west model boundary, and nearby unlined pits. Simulated flow from the South Platte River and unlined pits decreased drawdown resulting from dewatered pits, whereas the no-flow model boundary increased drawdown. Most drawdown occurs during the first year, and drawdown extent after 1 year is almost as large as after 15 years. Because dewatering typically occurs for multiple years and most drawdown occurs rapidly during the first year, groundwater-supported wetlands within the limit of 2-ft drawdown might be affected by the lower groundwater levels resulting from pit dewatering.

Groundwater budgets for simulations 6–9 indicate that the general effect of actively dewatered pits is to increase groundwater inflow from the upgradient ends of the South Platte River valley and leakage from the South Platte River and Big Dry Creek and to decrease or not affect most other components of the water budget. Simulated groundwater discharge to actively dewatered pits increased as the number of

pits increased and as the distance between two pits increased from 400 ft to 2,000 ft.

Simulated Effects of Pit Spacing and Configuration on Groundwater Levels Near Pits

Simulations of different hypothetical pit spacings and configurations are used to assess the effect that pit spacing and configuration might have on groundwater levels near reclaimed pits. Lined pits are used in all simulations related to pit spacing and configuration because lined pits generally resulted in greater groundwater-level changes than unlined pits in simulation 3 (see "Simulation 3—Reclaimed Pits in 2020"). Unlined pits would be expected to have an opposite but possibly lesser effect on groundwater levels near the pits. The model grid, time discretization, and all hydrologic conditions in simulations related to pit spacing and configuration are the same as those in simulation 3 (reclaimed pits in 2020) except for the addition of lined pits and different initial hydraulic-head conditions. Initial hydraulic-head conditions are taken from the final water table simulated at the end of simulation 3 so that simulated groundwater-level changes reflect only effects related to pit spacing and configuration. As with simulations of the cumulative hydrologic effects of reclaimed pits (simulations 3–5), lined pits are simulated by using inactive model cells at added pit locations, which act as barriers to groundwater flow. The direction of groundwater flow under initial head conditions is about N.15°E. at the location of simulated pits.

The effects of pit spacing and configuration on groundwater levels are simulated by using three pits in seven different configurations (fig. 42). Five configurations simulate different pit sizes aligned approximately cross gradient to the direction of horizontal groundwater flow, and two configurations simulate average-size pits (1,200 ft by 1,200 ft) offset upgradient or downgradient from each other. The distance between pits in each aligned configuration varies from 0 to 1,000 ft in 200-ft increments, depending on pit size. Pits aligned approximately cross gradient to groundwater flow obstruct groundwater flow to different extents based on pit size. Pit width in aligned configurations ranges from 1,000 to 1,800 ft in increments of 200 ft, and the combined width of the three aligned pits ranges from 3,000 to 5,400 ft, which represents 50–90 percent of the 6,000-ft distance between the west model boundary and the South Platte River at the location of simulated pits. Because the pits extend to bedrock and saturated thickness varies little at the aligned pit locations, the combined cross-sectional area of the pits consequently obstructs groundwater flow through about 50–90 percent of the aquifer on the west side of the river.

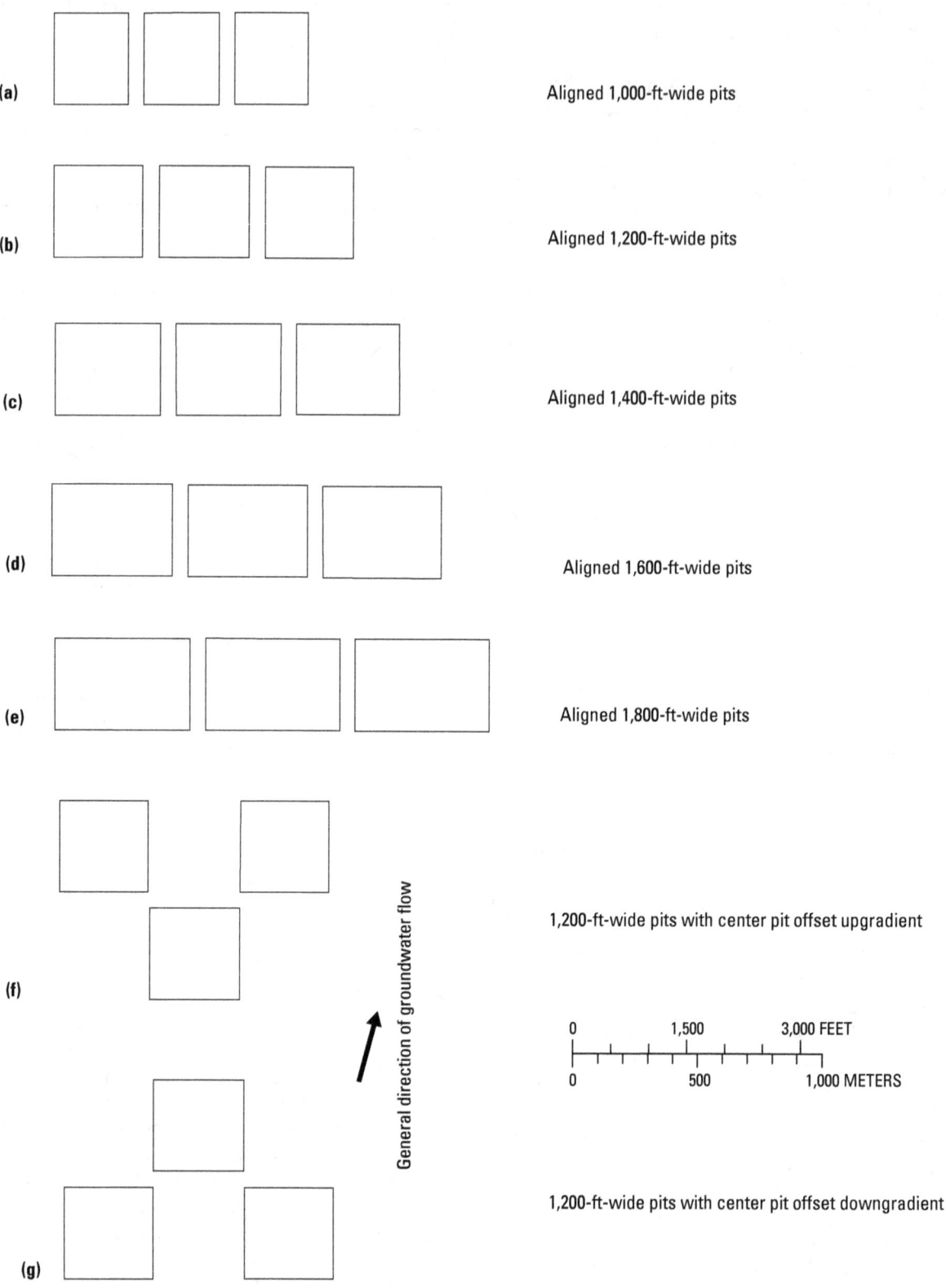

Figure 42.   Seven configurations used to simulate the effect of pit spacing and configuration on groundwater levels near reclaimed lined pits.

Simulated Effects of Three Aligned Pits

The magnitude and extent of groundwater-level decline and rise resulting from three 1,400-ft-wide pits (configuration c in figure 42) aligned approximately cross gradient to groundwater flow are shown in figures 43A–C to illustrate the general effect of pit spacing on groundwater levels. The maximum groundwater-level decline resulting from contiguous pits (no space between pits) is about 3.1 ft (fig. 43A) near the midpoint of the downgradient pit wall. The maximum groundwater-level rise resulting from contiguous pits is about 3.0 ft (fig. 43A), but the maximum occurs slightly west of the upgradient wall's midpoint because groundwater flow is not exactly perpendicular to pit alignment. The limits of 2-ft decline and rise occur about 1,000 ft downgradient and upgradient, respectively, of the contiguous pits (fig. 43A). The areal extent of groundwater-level decline decreases as the pits are separated, and the pattern of decline reflects the hydrologic effects of individual pits more so than when the pits are contiguous. The limit of 2-ft decline occurs about 500 ft downgradient from the center pit when pits are 200 ft apart (fig. 43B) and about 200 ft downgradient when the pits are 400 ft apart (fig. 43C). The limit of 2-ft groundwater-level rise resulting from groundwater mounding upgradient from pits exhibits similar reduction as the spacing between pits increases. Groundwater-level changes are less than 2 ft at nearly all locations when the pits are spaced 600 ft apart or more and are therefore not presented.

Pits of different sizes that are aligned approximately cross gradient to groundwater flow result in general patterns of groundwater decline and rise similar to those shown in figures 43A–C, but the magnitude and extent of groundwater-level change are different. The magnitude of groundwater-level decline and rise relative to pit spacing for five different pit widths is presented in figures 44A and 44B for locations 100 ft downgradient and 100 ft upgradient from the center pit. Fewer values are presented for larger pits because the distance between the South Platte River and the west model boundary limits the range of spacing available for larger pits. Groundwater-level decline and rise near the center pit represent maximum groundwater-level changes resulting from lined pits that are located in areas minimally affected by hydrologic boundaries. Groundwater-level decline and rise near the east pit generally are less than that indicated by figures 44A and 44B because of the hydrologic influence of the South Platte River. Groundwater-level decline and rise near the west pit generally are greater than that indicated by figures 44A and 44B because of the influence of the no-flow boundary on the west side of the simulated aquifer. Groundwater-level changes become greater as pit width increases because larger pits create larger obstructions to groundwater flow. The groundwater-level decline resulting from three contiguous 1,000-ft-wide pits is about 2.3 ft, whereas the decline resulting from three contiguous 1,800-ft-wide pits is about 3.9 ft. Similarly, the groundwater-level rise resulting from three contiguous 1,000-ft-wide pits is about 2.1 ft, whereas the rise resulting from three contiguous 1,800-ft-wide pits is about 3.8 ft.

The magnitude of groundwater-level decline and rise near pits decreases most as pit spacing is increased from 0 to 200 ft, and the magnitude of decline and rise decreases less as the distance between pits becomes greater. For average-size pits (1,200-ft wide), the magnitude of groundwater-level decline decreases by about 0.6 ft (from 2.7 to 2.1 ft) as the distance between pits is increased from 0 to 200 ft, but the magnitude of the decline decreases only by about 0.1 ft as pit spacing is increased from 800 to 1,000 ft. Because pit spacing has a progressively lesser affect on groundwater levels as the distance between pits increases, about 50 percent (0.6 ft) of the total reduction (1.2 ft) in the magnitude of the decline that occurs for a pit spacing of 1,000 ft is achieved by a pit spacing of only 200 ft, and about 75 percent (0.9 ft) of the total reduction in the magnitude of the decline is achieved by a pit spacing of 400 ft. Similarly, the magnitude of groundwater-level rise that occurs upgradient from 1,200-ft-wide pits decreases by about 0.5 ft (from 2.5 to 2.0 ft) as the distance between pits is increased from 0 to 200 ft, but it decreases only by about 0.1 ft as pit spacing is increased from 800 to 1,000 ft. About 42 percent (0.5 ft) of the total reduction (1.2 ft) in the magnitude of the rise that occurs for a pit spacing of 1,000 ft is achieved by a pit spacing of 200 ft, and about 67 percent (0.8 ft) of the total reduction in the magnitude of the rise is achieved by a pit spacing of 400 ft.

Simulated Effects of Three Offset Pits

Groundwater-level declines and rises resulting from average-size pits (1,200-ft wide) that are offset upgradient or downgradient (fig. 42, configurations f and g) from each other are simulated for five pit distances ranging from 0 to 800 ft (figs. 45A and 45B). Groundwater-level declines and rises represent conditions 100 ft downgradient and 100 ft upgradient from the center pit near the midpoint of the pit wall. Similar to pits aligned approximately cross gradient to groundwater flow, the magnitude of decline and rise resulting from offset pits decreases most as pit offset spacing increases from 0 to 200 ft, and the magnitude of decline and rise changes progressively less as the distance between pits increases. However, the magnitude of groundwater-level decline and rise decreases to a greater extent when pits are offset than when aligned pits are moved farther apart because the hydrologic effects of the offset pit are counteracted by the hydrologic effects of the other pits. In the configuration where the center pit is offset upgradient from other pits, the groundwater-level decline downgradient from the center pit is counteracted by the groundwater-level rise upgradient from other pits. Similarly, in the configuration where the center pit is offset downgradient from other pits, the groundwater-level rise upgradient from the center pit is counteracted by the groundwater-level decline downgradient from other pits. Offsetting the center pit 200 ft upgradient reduces the magnitude of groundwater-level decline by about 1.7 ft (from 2.7 to 1.0 ft), which is about 71 percent of the total reduction (2.4 ft) in the magnitude of the decline achieved by offsetting

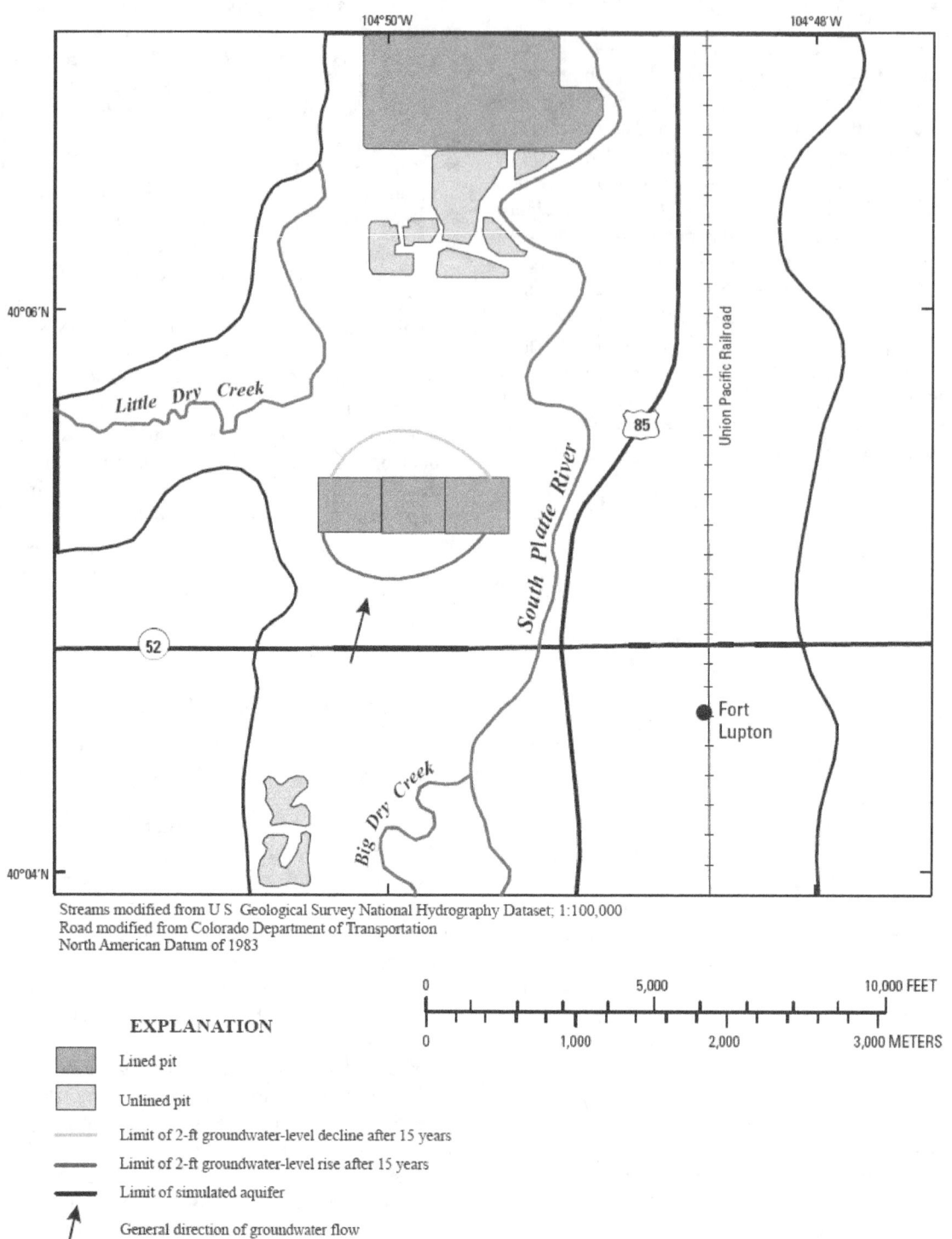

Streams modified from U S Geological Survey National Hydrography Dataset; 1:100,000
Road modified from Colorado Department of Transportation
North American Datum of 1983

EXPLANATION

Lined pit

Unlined pit

Limit of 2-ft groundwater-level decline after 15 years

Limit of 2-ft groundwater-level rise after 15 years

Limit of simulated aquifer

General direction of groundwater flow

Figure 43A. Simulated groundwater-level changes resulting from three 1,400-ft-wide lined pits with a spacing of 0 ft when pits are aligned approximately cross gradient to groundwater flow in the South Platte alluvial aquifer.

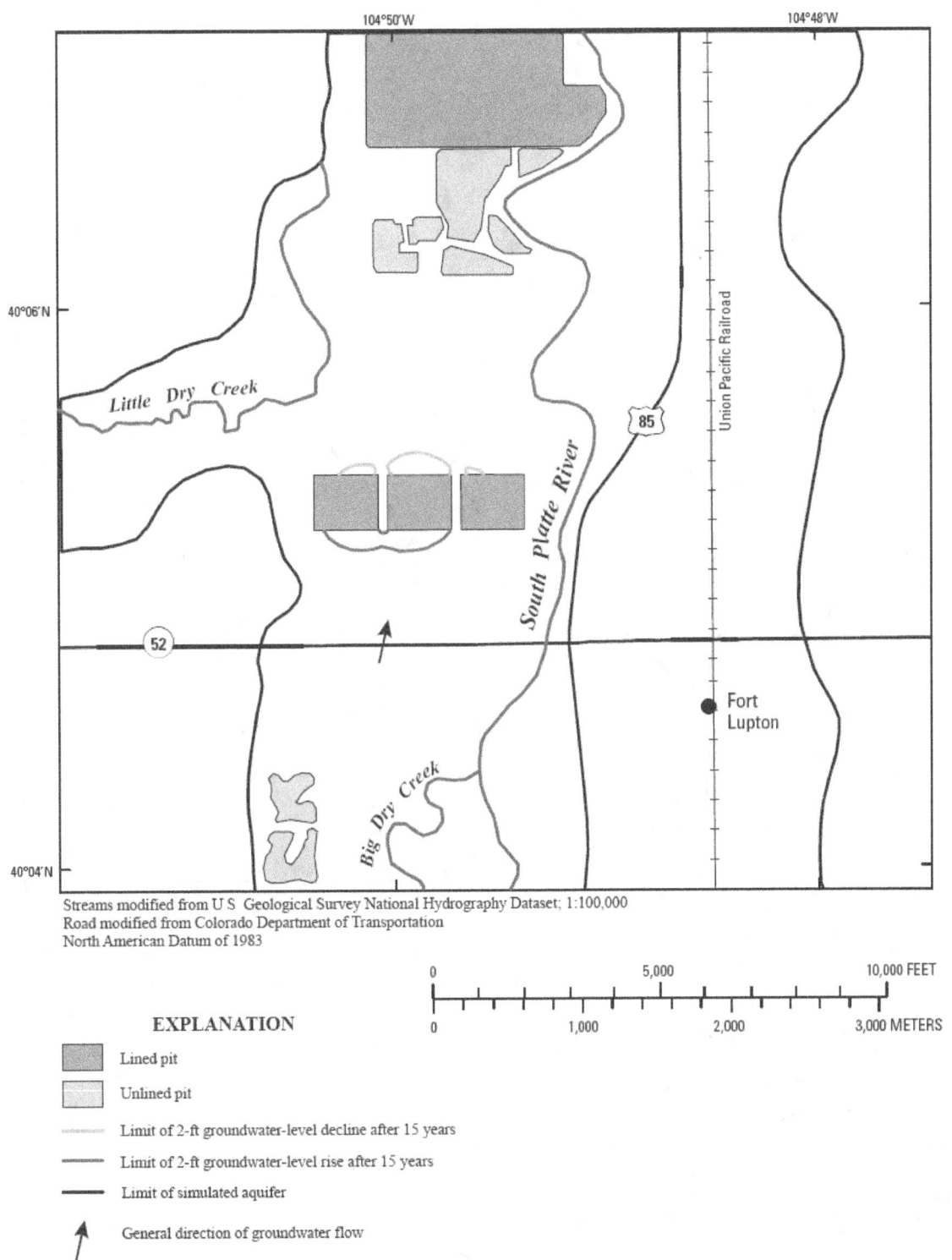

Streams modified from U S Geological Survey National Hydrography Dataset; 1:100,000
Road modified from Colorado Department of Transportation
North American Datum of 1983

EXPLANATION

- Lined pit
- Unlined pit
- Limit of 2-ft groundwater-level decline after 15 years
- Limit of 2-ft groundwater-level rise after 15 years
- Limit of simulated aquifer
- General direction of groundwater flow

Figure 43B. Simulated groundwater-level changes resulting from three 1,400-ft-wide lined pits with a spacing of 200 ft when pits are aligned approximately cross gradient to groundwater flow in the South Platte alluvial aquifer.

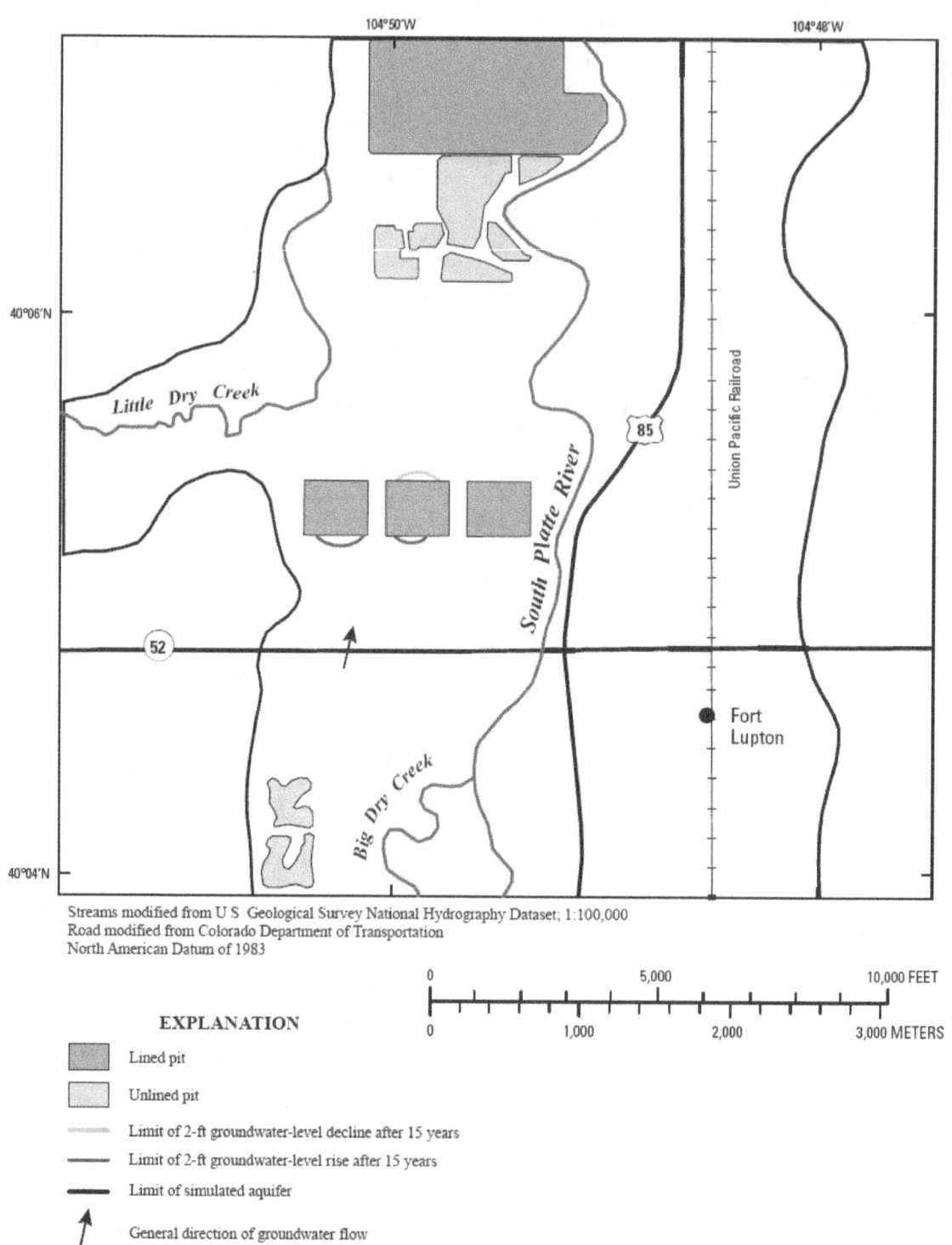

Streams modified from U S Geological Survey National Hydrography Dataset; 1:100,000
Road modified from Colorado Department of Transportation
North American Datum of 1983

EXPLANATION

◼ Lined pit

◻ Unlined pit

⋯ Limit of 2-ft groundwater-level decline after 15 years

— Limit of 2-ft groundwater-level rise after 15 years

▬ Limit of simulated aquifer

↑ General direction of groundwater flow

Figure 43C.   Simulated groundwater-level changes resulting from three 1,400-ft-wide lined pits with a spacing of 400 ft when pits are aligned approximately cross gradient to groundwater flow in the South Platte alluvial aquifer.

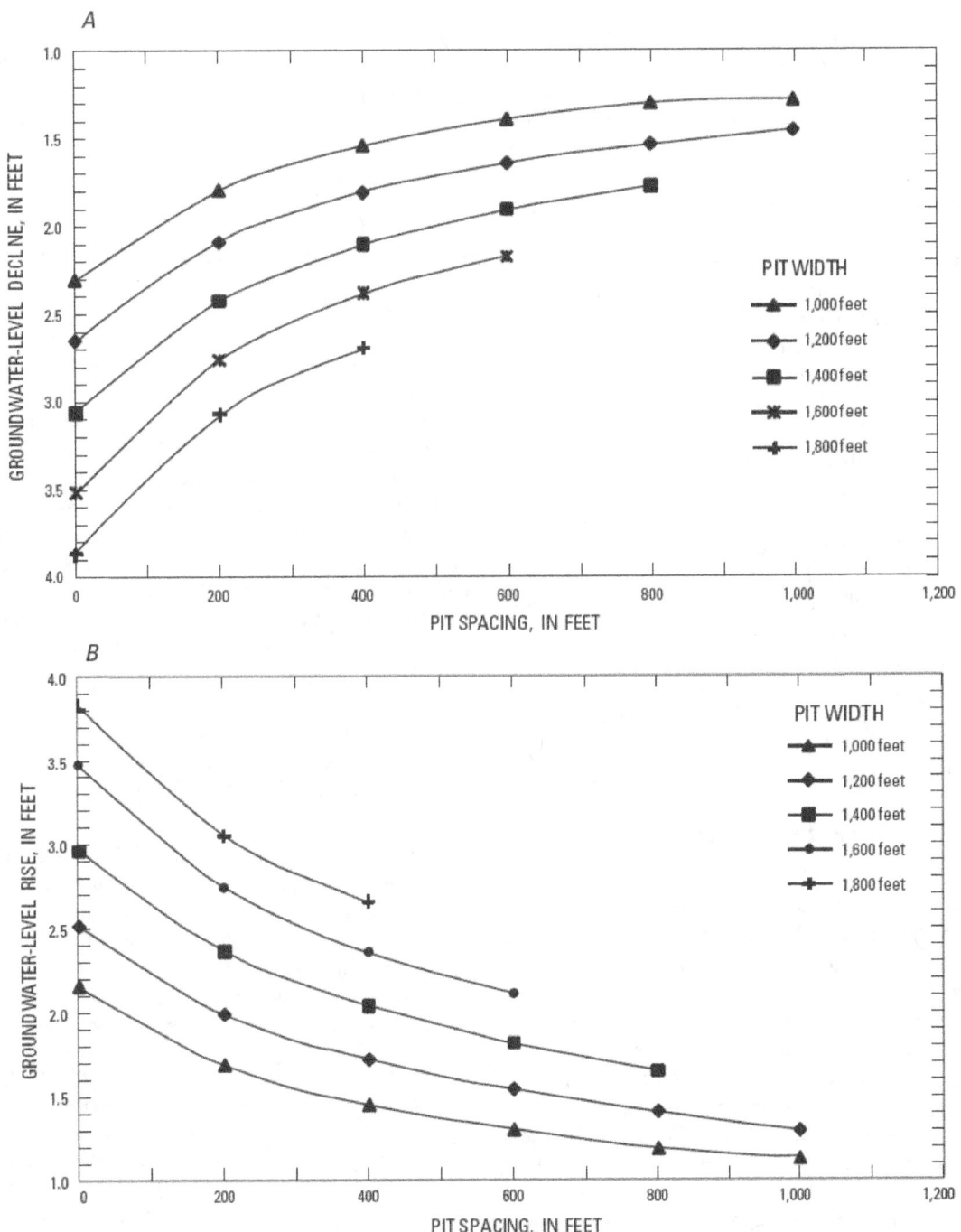

Figure 44. *A.* Relation of groundwater-level decline to pit spacing for five different pit sizes aligned approximately cross gradient to groundwater flow in the South Platte alluvial aquifer at a location 100 feet downgradient 15 years after pit reclamation. *B.* Relation of groundwater-level rise to pit spacing for five different pit sizes aligned approximately cross gradient to groundwater flow in the South Platte alluvial aquifer at a location 100 feet upgradient 15 years after pit reclamation.

the pit 800 ft upgradient. Increasing the offset distance of the upgradient pit from 600 to 800 ft reduces the magnitude of decline by less than 0.1 ft. Offsetting the center pit 200 ft downgradient reduces the magnitude of the decline by about 1.0 ft, which is about 91 percent of the total reduction (1.1 ft) in the magnitude of the decline achieved by an offset distance of 800 ft. Increasing pit offset distance more than 200 ft downgradient has little effect on reducing the magnitude of the decline (fig. 45A) because the downgradient end of the pit is beyond substantial hydrologic influence of the other pits.

The magnitude of groundwater-level rise upgradient from the center pit responds to offset distance in a manner similar to that for groundwater-level declines. The magnitude of groundwater-level rise decreases most as the center pit is offset from 0 to 200 ft and decreases less as pit offset distance increases beyond 200 ft. Offsetting the center pit 200 ft upgradient reduces the magnitude of groundwater-level rise by 1.3 ft (from about 2.5 to 1.2 ft), which is about 93 percent of the total reduction (1.4 ft) in the magnitude of the rise achieved by offsetting the pit 800 ft upgradient. Increasing pit offset farther than 200 ft upgradient has relatively little effect on reducing the magnitude of groundwater-level rise because the upgradient end of the pit is beyond substantial hydrologic influence of the other pits. Offsetting the center pit 200 ft downgradient reduces the magnitude of groundwater-level rise by 1.2 ft (from about 2.5 to 1.3 ft), which is about 71 percent of the total reduction (about 1.7 ft) in the rise achieved by an offset distance of 800 ft.

Summary of Simulated Pit Spacing and Configuration Effects

Comparison of simulations related to pit spacing and configuration indicates groundwater-level declines downgradient from lined pits and groundwater-level rises upgradient from lined pits increase as pit size increases and decrease as pit spacing increases. The magnitude of groundwater-level decline and rise decreases most as the spacing between pits is increased from 0 to 200 feet, and the magnitude of decline and rise decreases by successively lesser amounts as the distance between pits is increased beyond 200 feet. For 1,200-ft-wide pits aligned approximately cross gradient to groundwater flow, about 75 percent of the total reduction in the magnitude of groundwater-level decline obtained by a pit spacing of 1,000 ft was achieved by a spacing of 400 ft. About 67 percent of the total reduction in the magnitude of groundwater-level rise obtained by a pit spacing of 1,000 ft was achieved by a pit spacing of 400 ft. Offsetting the center pit upgradient or downgradient from other pits decreases the magnitude of groundwater-level decline and rise more so than increasing the distance between aligned pits. For 1,200-ft-wide pits, offsetting the center pit 200 ft upgradient from adjacent pits achieves about 71 percent of the total reduction in the magnitude of the decline and about 93 percent of the total reduction in magnitude of the rise that was obtained by offsetting the pit 800 ft upgradient. Offsetting the center pit 200 ft downgradient from

adjacent pits achieves about 91 percent of the total reduction in the magnitude of the decline and about 71 percent of the total reduction in magnitude of the rise that was obtained by offsetting the pit 800 ft downgradient. Offset pits with a spacing of 200–400 ft provided a configuration that reduced the hydrologic effects of lined pits by the greatest amount while minimizing the distance between pits.

Model Limitations and Transferability of Results

The numerical groundwater flow model presented by this study is a representation of a real hydrologic system. The accuracy of model simulations depends on the accuracy of parameter values input to the model and the extent to which important aspects of the hydrologic system are appropriately represented. Because parameters were estimated based on available data, measurement errors associated with the data are incorporated in the model. Because parameters representing recharge beneath irrigated land (RCH_irr), inflow along the east side of the model (Q_ReturnE), and hydraulic conductivity of zone 2 (LPF_Par2) have the highest composite scaled sensitivities in the model, errors associated with these parameters likely have the largest influence on simulation results. Errors associated with these parameters are estimated as small to moderate based on available data. The following limitations also need to be considered when interpreting simulation results provided by the model:

1. Model input parameters (such as hydraulic conductivity and recharge) and boundaries (such as the altitude of the top and base of the aquifer) are simulated as uniform within each model cell. Variability in parameters and boundaries smaller than the model cell size are not represented. Simulations that incorporate smaller-scale variability could produce results different than those shown.

2. Hydraulic head is computed at the center of each model cell as the average of head conditions within the cell. Analysis of the hydrologic effects of land-use change and aggregate mining at a scale finer than the model cell size (500 ft by 500 ft and 200 ft by 200 ft, respectively) used in this study would require simulations with a finer grid spacing.

3. The model is calibrated to steady-state average seasonal water-table and groundwater-flow conditions by using average seasonal parameter values. Although the model simulates the dynamic seasonal nature of the aquifer, the South Platte alluvial aquifer is a system with a continuous response to hydrologic stresses. A fully transient calibration to hydrologic conditions of the aquifer could produce results somewhat different than those shown.

4. The predicted effects of land-use change and aggregate mining assume hydrologic conditions such as precipita-

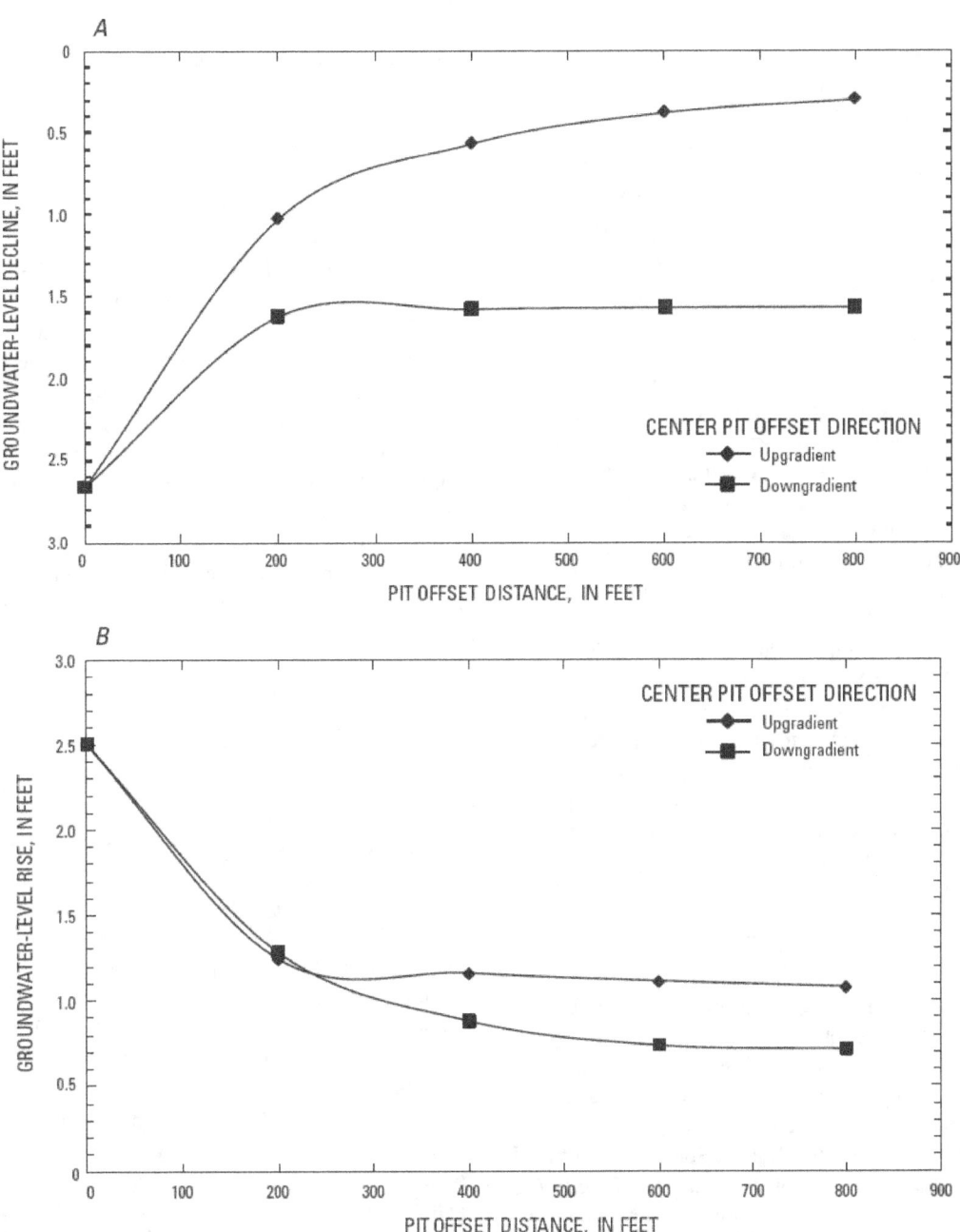

Figure 45. *A.* Relation of groundwater-level decline to pit offset distance for three 1,200-ft-wide lined pits in the South Platte alluvial aquifer at a location 100 feet downgradient 15 years after pit reclamation. *B.* Relation of groundwater-level rise to pit offset distance for three 1,200-ft-wide lined pits in the South Platte alluvial aquifer at a location 100 ft upgradient 15 years after pit reclamation.

tion, streamflow, and water use are the same during future simulation periods as they were during 2000. Substantial changes to these hydrologic conditions in the study area could alter the effects of land-use change and aggregate mining.

5. Simulations of the hydrologic effects of land-use change and aggregate mining indicate areas where groundwater-level changes might affect groundwater-supported wetlands. However, determination of the specific effects of groundwater-level changes on wetlands in the study area would require site-specific investigation beyond the scope of this report.

Simulation results presented by this study indicate the potential hydrologic effects of land-use change and aggregate mining on groundwater flow in the South Platte River valley between Brighton and Fort Lupton and are specific to the conditions described for each simulation. However, some of the simulation results might be transferable to other areas having hydrologic conditions similar to those of the study area. Simulation results also provide general information about the hydrologic effects of land-use change and aggregate mining that could be applicable to other hydrologic systems. The extent to which simulation results are transferable to other areas depends on the extent to which conditions in other areas are similar to those simulated. Knowledge of parameter sensitivity can be used to help determine transferability of results. Similarity between aquifers for parameters with high sensitivity, such as irrigation recharge, likely is more important than similarity for parameters with low sensitivity.

Summary and Conclusions

To improve understanding of land-use change and the potential effects of land-use change and aggregate mining on groundwater flow, the U.S. Geological Survey, in cooperation with the city of Fort Lupton and the city of Brighton, analyzed socioeconomic and land-use trends and constructed a numerical groundwater flow model of the South Platte alluvial aquifer in the Brighton–Fort Lupton area. As part of the study, wetlands in the Brighton–Fort Lupton area were mapped using false-color aerial photography and field investigations to indicate locations where groundwater-level changes resulting from land-use change or aggregate mining might affect wetlands.

Comparison of land use in 1957, 1977, and 2000 indicated little change in the general distribution of irrigated agricultural land and non-irrigated land over time, but both land uses decreased slightly between 1957 and 2000. Irrigated land use decreased 6 to 7 percent between 1957 and 1977 and between 1977 and 2000, whereas non-irrigated land use decreased about 4 percent during each time period. By contrast, urban land use increased about 165 percent between 1957 and 1977 and about 56 percent between 1977 and 2000. In 2000, urban land represented about 13 percent of the total Brighton–Fort Lupton area, whereas irrigated agricultural land

represented about 38 percent and non-irrigated land represented about 50 percent. Urban growth of Brighton and Fort Lupton between 1957 and 2000 primarily has been east of the South Platte River and along major transportation corridors. As of late 1999, five aggregate mining operations were evident in the Brighton–Fort Lupton area.

The urban-growth modeling program SLEUTH (Slope, Land cover, Exclusion, Urbanization, Transportation, and Hillshade) was used to predict future urban extent in the study area in 2020 and 2040 based on historical urban extent and growth in 1937, 1957, 1977, and 2000. SLEUTH simulations predicted urban growth will continue to occur predominantly to the east of Brighton and Fort Lupton and along major transportation routes. However, substantial growth also was predicted to the south and west of Brighton as areas of low urban density are filled in. The potential extent of aggregate mining in 2020 was estimated on the basis of existing mining and reclamation plans. The potential extent of aggregate mining in 2040 was estimated on the basis of the size, spacing, and density of pit development in 2020 and represents conditions when aggregate mining in the Brighton–Fort Lupton area is approximately fully developed.

Wetlands in the study area were mapped by the U.S. Geological Survey and U.S. Bureau of Reclamation during July–August, 2004. False-color infrared aerial photographs were obtained at 18 locations in the central and western parts of the study area at a scale of 1:24,000. Preliminary photo interpretation was performed to identify probable wetland areas, and those areas were subsequently verified by field inspection.

The numerical groundwater flow model used to simulate the hydrologic effects of land-use change and aggregate mining was calibrated to steady-state groundwater-level and flow conditions of the South Platte alluvial aquifer during the irrigation and non-irrigation seasons of 1957, 1977, and 2000 by using the inverse modeling capabilities of MODFLOW-2000. The calibrated model was used to simulate (1) steady-state hydrologic effects of predicted land-use conditions in 2020 and 2040, (2) transient cumulative hydrologic effects of the potential extent of reclaimed aggregate pits in 2020 and 2040, (3) transient hydrologic effects of actively dewatered aggregate pits, and (4) the effects of different hypothetical pit spacings and configurations on groundwater levels.

Calibration statistics indicated residuals likely are independent, random, and normal, and the calibrated model regression likely is valid. However, the model is highly non-linear, and linear confidence intervals on predictions would not accurately represent prediction uncertainty. Composite scaled sensitivities were calculated for parameters used in the calibrated model to evaluate the influence of each parameter on the calibrated model. Composite scaled sensitivity was largest for recharge beneath irrigated areas and lowest for recharge beneath urban areas. All components of the simulated groundwater budgets for the calibrated model represent reasonable values compared to available data.

Steady-state simulations of the hydrologic effects of land-use conditions in 2020 (simulation 1) and 2040 (simulation 2) indicated groundwater-level declines resulting from conversion of irrigated and non-irrigated land to urban areas were less than 2 ft relative to the irrigation-season water table in 2000. Groundwater-level declines were largest where irrigated agricultural land is converted to urban area because of the large difference (about 12 in. during the irrigation season) in recharge between the two land uses. Groundwater levels changed little where non-irrigated land was converted to urban area because estimated recharge beneath non-irrigated land (about 0.4 in.) was only slightly greater than that assumed for urban areas (0 in.). Groundwater-level declines resulting from land-use conditions in 2020 and 2040 were predicted to not substantially affect wetlands mapped by this study or areas of riparian herbaceous vegetation mapped by the Colorado Division of Wildlife in the study area because the declines were small and mapped wetlands and areas of riparian herbaceous vegetation generally are located where little or no simulated decline occurred. The larger urban extent in simulations of land-use change in 2020 and 2040 decreased recharge to the simulated aquifer by 17.9–31.6 percent, and the resulting lower water table increased groundwater inflow from the upgradient ends of South Platte River valley and its tributaries by 2.7–4.2 percent and leakage from the South Platte River and Big Dry Creek by 3.9–7.1 percent. Similarly, discharge was decreased to the South Platte River and Big Dry Creek (4.7–8.3 percent), Little Dry Creek and Third Creek (3.9–8.7 percent), and the downgradient end of the South Platte valley (1.6–3.3 percent).

Transient simulations of the cumulative hydrologic effects of reclaimed pits in 2020 (simulation 3), reclaimed lined pits in 2040 (simulation 4), and reclaimed unlined pits in 2040 (simulation 5) indicated lined pits caused groundwater levels to rise upgradient from pits and decline downgradient from pits, whereas unlined pits had an opposite effect on groundwater levels. The hydrologic effects of pits backfilled with fine-grained sediments were similar to but less than those of lined pits because the pits created less of a barrier to groundwater flow than lined pits. The hydrologic effects of lined, unlined, and fines-backfilled pits interacted to increase the magnitude of groundwater-level changes at some locations and decrease it at others, depending on the relative position of the pits. The maximum simulated groundwater-level decline resulting from the extent of reclaimed pits in 2020 was about 9 ft in 2035, 15 years after reclamation. The maximum simulated groundwater-level rise upgradient from lined pits was about 6 ft in 2035, 15 years after reclamation. Groundwater levels changed most during the first year after pits were reclaimed, and groundwater levels ceased to change substantially in most areas of the simulated aquifer within about 10 years. The addition of lined pits in 2040 resulted in a general increase in the magnitude and extent of groundwater-level rise relative to simulated conditions for 2020 because groundwater flow was obstructed over a larger part of the simulated aquifer. The maximum simulated groundwater-level decline and rise

resulting from the addition of reclaimed lined pits in 2040 was about 9 ft in 2055, 15 years after reclamation. The addition of unlined pits in 2040 resulted in a general increase in the magnitude and extent of groundwater-level decline relative to simulated conditions for 2020 because groundwater levels declined to lake levels in unlined pits over a larger area of the simulated aquifer. The maximum groundwater-level decline resulting from the addition of reclaimed unlined pits in 2040 was about 11 ft in 2055, 15 years after reclamation. Maximum groundwater-level rise resulting from the addition of reclaimed unlined pits in 2040 was about 5 ft after 15 years.

Wetlands mapped by this study generally are located where simulated groundwater-level changes resulting from reclaimed pits in 2020 were less than 2 ft, but some areas of riparian herbaceous vegetation mapped by the Colorado Division of Wildlife are located where simulated groundwater-level changes were more than 2 ft. Mapped wetlands and areas of riparian herbaceous vegetation are both located where simulated groundwater-level changes resulting from reclaimed pits in 2040 were more than 2 ft. Wetlands and riparian herbaceous vegetation located where groundwater-level changes are more than 2 ft might be affected by the changes. Some areas where groundwater levels were simulated to rise more than 2 ft at locations where the depth to water was less than 5 ft could create conditions favorable to the formation of new wetlands.

The groundwater budgets for simulations of reclaimed pits in 2020 and 2040 were greater than the budget for the calibrated model or simulations of the effects of land-use change because of additional groundwater inflow and outflow at unlined pits simulated as lakes in 2020 and 2040. The conversion of land area to pits (lined and unlined) in 2020 decreased distributed recharge at the land surface by 16.8 percent relative to the 2000 irrigation season because the simulated pits do not contribute distributed recharge. Groundwater-level declines resulting from the extent of reclaimed pits in 2020 increased leakage from the South Platte River and Big Dry Creek by 19.0 percent, and lined pits obstructed groundwater outflow at the downgradient end of the South Platte River valley, causing outflow to decrease by 14.0 percent. The general effect of adding lined pits in 2040 was to decrease leakage from unlined pits (22.9 percent), distributed recharge at the land surface (14.6 percent), groundwater discharge to unlined pits (21.3 percent), and groundwater discharge to the South Platte River and Big Dry Creek (7.0 percent) because the additional lined pits obstruct groundwater flow in the simulated aquifer. The general effect of adding unlined pits in 2040 was to increase leakage from unlined pits (204 percent), leakage from the South Platte River and Big Dry Creek (15.3 percent), discharge to unlined pits (207 percent), and discharge to the South Platte River and Big Dry Creek (3.9 percent) and to decrease groundwater entering storage (25.4 percent).

Transient simulations of the hydrologic effects of actively dewatered pits (simulations 6–9) indicated that the magnitude and extent of drawdown increased as the number of dewatered pits increased because the drawdown effects of each pit were additive. Increasing the distance between two actively dewatered pits from 400 ft to 2,000 ft did not reduce draw-down extent, because the drawdown resulting from each pit combined to create a single larger drawdown extent. Maximum drawdown in all simulations of actively dewatered pits was 37 ft. Drawdown decreased to 20 ft within 100–600 ft of actively dewatered pits and decreased more gradually farther from the pits. Maximum drawdown extent defined by the limit of 2-ft drawdown was about 12,400 ft for a single dewatered pit, 12,800 ft for two pits spaced 400 ft apart, 12,900 ft for two pits spaced 2,000 ft apart, and 13,100 ft for three pits spaced 400 ft apart. Drawdown was affected by the presence of the South Platte River, the no-flow west model boundary, and nearby reclaimed pits. Simulated flow from the South Platte River and unlined reclaimed pits decreased drawdown resulting from dewatered pits, whereas the no-flow west model boundary increased drawdown. Most drawdown occurred during the first year, and drawdown extent after 1 year was almost as large as after 15 years. Because dewatering typically occurs for multiple years and most drawdown occurred during the first year, groundwater-supported wetlands overlying areas of drawdown resulting from dewatered pits might be affected by drawdown resulting from the pits. The general effect of actively dewatered pits was to increase groundwater inflow from the upgradient ends of the South Platte River valley and its tributaries, increase leakage from the South Platte River and Big Dry Creek, and decrease most other components of the water budget.

Transient simulations of the hydrologic effects of different hypothetical pit spacings and configurations indicated that groundwater-level declines and rises resulting from reclaimed lined pits increased with pit size and decreased as the distance between pits increased. Groundwater-level decline and rise resulting from three contiguous 1,000-ft-wide pits aligned approximately cross gradient to groundwater flow were about 2 ft near the center pit, whereas groundwater-level decline and rise resulting from three contiguous 1,800-ft-wide pits were about 4 ft. The magnitude of groundwater-level change near pits decreased most as pit spacing was increased from 0 to 200 ft, and the magnitude decreased less as the distance between pits became larger. For 1,200-ft-wide pits aligned approximately cross gradient to groundwater flow, about 50 percent of the total reduction in the magnitude of groundwater-level decline that was obtained by a pit spacing of 1,000 ft was achieved by a pit spacing of only 200 ft, and about 75 percent of the total reduction in the magnitude of the decline was achieved by a pit spacing of 400 ft. About 42 percent of the total reduction in the magnitude of groundwater-level rise that was obtained by a pit spacing of 1,000 ft was achieved by a pit spacing of 200 ft, and about 67 percent of the total reduction in the magnitude of the rise was achieved by a pit spacing of 400 ft.

Offsetting the center pit upgradient or downgradient of other pits decreased groundwater-level declines and rises to a greater extent than increasing the distance between aligned pits. For 1,200-ft-wide pits, offsetting the center pit 200 ft upgradient from adjacent pits achieved about 71 percent of the total reduction in the magnitude of groundwater-level decline and about 93 percent of the total reduction in the magnitude of groundwater-level rise that was obtained by offsetting the pit 800 ft upgradient. Offsetting the center pit 200 ft downgradient from adjacent pits achieved about 91 percent of the total reduction in the magnitude of groundwater-level decline and about 71 percent of the total reduction in the magnitude of groundwater-level rise that was obtained by offsetting the pit 800 ft downgradient. Offset pits with a spacing of 200–400 ft provided a configuration that reduced the hydrologic effects of lined pits by the greatest amount while minimizing the distance between pits.

Acknowledgments

Many individuals contributed to the completion of this study. Thanks are extended to Jim Sartoris of USGS and David Salas of the U.S. Bureau of Reclamation for their efforts mapping and verifying wetlands for the study. Thanks also are extended to USGS geographers Susan Guthrie, for compiling numerous Geographic Information System data sets that provided information for the numerical groundwater flow model, and Mark Feller, for running the SLEUTH urban-growth model to predict future urban extent in the study area. Special thanks are extended to Lafarge Mining Company for providing a tour of an aggregate mine site where operations could be observed directly. Carl Mount of the Colorado Division of Mining, Reclamation, and Safety provided useful information about mining regulations and the pit permitting process, as well as aggregate-mine records for the study area. Carl Eiberger of Black Bear Water Resources provided ground-water-level data and information concerning the location of lined water-storage facilities in the study area. Ned Banta of the USGS provided technical assistance that was helpful to the completion of the study. The contributions of each of these individuals are gratefully acknowledged.

References Cited

Anderson, M.P., and Woessner, W.W., 1992, Applied ground-water modeling—Simulation of flow and advective transport: San Diego, Academic Press, Inc., 381 p.

Argus Interware, 1997, Argus ONE user's guide, Argus Open Numerical Environments—A GIS modeling system, version 4.0: Jerico, N.Y., Argus Holdings, Limited, 320 p.

Arnold, L.R., Langer, W.H., and Paschke, S.S., 2003, Analytical and numerical simulation of the steady-state hydrologic effects of mining aggregate in hypothetical sand-and-gravel and fractured crystalline-rock aquifers: U.S. Geological Survey Water-Resources Investigations Report 02–4267, 56 p.

Arnold, T.L., and Friedel, M.J., 2000, Effects of land use on recharge potential of surficial and shallow bedrock aquifers in the upper Illinois River basin: U.S. Geological Survey Water-Resources Investigations Report 00–4027, 18 p.

Barfield, B.J., Warner, R.C., and Haan, C.T., 1981, Applied hydrology and sedimentology for disturbed areas: Stillwater, Okla., Oklahoma Technical Press, 603 p.

Bauer, H.H., and Vaccaro, J.J., 1990, Estimates of ground-water recharge to the Columbia Plateau regional aquifer system, Washington, Oregon, and Idaho, for predevelopment and current land-use conditions: U.S. Geological Survey Water-Resources Investigations Report 88–4108, 31 p.

Bolen, W.P., 2005, Construction sand and gravel: U.S. Geological Survey 2005 Minerals Yearbook, p. 64.1–64.21.

Char, S.J., and Arnold, L.R., 2002, Digital geospatial datasets in support of hydrologic investigations of the Colorado Front Range Infrastructure Resources Project: U.S. Geological Survey Open-File Report 02–338, accessed April 27, 2005, at *http://water.usgs.gov/lookup/getgislist.*

City of Brighton, 2003, Brighton comprehensive plan: Brighton Department of Community Development maps showing land-use plans and zoning for the city of Bighton, accessed September 22, 2006, at *http://www.brightonco.gov.*

City of Fort Lupton, 2006, City of Fort Lupton zoning map: Fort Lupton Department of Planning and Building map showing land-use zoning for the city of Fort Lupton, accessed September 22, 2006, at *http://www.fortlupton.org.*

Colorado Decision Support Systems, 2004, South Platte DSS Districts 1, 2, 3, and 64, 2001 irrigated parcels: Colorado Decision Support Systems spatial dataset, accessed June 19, 2006, at *http://cdss.state.co.us/DNN/GIS/tabid/67/Default. aspx.*

Colorado Division of Water Resources, 2006a, Colorado's decision support systems: Colorado Division of Water Resources monthly stream-flow data, accessed January 4, 2006, at *http://cdss.state.co.us/DNN/ViewData/ StationsStreamflow/tabid/74/Default.aspx.*

Colorado Division of Water Resources, 2006b, Colorado's Decision Support Systems: Colorado Division of Water Resources monthly diversion data, accessed January 4, 2006, at *http://cdss.state.co.us/DNN/Structures/tabid/75/ Default.aspx.*

Colorado Division of Wildlife, 2007a, Riparian vegetation data—block 39104-E1: Colorado Division of Wildlife spatial dataset, accessed June 2, 2005, at *http://ndis.nrel. colostate.edu/ftp/riparian/index.html.*

Colorado Division of Wildlife, 2007b, Riparian vegetation data—block 40104-A1: Colorado Division of Wildlife spatial dataset accessed, June 2, 2005, at *http://ndis.nrel. colostate.edu/ftp/riparian/index.html.*

Colorado State Demography Office, 2007, Historical census population data for the cities of Brighton and Fort Lupton: Colorado State Demography Office data, accessed July 18, 2007, at *http://www.dola.state.co.us/demog_webapps/popu-lation_census.*

Colton, R.B., 1978, Geologic map of the Boulder–Fort Collins–Greeley area, Colorado: U.S. Geological Survey Miscellaneous Investigations Map I–855–G, scale 1:100,000.

Cooley, R.L., and Naff, R.L., 1990, Regression modeling of ground-water flow: U.S. Geological Survey Techniques of Water-Resources Investigations, book 3, chap. B4, 232 p.

Cowardin, L.M., Carter, V., Golet, F.C., and LaRoe, E.T., 1979, Classification of wetlands and deepwater habitats of the United States: U.S. Fish and Wildlife Service FWS/ OBS–79/31, 103 p.

Cronk, J.K., and Fennessy, M.S., 2001, Wetland plants—Biol-ogy and ecology: Boca Raton, Fla., CRC Press, 462 p.

Crosby, E.J., 1978, Landforms in the Boulder–Fort Collins–Greeley area, Front Range Urban Corridor, Colorado: U.S. Geological Survey Miscellaneous Investigations Series Map I–855–H, scale 1:100,000.

Douglas County, 2002, About Douglas County: Douglas County facts and statistics, accessed October 31, 2002, at *http://www.douglas.co.us/DC/Facts.htm.*

Draper, N.R., and Smith, H., 1981, Applied regression analysis (2d ed.): New York, Wiley, 709 p.

Energy Information Administration, 2006, US crude oil, natural gas, and natural gas liquid reserves, 2006 annual report: Energy Information Administration, 162 p.

Fetter, C.W., 1994, Applied hydrogeology (3d ed.): New York, Prentice-Hall, 691 p.

Gaggiani, N.G., 1995, Ground-water flow and effects of agricultural applications of sewage sludge and other fertilizers on the chemical quality of sediments in the unsaturated zone and ground water near Platteville, Colorado, 1985–89: U.S. Geological Survey Water-Resources Investigations Report 94–4037, 41 p.

Haitjema, H., 2006, The role of hand-calculations in ground-water flow modeling: Groundwater, v. 44, no. 6, p. 786–791.

Hammer, D.A., ed., 1991, Constructed wetlands for waste-water treatment—Municipal, industrial, and agricultural: Chelsea, Mich., Lewis Publishers, 831 p.

Harbaugh, A.W., Banta, E.R., Hill, M.C., and McDonald, M.G., 2000, MODFLOW–2000, the U.S. Geological Survey modular ground-water model—User guide to modular-ization concepts and the ground-water flow process: U.S. Geological Survey Open-File Report 00–92, 121 p.

Harbor, J.M., 1994, A practical method for estimating the impact of land-use change on surface runoff, groundwater recharge and wetland hydrology: Journal of the American Planning Association, v. 60, no. 1, p. 95–108.

Healy, R.W., and Cook, P.G., 2002, Using groundwater levels to estimate recharge: Hydrogeology Journal, v. 10, no. 1, p. 91–109.

Helsel, D.R., and Hirsch, R.M., 1992, Statistical methods in water resources: Amsterdam, Elsevier, 522 p.

Hill, M.C., 1994, Five computer programs for testing weighted residuals and calculating linear confidence and prediction intervals on results from the ground-water parameter esti-mation computer program MODFLOWP: U.S. Geological Survey Open-File Report 93–481, 81 p.

Hill, M.C., 1998, Methods and guidelines for effective model calibration: U.S. Geological Survey Water-Resources Investigations Report 98–4005, 90 p.

Hill, M.C., Banta, E.R, Harbaugh, A.W., and Anderman, E.R., 2000, MODFLOW–2000, the U.S. Geological Survey modular ground-water model—User guide to the observa-tion, sensitivity, and parameter-estimation processes and three post-processing programs: U.S. Geological Survey Open-File Report 00–184, 209 p.

Hillier, D.E., Schneider, P.A., Jr., and Hutchinson, E.C., 1979, Hydrologic data for water-table aquifers in the greater Denver area, Front Range Urban Corridor, Colorado: U.S. Geological Survey Open-File Report 79–214, 68 p.

Hurr, R.T., Schneider, P.A., Jr., and Minges, D.R., 1975, Hydrology of the South Platte River valley, northeastern Colorado: Colorado Water Conservation Board, Colorado Water Resources Circular 28, 24 p.

Johnson, A.I., 1967, Specific yield—Compilation of specific yields for various materials: U.S. Geological Survey Water-Supply Paper 1662–D, 74 p.

Kendall, W.D., 2002, A brief economic history of Colorado: Denver, Colo., Center for Business and Economic Forecasting, Inc., 24 p.

Knepper, D.H., Jr., ed., 2002, Planning for the conservation and development of infrastructure resources in urban areas—Colorado Front Range Urban Corridor: U.S. Geological Survey Circular 1219, 27 p.

Langer, W.H., Drew, L.J., and Sachs, J.S., 2004, Aggregate and the environment: American Geological Institute Environmental Awarness Series, no. 8, 64 p.

Leake, S.A., and Lilly, M.R., 1997, Documentation of a computer program (FHB1) for assignment of transient specified-flow and specified-head boundaries in applications of the modular finite-difference ground-water flow model (MODFLOW): U.S. Geological Survey Open-File Report 97–571, 56 p.

Leopold, L.B., 1968, Hydrology for urban land use planning: A guidebook on the hydrologic effects of urban land use: U.S. Geological Survey Circular 554, 18 p.

Lerner, D.N., 2002, Identifying and quantifying urban recharge: a review: Hydrogeology Journal, v. 10, no. 1, p. 143–152.

Lindsey, D.A., Langer, W.H., Cummings, L.S., and Shary, J.F., 1998, Gravel deposits of the South Platte River valley north of Denver, Colorado, Part A—Stratigraphy and sedimen-tary structures: U.S. Geological Survey Open-File Report 98–148–A, 18 p.

Lindsey, D.A., Langer, W.H., and Knepper, Jr., D.H., 2005, Stratigraphy, lithology, and sedimentary features of Quaternary alluvial deposits of the South Platte River and some of its tributaries east of the Front Range, Colorado: U.S. Geological Survey Professional Paper 1705, 70 p.

Louisiana Coastal Wetlands Conservation and Restoration Task Force, 2007, Wetlands functions and values: Louisiana Coastal Wetlands Conservation and Restoration Task Force, accessed February 1, 2007, at *http://www.lacoast.gov/education/functions.htm.*

McConaghy, J.A., Chase, G.H., Boettcher, A.J., and Major, T.J., 1964, Hydrogeologic data of the Denver Basin, Colo-rado: U.S. Geological Survey, Colorado Water Conservation Board Basic-Data Report 15, 224 p.

McDonald, M.G., and Harbaugh, A.W., 1988, A modular three-dimensional finite-difference groundwater flow model: U.S. Geological Survey Techniques of Water-Resources Investigations, book 6, chap. A1, 586 p.

McMahon, P.B., Lull, K.J., Dennehy, K.F., and Collins, J.A., 1995, Quantity and quality of ground-water discharge to the South Platte River, Denver to Fort Lupton, Colorado, August 1992 through July 1993: U.S. Geological Survey Water-Resources Investigations Report 95–4110, 71 p., 1 pl.

Merritt, M.L., and Konikow, L.F., 2000, Documentation of a computer program to simulate lake-aquifer interaction using the MODFLOW ground-water model and the MOC3D solute transport model: U.S. Geological Survey Water-Resources Investigations Report 00–4167, 146 p.

Mitsch, W.J., and Gosselink, J.G., 2000, Wetlands (3d ed.): New York, Wiley, 920 p.

Mladinich, C.S., 2006, Regional landscape change in northern Colorado Front Range, *in* Acevedo, W., and others, eds., Rates, trends, causes, and consequences of urban land-use change in the United States: U.S. Geological Survey Professional Paper 1726, p. 139–152.

Parton, W.J., Gutmann, M.P., Travis, W.R., 2003, Sustainability and historical land-use change in the Great Plains: the case of eastern Colorado: Great Plains Research v. 13, no. 1, p. 97–125.

Prudic, D.E., 1991, Estimates of hydraulic conductivity from aquifer-test analyses and specific-capacity data, Gulf Coast regional aquifer systems, south-central United States: U.S. Geological Survey Water-Resources Investigations Report 90–4121, 38 p.

Rantz and others, 1982, Measurement and computation of streamflow: U.S. Geological Survey Water-Supply Paper 2175, 631 p.

Reed, P.B., 1988, National list of plant species that occur in wetlands: U.S. Fish and Wildlife Service Biological Report 88 (26.5), 73 p.

Roark, D.M., and Healy, D.F., 1998, Quantification of deep percolation from two flood-irrigated alfalfa fields, Roswell Basin, New Mexico: U.S. Geological Survey Water-Resources Investigations Report 98–4096, 32 p.

Robson, S.G., 1983, Hydraulic characteristics of the principal bedrock aquifers in the Denver Basin, Colorado: U.S. Geological Survey Hydrologic Investigations Atlas HA–659, 3 sheets, scale 1:500,000.

Robson, S.G., 1996, Geohydrology of the shallow aquifers in the Denver metropolitan area, Colorado: U.S. Geological Survey Hydrologic Investigations Atlas HA–736, 5 sheets, scale 1:50,000.

Robson, S.G., Heiny, J.S., and Arnold, L.R., 2000, Geohydrology of the shallow aquifers in the Fort Lupton-Gilcrest area, Colorado: U.S. Geological Survey Hydrologic Investigations Atlas HA–746–C, 5 sheets, scale 1:50,000.

Salas, D., 2005, Wetlands mapping of the corridor between Brighton and Fort Lupton, Colorado: U.S. Bureau of Reclamation Technical Memorandum 8260–05–03, 7 p.

Savini J., and Kammerer, J.C., 1961, Urban growth and the water regimen: U.S. Geological Survey Water-Supply Paper 1591–A, 43 p.

Scanlon, B.R., Reedy, R.C., Stonestrom, D.A., Prudic, D.E., and Dennehy, K.F., 2005, Impact of land use and land cover change on groundwater recharge and quality in the southwestern USA: Global Change Biology, v. 11, p. 1,577–1,593.

Scanlon, B.R., Keese, K.E., Flint, A.L., Flint, L.E., Gaye, C.B., Edmunds, W.M., and Simmers, I., 2006, Global synthesis of groundwater recharge in semiarid and arid regions: Hydrological Processes, v. 20, p. 3335–3370.

Schneider, P.A., Jr., 1962, Records and logs of selected wells and test holes, and chemical analyses of groundwater in the South Platte River basin in western Adams and southwestern Weld Counties, Colorado: U.S. Geological Survey, Colorado Water Conservation Board Basic-Data Report 9, 84 p.

Schneider, P.A., Jr., and Hillier, D.E., 1978, Hydrologic data for water-table aquifers in the Boulder–Fort Collins–Greeley area, Front Range urban corridor, Colorado: U.S. Geological Survey Open-File Report 78–567, 55 p., 1 pl.

Schupbach, S.A., and Lewis, L.E., 1996, CDSS rivers Division 1: Colorado Division of Water Resources spatial dataset accessed, April 4, 2006, at *http://cdss.state.co.us/ DNN/GIS/tabid/67/Default.aspx.*

Shaw, S.P., and Fredine, C.G., 1956, Wetlands of the United States, their extent, and their value for waterfowl and other wildlife: U.S. Fish and Wildlife Service Circular 39, 67 p.

Smith, R.O., Schneider, P.A., Jr., and Petri, L.R., 1964, Ground-water resources of the South Platte River basin in western Adams and southwestern Weld Counties, Colorado: U.S. Geological Survey Water-Supply Paper 1658, 132 p., 10 pls.

Susong, D.D., 1995, Water budget and simulation of one-dimensional unsaturated flow for a flood- and a sprinkler-irrigated field near Milford, Utah: U.S. Geological Survey Water-Resources Investigations Report 95–4072, 32 p.

Theis, C.V., Brown, R.H., and Meyer, R.R., 1963, Estimating the transmissibility of aquifers from the specific capacities of wells, *in* Bentall, Ray, ed., 1963, Methods of determining permeability, transmissibility and drawdown: U.S. Geological Survey Water-Supply Paper 1536–I, p. 331–341.

Townley, L.R., 1995, The response of aquifers to periodic forcing: Advances in Water Resources, v. 18, p. 4, 795–4812.

Trimble, D.E., and Machette, M.N., 1979, Geologic map of the greater Denver area, Front Range Urban Corridor, Colorado: U.S. Geological Survey Miscellaneous Investigations Map I–856–H, scale 1:100,000.

U.S. Department of Commerce, 1968, Climate atlas of the United States: Environmental Science Services Administration, Environmental Data Service, 80 p.

U.S. Department of Commerce, 2007, Historical employment data for Adams and Weld Counties: Bureau of Economic Analysis data, accessed June 5, 2007, at *http://www.bea.gov/regional/reis/*.

U.S. Geological Survey, 1999, Coverage LU90—High-Resolution Land Use and Land Cover 1996/1997 Front Range Infrastructure Resources Project Demonstration Area: U.S. Geological Survey spatial dataset, accessed May 19, 2004, at *http://rockyweb.cr.usgs.gov/frontrange/datasets.htm*.

U.S. Geological Survey, 2001a, Coverage LU30—High-Resolution Land Use and Land Cover 1937/1938 Front Range Infrastructure Resources Project Demonstration Area: U.S. Geological Survey spatial dataset, accessed May 19, 2004, at *http://rockyweb.cr.usgs.gov/frontrange/datasets.htm*.

U.S. Geological Survey, 2001b, Coverage LU50—High-Resolution Land Use and Land Cover 1953–1958 Front Range Infrastructure Resources Project Demonstration Area: U.S. Geological Survey spatial dataset, accessed May 19, 2004, at *http://rockyweb.cr.usgs.gov/frontrange/datasets.htm*.

U.S. Geological Survey, 2001c, Coverage LU70—High-Resolution Land Use and Land Cover 1977/1978 Front Range Infrastructure Resources Project Demonstration Area: U.S. Geological Survey spatial dataset, accessed May 19, 2004, at *http://rockyweb.cr.usgs.gov/frontrange/datasets.htm*.

U.S. Geological Survey, 2001d, Hydrography (FRIHY, FRIHYX)—(1997) Front Range Infrastructure Resources Project Demonstration Area: U.S. Geological Survey spatial dataset, accessed May 19, 2004, at *http://rockyweb.cr.usgs.gov/frontrange/datasets.htm*.

U.S. Geological Survey, 2001e, Railroads (FRIRR)—(1997) Front Range Infrastructure Resources Project Demonstration Area: U.S. Geological Survey spatial dataset, accessed May 19, 2004, at *http://rockyweb.cr.usgs.gov/frontrange/datasets.htm*.

U.S. Geological Survey, 2001f, Roads (FRIRD)—(1997) Front Range Infrastructure Resources Project Demonstration Area: U.S. Geological Survey spatial dataset, accessed May 19, 2004, at *http://rockyweb.cr.usgs.gov/frontrange/datasets.htm*.

U.S. Geological Survey and University of California at Santa Barbara, 2001, Project Gigalopolis-urban and land cover modeling: U.S. Geological Survey data, accessed September 14, 2006, at *http://www.ncgia.ucsb.edu/projects/gig*.

U.S. Geological Survey, 2006a, USGS surface-water data for Colorado: U.S. Geological Survey monthly streamflow statistics available from the National Water Information System Database, accessed January 4, 2006, at *http://waterdata.usgs.gov/co/nwis/sw*.

U.S. Geological Survey, 2006b, USGS ground-water data for Colorado: U.S. Geological Survey field water-level measurements available from the National Water Information System Database, accessed November 29, 2006, at *http://waterdata.usgs.gov/co/nwis/gw*.

VanKlaveren, R., Pochop, L.O., and Hedstrom, W.E., 1975, Evapotranspiration by phreatophytes in the North Platte basin of Wyoming: Wyoming Water Resources Data System Library Water Resources Series no. 56, accessed September 23, 2005, at *http://library.wrds.uwyo.edu/wrs/wrs.html*.

Verhoeven, J., 2003, Wetlands and water resources: a valuable linkage: Water Environment, v. 21, p. 52–53.

Wagner, A., 2002, Adams County, Colorado: a centennial history, 1902–2002: Virginia Beach, Va., The Donning Company Publishers, 192 p.

Weld County, 2006, Weld County zoning map: Weld County Department of Planning Services map showing land-use zones for Weld County, Colorado, accessed September 22, 2006, at *http://www.co.weld.co.us*.

Western Regional Climate Center, 2007, Historical climate information: Western Regional Climate Center data, accessed September 25, 2007, at *http://www.wrcc.dri.edu/CLIMATEDATA.html*.

Wilson, W.W., 1965, Pumping tests in Colorado: Denver, Colorado Water Conservation Board Groundwater Circular 11, 361 p.

Winston, R.B., 2000, Graphical user interface for MODFLOW, Version 4: U.S. Geological Survey Open-File Report 00–315, 27 p.

Appendix—Color infrared aerial photographs used by this study to map wetlands and surface water in the South Platte River valley, Brighton to Fort Lupton, Colo.

(Locations of aerial photograph centroids are shown in figure 20.)

The date (mm–dd–yy), time (photographs 1–1, 1–9, 2–1, and 2–9 only), scale at which photographs were taken, photograph project name, and photograph number are shown at the top of each photograph.

Photograph 1–1.

Photograph 1–2.

Photograph 1–3.

Photograph 1–4.

Photograph 1–5.

Photograph 1–6.

Photograph 1–7.

Photograph 1–8.

Photograph 1–9.

Photograph 2–1.

Photograph 2–2.

Photograph 2–3.

Photograph 2–4.

Photograph 2–5.

Photograph 2–6.

Photograph 2–7.

Photograph 2–8.

Photograph 2–9.